The Complete Book Of Talismans, Amulets And Magic Gemstones
William Thomas Pavitt and Kate Pavitt

Revised And Updated Edition
With Additional Material By
Brad Steiger, Diane Tessman
and Shelley Kaehr, Ph.D.
And A Special Introduction By
Timothy Green Beckley

The Complete Book Of Talismans, Amulets And Magic Gemstones

by William Thomas Pavitt and Kate Pavitt

Additional Material By Brad Steiger, Diane Tessman and Shelley Kaehr, Ph.D.

With A Special Introduction By Timothy Green Beckley

Covers By William Kern

THE COMPLETE BOOK OF TALISMANS, AMULETS AND MAGIC GEMSTONES
by William Thomas Pavitt and Kate Pavitt

Additional Material By Brad Steiger, Diane Tessman and Shelley Kaehr, Ph.D.
With a Special Introduction By Timothy Green Beckley

This edition Copyright 2008 by Global Communications/Inner Light

All rights reserved. No part of these manuscripts may be copied or reproduced by any mechanical or digital methods and no exerpts or quotes may be used in any other book or manuscript without permission in writing by the Publisher, Global Communications/Inner Light, except by a reviewer who may quote brief passages in a review.

Revised Edition

ISBN   1-60611-045-4
EAN   978-1-60611-045-4

Published by
Global Communications/Inner Light
Box 753 · New Brunswick, NJ 08903

Printed in United States of America

Staff Members
Timothy G. Beckley, Publisher
Carol Ann Rodriguez, Assistant to the Publisher
Sean Casteel, General Associate Editor
Tim R. Swartz, Graphics and Editorial Consultant
William Kern, Editorial and Art Consultant

Sign Up On The Web For Our Free Weekly Newsletter
and Mail Order Version of Conspiracy Journal
and Bizarre Bazaar
www.ConspiracyJournal.com

Order Hot Line: 1-732-602-3407

A SPECIAL INTRODUCTION

JUST LIKE

WISHING ON A RAINBOW

By Timothy Green Beckley

In this day and age everyone wants to get rich!

And quickly!

We all want the best for ourselves and our family – and we'd better get on the ball and do it lickity split.

If we don't have a super paying job or a rich daddy, or a boyfriend who is in the mob, we have to go about finding the end of the rainbow in some other way.

Good luck charms have been with us since the beginning of recorded history. People have come to put their faith in that which they believe to be magical. It could be something as "simple" as a good luck gemstone, or as "complicated" as using a word from the Kabala. But there is a strong belief that these talismans and amulets really work.

The book you are now beginning to read is perhaps the best reference work on the subject, and includes a variety of "magical tools" that are practical and helpful. We have updated this terrific study guide and work book with added material by Brad Steiger and Diane Tessman. We truly believe you hold a valuable elixir for improving your life in your hands.

If you wish counseling and help in any of life's problems we can refer you to our own Dragonstar as well as Diane Tessman for private counseling. You need but drop me a line either through the mail or by e mail if you are on line.

And above all else in life – GOOD LUCK!

Timothy Green Beckley

MRUFO8@hotmail.com

The Complete Book of Talismans, Amulets and Zodiacal Gems

by William Thomas Pavitt and Kate Pavitt

This is a study of the symbolism of precious stones, and how they have been used as magical objects through the ages, both intrinsically, and as a vehicle for symbolic engravings. The Pavitts cover Hindu, Jewish, Chinese, Egyptian, Roman, Gnostic, and Christian lore of gems. The final section discusses the astrological connections of key gems, sign by sign. This work also includes quite a bit of history of important (and often 'cursed') stones such as the Hope diamond, and practical advice about purchasing gems. Anyone interested in the symbolism of gemstones will find this a great reference and a fascinating read.

TABLE OF CONTENTS
Title Page
Preface
Contents
List of Plates

Part I. Amulets and Talismans
Chapter I
Chapter II
Chapter III
Chapter IV
Chapter V
Chapter VI
Chapter VII
Chapter VIII
Chapter IX
Chapter X
Chapter XI
Chapter XII

Part II. The Gems of the Zodiac
Chapter I. Aries—The Ram
Chapter II. Taurus—The Bull
Chapter III. Gemini—The Twins
Chapter IV. Cancer—The Crab
Chapter V. Leo—The Lion
Chapter VI. Virgo—The Virgin
Chapter VII. Libra—The Balance
Chapter VIII. Scorpio—The Scorpion
Chapter IX. Sagittarius—The Archer
Chapter X. Capricorn—The Goat
Chapter XI. Aquarius—The Water-Bearer
Chapter XII. Pisces—The Fishes

Real and Artificial Gems and How to Test and Select Them
Bibliography For Talismans

Using Charms, Amulets and Rings to Enhance Your Life

LIST OF PLATES
Gems, Symbols, and Glyphs of the Zodiac
Frontispiece—Page 6
DESCRIPTION.

1. Aries the Ram, Diamond, Iron.
7. Libra the Balance, Opal, Copper.
2. Taurus the Bull, Sapphire, Copper.
8. Scorpio the Scorpion, Aquamarine, Iron.
3. Gemini the Twins, Agate, Silver.
9. Sagittarius the Archer, Topaz, Tin.
4. Cancer the Crab, Emerald, Silver.
10. Capricorn the Goat, Ruby, Lead.
5. Leo the Lion, Chrysolite, Gold.
11. Aquarius the Water-bearer, Garnet, Lead.
6. Virgo the Virgin, Cornelian, Silver.
12. Pisces the Fishes, Amethyst, Tin.

PLATE	DESCRIPTION	PAGE.
I.	Primeval Talismans; Chinese, Indian, and Thibetan Talismans	7
II.	Indian and Thibetan Talismans (continued)	16
III.	Chinese and Japanese Talismans	23
IV.	Egyptian Talismans	33
V.	Egyptian Talismans	37
VI.	Egyptian Talismans	41
VII.	Egyptian and Gnostic Talismans	47
VIII.	Etruscan, Greek, Roman, and Oriental Talismans	56
IX.	Early Christian and Mediæval Talismans	61
X.	Mediæval Talismans	71

GEMS, SYMBOLS, AND GLYPHS OF THE ZODIAC.
Frontispiece.

viii

THE COMPLETE BOOK OF TALISMANS, AMULETS AND MAGIC GEMSTONES

by
WILLIAM THOMAS PAVITT & KATE PAVITT
Updated and Revised Edition
With Additional Material by Brad Steiger,
Diane Tessman and Ellie Crystal

With Frontispiece and Ten Plates

© 2008 Global Communications/Inner Light

Conspiracy Journal
PRODUCTIONS

PREFACE

The subject of Talismans and Gems of the Zodiac covers a wide area, and the difficulty of arriving at a definite conclusion is increased because of the varying opinions between writers on these subjects as to the stones referred to, or intended by the Ancients, complicated still further by the different languages from which these records have been translated, and where Month or Zodiacal gems are referred to by many of the writers who are obviously unacquainted with Astrology or Astronomy.

The present volume being the result of many years of study and research, it is not easy in all cases to specify the original source of our information, which has been collected, not only from ancient and modern writings, but also from personal experience and experiments, noted at the time they occurred, long before this book was contemplated. Again, we find that many, and more especially modern authors, quote from one another in places, and the original source of the information is obscure; we have, therefore, endeavoured to give, as far as possible, our authorities, although, owing to the antiquity of the subject, much is necessarily left to deduction and conjecture; and there may be unintentional omissions, the remedy of which we give a list of books that we have at different times consulted and studied with advantage.

We have endeavoured throughout to make the subjects dealt with as interesting as possible, believing that the symbols expressing the faiths of bygone days form the basis of occult forces, a proper understanding of which is becoming more and more recognised by scientists as necessary in the interests of progress at the present day.

It will be noticed that many of the gems have similar qualities attributed to them which, according to the ancient authorities, were specifically arranged for the benefit of those types whose planetary aspects brought them into harmony with the particular stone specified.

With regard to characteristics dealt with in the latter part of the book, this must be regarded as general, and liable to variation according to the remaining Planetary influences, which would be indicated in a horoscope. With this proviso, the information given will be found reliable and very helpful in giving a knowledge of our dispositions and those of our friends and associates and should pave the way to a sympathy and understanding impossible without this knowledge. It will also afford a simple and easy means of at least proving there is something in Astrology, and if interest is aroused the fullest information may be obtained by a study of the books mentioned, dealing with the subject.

We have greatly benefited from the assistance given as by Mrs. G. M. Walker in lending us scarce and valuable books for reference, and by G. H. Greenop, Esq., kindly translating many old Greek and Latin writings; we should also like to acknowledge our obligations to the Directors of the British Museum for the facilities given in obtaining information, and their permission to make drawings from the actual Talismans in their collections.

WM. THOS. PAVITT
17, HANOVER SQUARE. LONDON W.
3rd August, 1914.

CONTENTS
PART I

CHAPTER I
The Psychic and Magnetic Influence of Talismans and Gems 1

CHAPTER II
Talismans of Primitive Races—The Axe—Arrow-head—The Swastika—The Serpent—The Interlaced Triangles..6

CHAPTER III
The Tau Cross—Aum Ma Ni Pad Me Hum—Indian Talismans—Ganesa the Elephant-headed—Hanuman the Monkey God—The Eight Glorious Emblems of Buddha—The Wheel of Life—The Conch Shell—The Two Fishes—The Lucky Diagram—The Lotus—The Frog—The Three Gems..12

CHAPTER IV
Talisman for Wisdom—Buddha's Footprints—The Doric.—Knots—Chinese Talismans—The Trigrams—The Five Bats—The Goose—Stork—Pine Tree—Peach—Lucky Sentence—The Phoenix—The Dragon—Horse Hoof—Siva's Charm—The Money Sword—Red in Talismans—The Lock—Bells—The Tortoise—The Tiger—Pigs—The Black Cat..19

CHAPTER V
The Pear Charm—Show Fu—Jade—The Blue Gown for Longevity—Japanese—The Tiger—Wolf—Fox—The Thunder, Fire and Echo—The Fan of Power—Hotei, the God of Contentment—The Eagle—The Millet Dumpling—Carp—Sacred Dog—Stork—Tortoise—Crane—Child's Hand—Mitsu-Domoe—Hammer of Daikoku—The Keys—Anchor—Crystal Ball—Leaf Talisman—Ota-fu-ku—Bow—Temple at Ise 25

CHAPTER VI
Egyptian Beliefs—Crux Ansata—The Menat—The Two Plumes—The Single Plume—The Nefer—The Cartouche—The Angles and Plummet—The God Bes—Aper—The Tat—The Heart..30

CHAPTER VII
The Buckle of the Girdle of Isis—The Scarab—The Eye of Osiris—The Two Fingers—The Collar—The Hawk—The Sma—The Ladder and Steps—The Snake's Head—The Serpent—The Sun's Disc—The Frog—The Fish—The Vulture—The Sa, or Tie..36

CHAPTER VIII

Gnosticism—Abraxas—Sacred Names—Khnoubis—The Seven Vowels—The Magic Symbols—The Archangels—Lion-headed Serpent—Aum—The Ineffable Name—Horus—Osiris—Isis—Etruscan, Greek, and Roman—The Crescent Symbol—The Horseshoe—Tusk, or Horn—Stable Keys—Amalthaea's Horn, or Cornucopia—Serapis—Bull's Head—Diana—Harpokrates—Anubis—Bellerophon—Salus Ring—Hygieapage...44

CHAPTER IX

The Bulla—The Tusk—Pine Cone—The Frog—Skull of an Ass—Key Talismans—Grylli, or Chimerae—Goat—The Ox—Lion—Eagle—The Caduceus—Mercury—Health Rings—Boar's Head—Clenched Hand—Open Hand—Figured Hands—The Lizard—The Spider—The Fish—Snails..51

CHAPTER X

The Orient—The Koran—Jochebed—Bead Necklaces—Mashallah—Hassan and Hussein—Hand of the Lady Fatima—Five Principal Commandments—Zufur Tukiah—Nasiree—Gadiri—Mohammed—Merzoum—The Diamond—Cube of Amber—Scorpion-charming—Early Christian and Mediaeval Talismans—Clement of Alexandria—The Fish—Dag—Palm Branch—The Ship—Sacred Monogram—Shen—Constantine the Great—Thoth—The Cross—Household Cross—Yucatan—Hand and Cross—Wheel Cross..57

CHAPTER XI

The Agnus Dei—The Coventry Ring—Ananizapta—Tau Cross—Cross of St. Benedict—Byzantine Ring—Simsum Ring—Abracadabra—Pentalpha, Pentacle, Pentagram, or Five-pointed Star—The Kabala—The Table of Jupiter—The Ten Divine Names—The Planetary Angels—The Agla—Dr. Dee..................................63

CHAPTER XII

Tetragrammaton—Phylactery—Talismans against all mischiefs, the Magus—Venus Talisman—Totaphoth—Abraxas—Eye of a Cock—Bells—Gargoyles—Cramp Rings—Blessing of Rings—Musseltaub—Posie Rings—Gemmel Rings—Zodiacal Rings—The Signs of the Zodiac in Rhyme—General Talismans—The Lee Penny—Crystal—The Moon Talismans—Peacock—Juno—Fire Talismans—Gold Nugget—Coins—Card Talismans—Badger's Tooth—Four-leaved Clover..........................69

PART II
CHAPTER I
ARIES—THE RAM
The Zodiac—Zodiacal and Calendar Months—The New Year—The Constellation—Hamal—The Passover—Characteristics of Aries People—Gems of Aries—The Bloodstone and Heliotrope—Mars the Ruling Planet—Marbodeus Gallus—The Diamond—The Qualities of the Diamond—Tavernier—The Regent—The Koh-i-Noor—The Hope Diamond... 77

CHAPTER II
TAURUS—THE BULL
The Constellation—Aldebaran—The Chaldeans—The Temples—Apis Bull—Aphrodite—Characteristics of Taurus—Training—Gems of Taurus—The Sapphire—Bishop's Ring—St. Jerome—Qualities of the Sapphire—Star Sapphire—Solomon's Seal—Charlemagne's Talisman—The Turquoise—Boetius de Boot—Horseman's Talisman—Qualities of the Stone..84

CHAPTER III
GEMINI—THE TWINS
Period—The Twins, Castor and Pollux—The Argonauts—King Solomon's Pillars—Maia—Ovid and Wedding of Mary Queen of Scots—Gemini Number—Characteristics—Agates and their Virtues—Orpheus—Chrysoprase—Alexander the Great—Virtues of the Stone... 89

CHAPTER IV
CANCER—THE CRAB
The Dark Sign—Its Duration—Origins—Summer Solstice—Hercules and the Crab—Characteristics—Goddess Esmeralda and the Ancient Peruvians—The Emerald Isle—Moonstones—Blue Moon—Pearls—Cat's Eyes—Rock Crystals—Crystal-gazing—Virtues of the Crystal..95

CHAPTER V
LEO—THE LION
Period—Constellation—The Fiery Sign—Hercules and the Lion—Characteristics—Personal Magnetism of the Type—Disposition—Money-makers—Entertainers—Health Defects—Marriage and Love Affairs—Artistic Tendencies—Gems of the House—The Sardonyx Qualities of the Stone—The Chrysolite and the Romans—The Tourmaline—Peculiarities of the Stone—Amber—Virtues and Medicinal Uses—The Topaz 101

CHAPTER VI
VIRGO—THE VIRGIN
Period—Constellation—Mythology—Symbols—Paris under Virgo—Reflecting Qualities of the Sign—Characteristics—Marriage—Professions—Ailments—Harmonious Types—Gems of the House—Cornelian—Virtues of the Cornelian—Napoleon's Seal Talisman—Clairvoyant Properties of the Stone—Jade—New Zealanders' Faith—The Tiki—Jade as Racing Talisman..................107

CHAPTER VII
LIBRA—THE BALANCE
Period—Constellation—Origin of the Sign—The Yoke—The Altar—Characteristics of the Type—Influence of Saturn—Inclination for Companionship—Marriage—Moods—Partnership—Professions—Health Defects of the Type—Gems of the House—The Opal—Coral—Lapis Lazuli—The Modern Ill-luck of the Opal—Its Ancient Virtues—Sensitiveness of the Opal—Its Virtues as a Libra Gem—Coral—Virtues—As Infant's Talisman—Lapis Lazuli—Egyptian Talisman—Qualities of the Stone..................113

CHAPTER VIII
SCORPIO—THE SCORPION
Period—Ruling Planet—Mythology—Symbology—Characteristics of the Type—Effect of the Malefic Aspects—Health Defects—Professions—Religion—Marriage—The Gems of the House—The Beryl and Aquamarine differing only in Colour—Qualities of the Beryl—Clairvoyant Properties—The Carbuncle as Transmitter of Light—Noah's Lamp—Talisman against Infection—The Lodestone—Magnetic Qualities as an Amulet against Shipwreck and Gout..................118

CHAPTER IX
SAGITTARIUS—THE ARCHER
Period—The Constellation—The Bow in the Cloud—Mythology—Characteristics of the Type—Appropriateness of the Symbol—Fresh Air a Necessity—Professions—Ailments—Marriage Relations—Gem of the House—The Topaz—Nan Ratan—Pliny and the Topaz—Discovery of the Stone—The Emperor Hadrian and his Ring—Appropriateness of the Stone to the Type—The Stone of Strength—As a Talisman against Asthma—Marbodus and the Topaz—Chrysolite also Favourable 123

CHAPTER X
CAPRICORNUS—THE GOAT
Constellation—Period—Ruling Planet Saturn—Mythology—The Symbol of the Goat—Characteristics—Constitution and Health Defects—India under the Rule of

Capricorn—Professions—Marriage—Saturn favourable for the Elderly—Gems of the House—The Ruby—Spinel—Qualities of the Gem—Sensitiveness for Good or Evil—The Malachite—Copper as a Talisman against Colic and Cholera—Black Onyx—Favourable and Unfavourable Influence of the Stone—Jet—The Afflictions of Saturn—Effects on other Types..128

CHAPTER XI
AQUARIUS—THE WATER-BEARER
Constellation—Period—Symbol—Early Religious Teachings—The Glyph—Rulers of the House—Saturn and Uranus—Characteristics of the Type—Temper—Professions—Health Defects—Marriage and Friendships—Gems of the House—Garnets and Zircons—The Garnet and Ruby—Qualities of the Stone—Virtue, as a Keepsake—The Zircon—The Hyacinth—The Jargoon—The Jacinth as a Talisman for Sleep—Set in Gold for Restlessness—The Lyncurion of the Ancients: its Virtues 134

CHAPTER XII
PISCES—THE FISHES
Period—Constellation—Precession of the Equinoxes—Ichthyes the Fishes—Mythology—Symbol—The Rulers of the House—Characteristics—Ailments of the Type—Professions—Friendship and Marriage—Harmonious and Inharmonious Types—The Gem of the House—The Amethyst—Virtues of the Stone—Talisman against Inebriety—Its Calming Influence—The Stone of St. Valentine—As a Lovers' Talisman—The Effect of Purple Rays—The Amethyst Beneficent to all Types 139

APPRAISING AND SELECTING GEMS..143

BIBLIOGRAPHY..146

USING CHARMS, AMULETS AND RINGS TO ENHANCE YOUR LIFE
Creating Charms with Candles
Using a Wax Image to Charm
The Ancient Lucky Seven Love Ritual
A Ritual for Summoning a Spirit of the Dead
The Love Ritual of the Seven Knots
A Tree Charm to Gain Strength
The Incredible Magic In Stones and Gems:
How to Use Them in Amulets and Rings
By Brad Steiger..148

ON TALISMANS
By Shelley Kaehr, Ph.D..155

GETTING THE MOST OUT OF YOUR GEMSTONES
By Diane Tessman..157

PART I
AMULETS AND TALISMANS
CHAPTER I

Introduction.—The Psychic and Magnetic Influence of Talismans and Gems.

From remotest times, back even to the birth of humanity, Precious Stones and Talismans have been held in high estimation by all nations; the former, primarily because of their beauty, and the latter on account of their virtues, as transmitters of good luck and to avert misfortune. The association of Gems with power, civil and religious, has ever been noticeable; and to the fascination of antiquity may be added the allurement of mystery. Moreover, of the many and varied signs of wealth and luxury, jewels have played a most important part in the lives of the great, not only on account of their beauty but because they contained in a small compass the equivalent to a large sum of money and in times of danger could easily be concealed and carried from place to place.

As tokens or symbols they conveyed joy and confidence to their owners, and were thought to give warning of coming events, inspiring courage and faith in the fearful, and the romances and tragedies in which they have played a part, together with their marked influence on the lives of individuals and nations, intensifies our interest in them so that it is little wonder that faith in the mysterious properties ascribed to them should have survived the growth of ages and still find so many believers in all countries. The philosophers of thousands of years ago, understanding their suitability as a medium for the transmission of astral forces and vibrations, invested them with much importance, attributing to them spiritual as well as material powers, special characteristics and medicinal and curative qualities.

In all probability gems had their origin in the very remote period of the Earth's history when it was still in a molten state subject to deluge and fire, before its solidification made it possible for vegetation to appear, and the translucent lustre of certain gems is due to the action of the floods which preceded the fiery volcanic period. The colouring which forms their greatest fascination is due to various metallic oxides in combination with oxygen which in varying quantities gives red, blue, yellow, or green colourings, as shown by the Ruby, Sapphire, Emerald, Topaz, and Amethyst.

It is most difficult to determine with any certainty in what country Precious Stones were first worn as ornaments, but the consensus of opinion seems to point to India, as far as recognised history is concerned, as their birthplace, for every rare and beautiful production of Nature, Gems and Pearls are associated with the East.

The earliest records of humanity do not, however, stop with known histories, for traces of man's love for gems are found in the discoveries of travellers and the traditions of South America, evidence proving an inheritance from past civilisations of great antiquity. There is an innate attraction to the marvellous in mankind, the imagination leading us to endow the rare and precious with peculiar qualities, particularly when the source of its beauty and rarity is not readily perceptible. It is akin to the extraordinary magnetic influence which one person may exercise over another without any tangible evidence of super-physical powers, or the mysterious attraction which the Magnet exercises over Iron, and establishes the inference that other minerals may be similarly endowed with properties at present unrecognised by our ordinary physical senses.

Modern research confirms the old teaching that the Universe was created from the four elements, Fire, Air, Water, Earth, in the order given, each growing as it were from its predecessor and all animated in turn by the Word breathed upon them at the Creation; this force, or energy, permeates all existing things from man, who is the highest of apparent physical manifestations down through the animal and vegetable kingdoms to the mineral, in which this energy, by reason of its very slow atomic changes, is least obvious. This Force manifests in the form of vibrations moving in waves through every composite part of the physical world, and, according to the condition of its medium, helping and giving power when in harmony, and thwarting or nullifying action when under unfavourable conditions. To this Force, or Etheric influence, is due the law of Evolution, or progress, which operates in every department of the Universe, not being confined to any one kingdom, but harmonising each with the other, being naturally most powerful in man whose evolution is the highest, and forms the medium through which man can act on the lower kingdoms and receive desired vibrations from them. We may thus interpret Plato's statement "that gems owe their origins to the stars" as an etheric influence acting on the auriferous matter which forms their composition.

Evidence of undoubted authenticity of wonderful occult powers and experiences has within recent years become readily accessible to all. Psychometry [the art of sensing past happenings to individuals from the handling of something belonging to them, such as a glove or jewel] may be said to be established as a fact; and that this power is not confined to human affairs but permeates also the lower kingdoms is aptly illustrated by a personal experience which occurred during the summer of 1912. Mr. J. Wedgewood of the Theosophical Society, who is much interested in sensing colours from the touch of Precious Stones, and with whom I have frequently experimented in this direction, called one day at my office with a lady friend, Mrs. Russak, also of the Theosophical Society, and a well-known occultist. In the course of conversation Mr. Wedgewood said, "If you want to know anything about any of your stones, this lady can tell you," and, being desirous of getting a real test, I selected two new stones that I knew had never been used, as will be seen by what follows:—I handed one to Mrs. Russak which she held in the palm of her hand for a moment or so, and then gave me what was, as far as I could judge, a description of the processes of its formation; then, holding it out to me, went on to say, "I am sorry I cannot give you any events connected with this stone, but within the last month you have changed its centre of gravity." The stone was a Jargoon that I had only just received back from the lapidary with whom I had left it in the rough to be cut; it was a very decided oval in shape whilst in its rough state, and the lapidary had advised me to have practically half of it cut away, leaving the stone quite circular and only about half its original size, although much more valuable and finer in colour than it would have been had it been cut as an oval twice the size.

The second stone was a piece of Lapis Lazuli, and after holding this for a while the Seer said, "I only get warm friendly vibrations from this stone, and as far as I can tell it has had no history as a finished stone; but it must have come into your possession under very kindly conditions." The stone in question had been cut from a large piece of Lapis Lazuli given to me in its natural rough uncut form by a client, in recognition of quite a slight service I had rendered her, but which had played a rather important part in her life.

This ability to gauge and come into touch with the soul of things is unfortunately at present only confined to the few, although innate in every human being, and must be regarded as a latent sense which will be common to coming generations, opening up realms hitherto undreamt of and making a decided forward step in human evolution.

Confusion and doubt have arisen as to the exact stones mentioned by the early writers, owing to their elastic methods of describing all red stones as Rubies, all green stones as Emeralds, and all blue stones as Sapphires; this confusion has not been lessened by reason of the complexity of the many languages of the East, to say nothing of the artistic liberties taken by modern poets and authors, (who, probably unaware of the necessity for astronomical or astrological knowledge as a basis for the Zodiacal placing of the stones,) have taken our calendar as it stands for the Month stones with such embellishments as their fancy dictated.

The Precious Stones ascribed to the twelve months of the year were those worn in the breastplate of the High Priest, and it was believed that the Divine revelations obtained by the shining or dullness of the stones in the Urim and Thummim, due to some virtue inherent in them, were indicative as to whether the atonement had been accepted or not. These twelve stones, engraved with twelve anagrams of the name of God, had a mystic power over the Zodiac, harmonising the twelve Angels and good Spirits who had affinity with the twelve tribes of Israel.

The origin of Talismans and Amulets is lost in the obscurity of the ages, but as far back as we can trace human records they are to be found; the terms Talisman and Amulet have become from indiscriminate use to be considered synonymous, but in his notes to the Archaeological Journal, the Rev. C. W. King says:—

"The meaning of these two words is entirely distinct. Talisman being the conception in the Arabic tongue of the Greek, meaning the influence of a planet, or the Zodiac, upon the person born under the same. A Talisman in olden times was, therefore, by its very nature a sigil, or symbolic figure, whether engraved in stone or metal, or drawn upon parchment or paper, and was worn both to procure love and to avert danger from its possessor. The latter purpose alone was the object of the Amulet, its Latin signification being to do away with, or baffle, its root being Amalior. Pliny cites the word as the country-folk name for the Cyclamen which ought to be planted in every human home, because where it is grown poisonous drugs have no power to harm, on which account they call it the flower, Amuletum."

The belief in them is by no means so universal as in olden times, and to the thoughtful person many of the attributes claimed for them cannot be admitted; at the same time, with the growing knowledge of finer forces opening up new powers to mankind and to which we are slowly coming into touch, many people are prepared to admit that there may be some active power in a thought made concrete in the form of a Talisman or Amulet which may be made for some specific purpose, or for particular wear, becoming to the wearer a continual reminder of its purpose and undoubtedly strengthening him in his aims and desires.

Symbols, frequently of a religious nature, have formed the basis of Talismans and Charms from earliest times, holding a very important place in the affairs of humanity, for symbolism was a power before civilisation was evolved, and by its recognition of a certain order in physical affairs it was undoubtedly a great factor in the establishment of human laws. In modern religions this law is recognised by the use of each symbol in accordance with the character of ceremonial worship, colour also playing a very important part in the service.

Too frequently one hears a religion condemned as idolatrous because its God or Gods were typified in human or animal form. That it was the virtue the figure represented, and not the figure itself that was venerated, is ignored; but Christians would be indignant if the use of the Lamb and Eagle as symbols in their services caused them to be accused of idolatrous worship of these emblems!

The force of the Spirit behind the symbol is very apparent with regard to the Cross, as may be understood when we think of the martyrs who have endured unflinchingly the most excruciating tortures human brain could devise, holding fast to their faith by this symbol.

The savage had his Totem, which he believed gave him certain virtues, and helped him to success in his combats and in his struggle for existence.

Those of our readers who have any knowledge of Astrology and Planetary influences will readily understand the sympathy between any metal, or stone, ruled by any particular planet, and any person coming under the influence of that planet.

In the writing of the philosophers and Alchemists of the Middle Ages directions are given that these Talismans should be made, or commenced, under favourable aspects, so that the Work may receive the vitalising rays proceeding from the planet represented.

THE COMPLETE BOOK OF TALISMANS, AMULETS AND MAGIC GEMSTONES

CHAPTER II
Talismans of Primitive Races—The Axe—Arrow-head—The Swastika—The Serpent—The Interlaced Triangles.

Amongst primitive races the Axe was the symbol for Chief, God, or Divine Being, and had its origin in the Neolithic or later Stone Age, which ended in Europe about 2000 B.C.

It was doubtless the earliest weapon of prehistoric man, and in addition to its uses as a weapon would have been in constant service in clearing the way when moving from place to place, and in cutting and shaping the wood used in forming his shelters. This being so, it is easy to conceive of its association with strength, power, and utility; and its symbolic use to express these virtues is a logical conclusion, whilst from remains found in various parts of the world it is evident that its use for this purpose was universal, and amongst primitive races the Axe became the recognised hieroglyphic for God, Chief, or Ruler; moreover, as a symbol of power, its place is taken by the State Sword which is carried before the King at important ceremonies even to the present day.

Amongst the remains of the Stone Age, Talismans formed in the shape of Axeheads have been found pierced with holes for suspension, and Illustration No. 13 (Plate I) is an example in Slate of the Neolithic period found in Portugal, and its ornament is the Divine in its feminine aspect as represented by prehistoric man, who placed the feminine first in his beliefs, tracing his own descent and his position in the tribe through the Mother.

Illustration No. 16 (Plate I) is of a blue flint Talisman from Egypt; and No. 15 (Plate I) is in Haematite, and comes from the Upper Congo, where the natives of the present day regard it as an effective Talisman against disease.

The Arrow-head in its symbolism had a similar significance to that of the Axe, and in Japan flint Arrow-heads were thought to have been rained from Heaven, or dropped by flying spirits. They were very popular in the early days of the present civilisation as Amulets to protect the wearer from disease and to avert the Evil Eye; whilst throughout Europe they were regarded as the product of Elves (Elf-shots, or fairy weapons), water in which they had been dropped or dipped, being considered very efficacious in curing feminine ailments (see Illustration No. 17, Plate I).

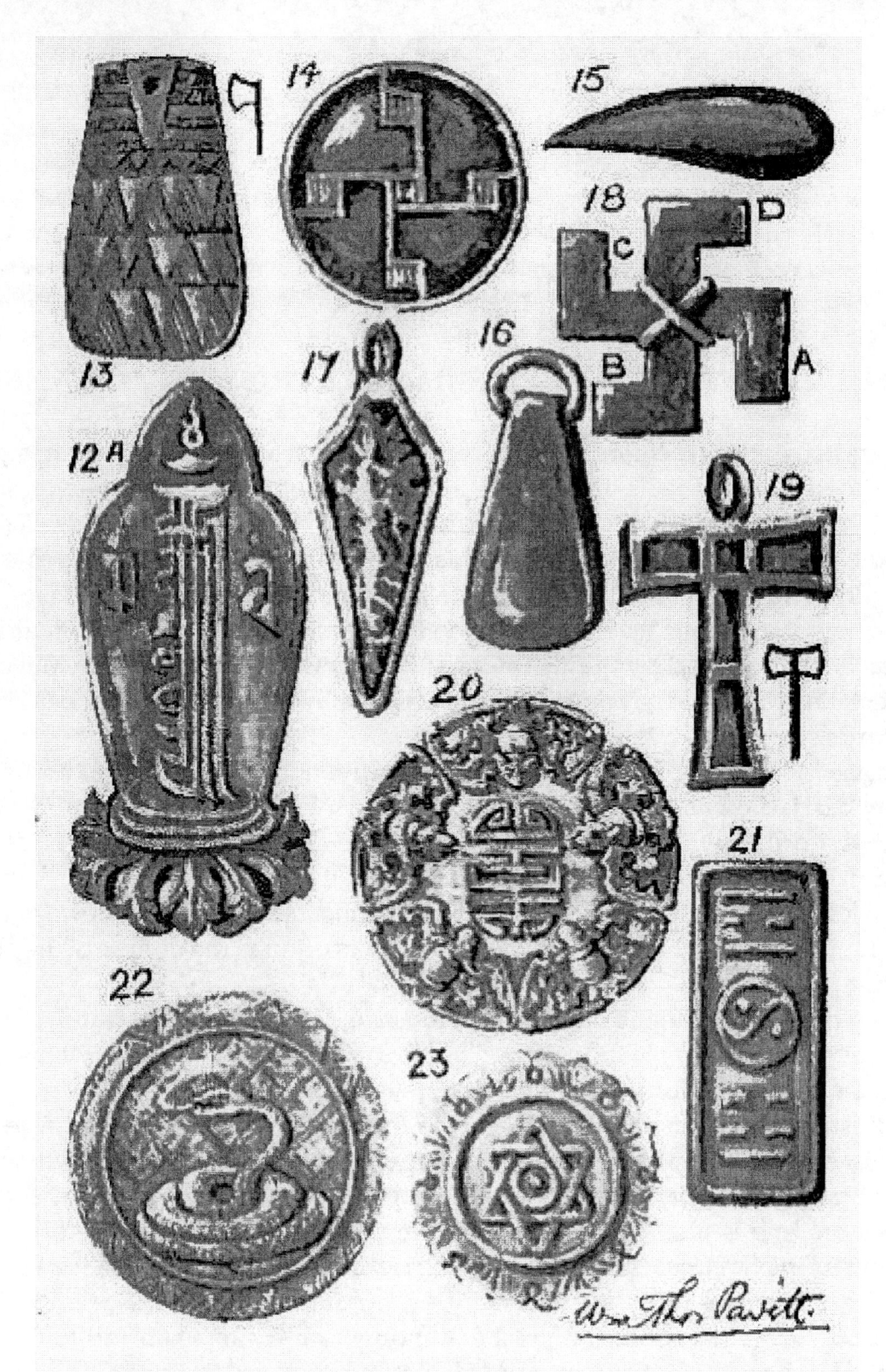

THE COMPLETE BOOK OF TALISMANS, AMULETS AND MAGIC GEMSTONES

PRIMEVAL, CHINESE, INDIAN AND THIBETAN TALISMANS.

PLATE 1.

THE COMPLETE BOOK OF TALISMANS, AMULETS AND MAGIC GEMSTONES

PLATE I. PRIMEVAL, CHINESE, INDIAN AND THIBETAN TALISMANS.

The Swastika, one of the oldest and certainly the most universal Talisman known, can be traced back to the Neolithic Age, and it has been found engraved on stone implements of this period. It is to be met with in all parts of the Old and New Worlds and on the most ancient ruins and remains, it thus living through the Ages in active use down to the present time. In spite of its antiquity and the fact that some writers quote it as being in use among the Egyptians, we have not been able to find it, as a symbol used by them, amongst their remains in the British Museum, and authorities whom we have consulted are also unaware of its existence in Egyptian records.

It was used long before its present name was given it, and extensive discussion has been carried on as to whether its correct form is with its arms turned to the left, or to the right, without, as far as we have been able to ascertain, any definite conclusion being arrived at. Both forms seem equally popular, and are so found in all countries; whilst on the rock walls of the Buddhist caves of India they are used in great numbers, with their arms turned both ways often in the course of the same inscription.

In Sanskrit its name means Happiness, Pleasure, Good Luck, Su—good, or well; Asti—being, making it = "Good Being"; and it is still used in India, China, and Japan as an Amulet for long life, good fortune, and good luck.

The illustration shown on Plate I, No. 14 is from a shield of the Bronze Age, the background being of dull red enamel, and the arms turned to the left; whilst No. 18, which turns to the right, is taken from between the feet of a statue of Buddha from Ceylon, and is also commonly found in the footprints of this Deity, sometimes both forms being used in the same impression. In China the Swastika sign is pronounced Wan, meaning a great number, a multitude, great happiness, longevity; both forms are used, but most commonly that which is turned to the left. The Jains of India regard it as a symbol of human progress, the right arm A (Illustration No. 18) representing the lowest stage of life, as protoplasm; the lower arm B indicating the soul's evolution, and through plant and animal life C representing human evolution, and D the spiritual life, the plane on which the soul is entirely freed from matter by the practice of the three jewels, right belief, right knowledge, and right conduct. In their temples at their service of baptism or its equivalent rite, this symbol is traced on the forehead of the candidate as a benediction for protection from evil influences. It is used as an emblem of the highest of all, the Almighty maker of the heavens and earth, indicating the Divine Force radiating through the Universe; it is also regarded as a sign of Benediction and good augury amongst Buddhists and all Eastern nations, and as a symbol of the Sun, when represented turned to the left, the Autumnal period, and when turned to the right the Vernal.

It has been identified as the Hammer of Thor, the Lord of Thunder and Lightning, the God of the Air; and amongst the Scandinavians was believed to have dominion over the Demons of the Air, and the coat-of-arms of the Isle of Man—a Swastika formed of three human legs, is a legacy from the early settlers of their race. It may occasionally be met with, having five or six limbs, and is then probably intended to represent the Wheel of the law, or Buddha's Wheel; whilst a three-limbed figure is much used in the Punjaub and other parts of India by the Mohajin Log (the banking, or moneyed class) as a charm which was not only worn, but used as an ornament in their houses, generally over the door.

It is also the symbol indicated by the silent ascetic sitting with arms folded over the breast, the legs crossed, and each foot placed on the opposite thigh, which accounts for this pose, so familiar amongst the images of the Indian gods.

Dr. Eitel says this symbol was frequently cast on bells during the Middle Ages, and the instances as being still in existence those of Appleby, Scotheim, Waldingham, Bishop's Norton, and Barkwith in Lincolnshire, Hathersage in Derbyshire, Maxborough in Yorkshire and many others.

The fact that this symbol is found universally throughout India, Africa, North and South America, Asia and Europe forms a very strong argument for a common origin lost in the far distant past, and is considered by some writers as evidence of a connection between these continents and the lost continent of Atlantis.

The Serpent throughout all ages has appealed to the imagination of man, to whom its various characteristics afforded opportunities for symbolic expression; from its length of life it has been used as the symbol of Eternity, and as a Talisman for Longevity, Health, and Vitality, and when depicted with its tail in its mouth (this form being particularly noticeable in ancient rings) it indicates perpetual union, whilst to the Aztecs, who used it in this way as a symbol of the Sun, it signified unending Time, ever beginning, ever creating, and ever destroying, and was considered to have great protective and enduring virtues.

When shown coiled, its folds signify succession of ages, and if the tail is hidden, unfathomable antiquity (see Illustration No. 22, Plate I, which is taken from an ancient Japanese example in the British Museum).

In primeval days, serpents of the Python family attained huge dimensions, and

THE COMPLETE BOOK OF TALISMANS, AMULETS AND MAGIC GEMSTONES

would naturally be held in dread and awe by early man; and in all primitive religions we find the belief held that the soul of man passed at death into a serpent to undergo regeneration and renewal, so symbolised because the serpent casts its skin once a year and becomes a new serpent.

To the Eastern mind the Sun in its passage through the heavens formed a curve similar to that of the Snake, and by its progression spirally, with great quickness at will, though without feet and hands or organs by which other animals perform their movements, it was supposed to symbolise lightning or fire, the vitalising principle of life in its good aspect, and, when antagonistic, it became typical of evil and misfortune.

In Egypt the Serpent in the form of the Uraeus was worn round the head as a mark of Royalty, and to symbolise Divine Power, Wisdom, and Energy, every tomb of the Kings yet opened has the Serpent sculptured erect on each side of the doorway to guard and protect the body within. It first became a type of the Evil One when this form was assumed by Sut (after killing Osiris) in his endeavour to escape from the vengeance of Horus.

In Indian religions the Serpent is known as Ananta, or endless, a symbol of infinite duration and Eternity; Vishnu, the Creator, is represented sleeping on this serpent whose numerous heads form a canopy over the God, each giving constant attention to his expected awakening, when new creations and a new order of things will be established, and was valued as a talisman for Knowledge, Wisdom, and Understanding.

Serpents were sacred to the Great God of Medicine because of the idea that they have the power of renewing their youth by casting their skins, hence the wand of Aesculapius is represented as entwined by two serpents, the emblem of Medical Science, and in the temple of Epidaurus, the most important sanatorium of the Metropolis, a large serpent was kept, typical of Health and Vitality. As a symbol, it was used in connection with Ceres, Mercury, and Diana in their most beneficent qualities; whilst Python in monstrous form represented all that was evil.

Solomon's Seal, also known as the Interlaced Triangle, is another ancient Talisman that has been universally used in every religion; but though it is said to have been the symbol by which the wise King ruled the Genii, it could not have originated with him as its use dates back much further than the Jewish Dispensation.

As a Talisman it was considered all-powerful, being the perfect sign of the Absolute, and was worn for protection against all casualties, dangers, and mischief, and to preserve its wearer from all evil.

In its composition the Triangle with its apex upwards symbolises Good, and with the inverted Triangle, Evil: the Triangle with its apex up being typical of the Trinity that exists in all religions; in India, China, and Japan its three angles represent Brahma, Vishnu, and Siva, the Creator, Preserver, and Destroyer or Regenerator; in Egypt it represented Osiris, Isis, and Horus, and in the Christian Church the Holy Trinity. As a whole it stood for the elements of fire and spirit, composed of the three virtues, Love, Truth, and Wisdom. The Triangle with its apex downward represented the element of water, and typified the material world, or the three enemies of the soul, the World, the Flesh, and the Devil, and the cardinal sins, Envy, Hatred, and Malice.

Therefore, the meaning of the two Triangles interlaced, is the triumph of spirit over matter, and at the commencement of our present civilisation was considered an all-powerful Talisman, particularly when used with either a Tau Cross, the Hebrew Yod, or the Crux Ansata in the centre.

The Illustration No. 23, Plate I, is from an Indian form of the Talisman, and has the Sun's symbol in the centre.

THE COMPLETE BOOK OF TALISMANS, AMULETS AND MAGIC GEMSTONES

CHAPTER III

The Tau Cross—Aum Ma Ni Pad Me Hum—Indian Talismans—Ganesa the Elephant-headed—Hanuman the Monkey God—The Eight Glorious Emblems of Buddha—The Wheel of Life—The Conch Shell—The Two Fishes—The Lucky Diagram—The Lotus—The Frog—The Three Gems.

OF the many and various Symbols and Talismans which have come down to us through the ages, the Tau Cross is one of the most ancient, and is undoubtedly the prototype of all modern crosses; it probably had its origin in the double-axe hieroglyphic used by primitive man, and symbolised the Divine attributes of rule and power appertaining to the single axe as mentioned in the previous chapter, and is still recognised as an emblem of authority in the form of the Gavel, or Mallet, with which the auctioneer conducts sales of property and the chairman controls meetings both in public and in the various lodges of secret societies. Formerly it was also universally worn as a talisman of powerful efficacy to protect its wearer from diseases of an inflammatory nature and against bites of serpents and other venomous reptiles (see Illustration No. 19, Plate I). Moses, who from his training in the Egyptian temples would be familiar with its symbolic significance, also used this cross, with the brazen serpent attached, to save the Israelites in the Wilderness when they were afflicted by the fiery serpents. This form of cross is to be found in all known religions of both hemispheres, and has ever been regarded as the symbol of eternal life and of regeneration, and in relation to this, John Dudley, writing in 1846, says: "that such deep mysterious meaning was possibly intended by our Saviour dying upon the Cross, giving spiritual life and immortality to all mankind." It was also the mark mentioned in Ezekiel ix. 4 which was set in the foreheads of those destined for exemption from Divine punishment in Jerusalem; and the Tau is conspicuous in various old stained-glass representations of the subject depicted as described in Scripture. A further instance of significance is that it also figured on the roll-call of the Roman Legions, a Tau Cross being placed against the names of all those who had survived the battle, and a Theta against the slain.

The Tau Cross was also the sign adopted by Anthony the Copt, an Egyptian hermit gifted in the cure of Erysipelas (a diffusive inflammatory affection of the

THE COMPLETE BOOK OF TALISMANS, AMULETS AND MAGIC GEMSTONES

skin) and as an Amulet against St. Anthony's Fire, as this disease was subsequently called, this cross came into great favour, particularly among the Jews, who used it in conjunction with various magical formulas both for Erysipelas and Epilepsy, or the falling sickness, as stated by the Rev. C. W. King. We also learn from Grose that a brotherhood known as the Order of St. Anthony was instituted in 1095 by one Gaston Frank. The friars of this order made it their object in life to minister to those afflicted with St. Anthony's Fire, the relics of this saint being believed to be most efficacious in the cure of this complaint. We are also told that this fraternity wore a black habit with the letter T in blue on their breasts, this symbol being known as St. Anthony's Cross. As this saint was habitually invoked for the cure of Epilepsy as well as Erysipelas, the Tau Cross became regarded as a Talisman against both maladies.

In the Archaeological Journal we note the following

"Among Stothard's effigies are those of Sir Roger de Bois and lady, each of whom wears on the right shoulder a circular badge graven with a Tau Cross on which appears the word ANTHON," thus testifying to the fact that Sir Roger also belonged to the Brotherhood, whilst in Ireland to this day St. Anthony's Cross is still used as a charm against sickness.

Aum, the mystic emblem of the Deity, was first introduced into Europe by the translation of the Gita, in which we are told it is forbidden to be pronounced aloud, and in its complete expression is still in universal use as a Talisman throughout Asia. It is usually spelt om, but being tri-literal seems, according to most Sanskrit scholars, better expressed by AUM, or AOM, or AWM, being formed of the three Sanskrit letters that are best so expressed. The date generally believed for its universal use is the thirteenth century B.C. It represents the Hindu Triad, or triform Deity, three in one, A the Creator, U the Preserver, and M the Destroyer, or Transformer, and is the image of the Ancient of Days; and in the Book of the Pitris it is written: "The husband is as ancient as the wife, and the wife is as ancient as the husband, and the son is also as ancient as the husband and wife, and the one that contains all these is called AUM."

The signification of the invocation AUM MA NI PAD ME HUM (AUM! the Jewel in the Lotus HUM) is therefore very important, and accounts for the great veneration in which it is held (see Illustration No. 12a, Plate I), and in Buddhism in Thibet, by Waddell, we note that it is stated in the MANI KAHBUM that this charm will bring the greatest happiness, prosperity, all knowledge, and the means of deliverance from enemies and all evil on earth, whilst the devout firmly believe that as they revolve the magical sentence within their prayer-wheels by day and night they are preventing the series of re-births otherwise inevitable, and that when their lives have ended here they will pass straightway to the Paradise of Buddha, for the

"Aum closes re-birth among the gods,
Ma among the Titans,
Ni as a man,
Pad as a beast,
Me as a Tantalus, and
Hum as an inhabitant of Hell."

To each of these words is given the distinctive colour of these six conditions of re-birth:

"Aum the godly white,
Ma the Titanic blue,
Ni the human yellow,
Pad the animal green,
Me the tantalic red,
Hum hellish black."

There is also a special Rosary used for the repetition of this charm, composed either of the Conch Shell, or crystal beads; in use, the right hand is passed through the Rosary, which hangs down knotted end up, and the hand with the thumb upward is carried to the breast and held there. On the first syllable AUM being pronounced, the first bead is grasped by raising the thumb and quickly depressing the tip to reach the bead against the outer side of the second joint of the first finger, during the remainder of the sentence the bead, still grasped, is gently revolved to the right, and on conclusion of the invocation is dropped down the palm side of the string; and with another AUM, the next bead is proceeded with until, on conclusion of each cycle of the rosary, each of the keeper beads are touched, saying respectively,

Om!   Ah!   Hum!

In countries where Buddhism is practised, particularly in Thibet and India, this charm is depicted on silk flags, flown from lofty flagstaffs, so that when the flag is blown out by the wind the sentence may be wafted to heaven to bring down blessings to the entire district.

The prayer-wheel, which contains this mystic sentence printed on long lengths of silk ribbon coiled on cylinders, is revolved by the Lama priest sunwise, and he is very strict in this observance, believing that the reversing of the prayer would also reverse the results of the invocation.

Aum is recognised throughout India as an emblem of the Deity, carrying with its pronunciation a thousand good things to the faithful; and a Brahmin teacher when addressing an assembly will use this word when commencing his discourse, and also at the close, so that he may not lose his knowledge and understanding.

THE COMPLETE BOOK OF TALISMANS, AMULETS AND MAGIC GEMSTONES

Indian Talismans.—In India we find, as in most countries, that Talismans very frequently have religious origins, and representations of the Deities are in common use for the protection of their wearers, as well as for their spiritual and material well-being. A belief in a Trinity of gods is universal, with Brahma as the Creator, Vishnu the Preserver and Restorer, and Siva the Destroyer or Regenerator. In the course of the developments of the various sects Vishnu, originally regarded as a manifestation of Solar energy, became the supreme god, and the worshippers of Vishnu attribute to him all the qualities of the triune gods, his image and various symbols being amongst the most common of Indian Talismans. He is believed to have ten Avataras, or Incarnations, in which his spirit descended in human form to effect great reformations and to regenerate the world; the tenth incarnation, yet to come, is for the final destruction of the wicked, and to regenerate and purify the world.

Gotama Buddha, the founder of Buddhism, was Vishnu's ninth incarnation, and his images and symbols are extremely popular Talismans for protection and good fortune. Buddhism, which was founded about the fifth century B.C., has established itself throughout India, China, Ceylon, Japan, Thibet, and Central Asia, inculcating a very high system of theology, the ultimate end of which is Union with the Divine. The Brahmins place Buddha foremost amongst the gods, as opposed to Brahma of the Hindus.

Amongst other sects, Siva is regarded as the greatest of the gods, and there is much overlapping amongst these beliefs, and numerous minor gods exist, typifying various virtues and gifted with powers and attributes which bring them into intimate relations with humanity, for which reason their symbols and personifications are in common use as Talismans. Talismans of Ganesa, the elephant-headed god, the son of Siva, (who is regarded as the God of Wisdom and Prudence, and the Remover of obstacles,) are always worn when any important undertaking is begun. He is represented with four arms holding respectively a Lotus, a Shell, a Goad or Club, and the Discus or Wheel, and the rotundity of his body is symbolic of his high importance and good standing, and not, as might be supposed, intended as evidence of good living (see Illustration No. 28, Plate II).

THE COMPLETE BOOK OF TALISMANS, AMULETS AND MAGIC GEMSTONES

INDIAN AND THIBETAN TALISMANS.

PLATE 2.

THE COMPLETE BOOK OF TALISMANS, AMULETS AND MAGIC GEMSTONES

PLATE 2. INDIAN AND THIBETAN TALISMANS.

Hanuman, the Monkey god, is the most popular form of Talisman for Luck, Health, and Good Fortune amongst the Hindus, and his wonderful exploits are a constant theme of interest from childhood to old age.

He was unequalled in learning, knowledge of medicine, and magic, and his skill and cunning in defeating his enemies were superhuman; he fought for Rama, who was an incarnation of Vishnu, performing on his behalf prodigious feats of valour. On one occasion, whilst fighting against Ravana the King of Demons, his enemies greased his enormous tail and set it on fire, but only to their own discomfiture, for with it Hanuman burnt down Lanka, their capital city (see Plate 2, No. 29). The eight glorious emblems of Buddha are all used as Talismans; they consist of the Wheel of the Law, the Conch Shell, the Golden Fish, the Lucky Diagram, the Lotus, the Umbrella, the Vase, and the Trumpet of Victory.

Buddha at his birth had the marks of two feet upon his head and a wheel, or disc, in his hand, by which symbols the Pandits foretold that he would become a great ruler.

The Wheel of Life was drawn by Buddha in a rice field from grains of rice, to illustrate his teaching that the perpetual succession of cause and effect during life resembles the turning of a wheel; and the symbol is worn as a wheel of fortune, so that misfortunes may roll by and good fortune come uppermost. The wheel was also used to explain the vision seen by a disciple on other spheres, the five spokes divided the Hells, the place of Animals, Ghosts, or evil spirits, Gods, and men (illustrated Plate II, No. 34).

The Conch Shell was taken from a demon of the sea by Krishna, who used it for a horn (see Illustration No. 35, Plate II), and is prized as a Talisman for oratory and learning, as well as a bringer of wealth, the latter being no doubt suggested by the fact that shells were the current coin of primitive people.

The Fish is the symbol of the first incarnation of Vishnu, who in this form saved Manu from the Flood to become the progenitor of the new race. Because of its fertility it is used as a Talisman for increase of riches, and is illustrated on Plate II, No. 32.

The Lucky Diagram is very common in Thibet, and is worn as a Talisman for Longevity (see Illustration No. 30, Plate II).

The Lotus expresses the idea of superhuman origin, as it grows from the body of the water without contact with the solid earth, and no matter how muddy the water may become still preserves its purity undefiled. It is one of the symbols of Lakshmi, the consort of Vishnu, who is the goddess of Fortune and of Beauty; it is worn as a Talisman of Good Luck and Good Fortune, and as Lakshmi is particularly favourable for children it is worn to avert all childish diseases and accidents, as well as to protect from the Evil Eye (see Illustration No. 33, Plate II).

Frogs made of amber or gilded metal are also frequently worn as amulets by children in Burmah, that they may not decline in health through the evil glance. Brightly coloured ribbons are hung upon houses and attached to the heads and tails of horses to distract the attention of the Evil Eye, and protect the animals from harm, which probably accounts for the origin of the gaudy decorations we frequently see in our own country tied to the heads and tails of fine cart-horses on their way to the fair or horse show.

The Three Gems Talisman (Illustrated on Plate II, No. 31) is to be met with wherever Buddhism is established, and symbolises Buddha His Word, and the Church; it is worn to promote the three virtues, Endurance, Courage, and Obedience, the Buddhist Law.

CHAPTER IV

Talisman for Wisdom—Buddha's Footprints—The Dorje—Knots—Chinese Talismans—The Trigrams—The Five Bats—The Goose—Stork—Pine Tree—Peach—Lucky Sentence—The Phoenix—The Dragon—Horse Hoof—Siva's Charm—The Money Sword—Red in Talismans—The Lock—Bells—The Tortoise—The Tiger—Pigs—The Black Cat.

Illustration No. 24, Plate II is a Talisman for Wisdom and Perseverance, and is of great power amongst the Hindus; the circle is indicative of infinity, the border of triangles signifies that all nature is subject to the laws of the Trinity, Brahma, Vishnu, and Siva; the serpent is the symbol of Wisdom and Perseverance, and indicates that without these attributes the revelation of the higher truths cannot be attained. The seven-knotted Bamboo represents the seven degrees of power of invocation which Initiates must acquire.

Impressions of Buddha's Footprints, another very popular Talisman (see Illustration No. 25, Plate II), are to be met with not only in the form of personal ornaments, but in gigantic proportions of which an example may be seen at the British Museum, beautifully carved and ornamented with numerous sacred emblems. The most celebrated "footprint" is on Adam's Peak, near Colombo, which attracts from all countries pilgrims who have adopted the religion of Buddha, Mohammed, or the Hindu gods, each claiming it as the Impression of their respective Deities.

Sir Gardiner Williamson says that the Mohammedans of Egypt show a footprint of the Prophet which gives the name to a village on the banks of the Nile—Attar a Nebbee. Herodotus mentions the impression of the foot of Hercules, two cubits in length, on a rock near the bank of the River Tyras, in Scythia. In Italy, tablets dedicated to Isis have been found. From this we gather that this practice of carving footprints on rocks and stone is one which dates from the remote Bronze Age, and that the area over which they are found embraces the whole world.

In Thibet, the Lamaist Sceptre, or Dorje, the thunderbolt of Indra, is greatly valued as a Talisman (see Illustration No. 26, Plate II). This symbol is prized as a Talisman against Demons, and to bring fruitfulness. Indra, as the deity of the atmosphere, governs the weather and dispenses the rain, sending forth lightnings and thunder against Ahi the demon of drought, whom he overcomes with his thunderbolt, compelling him to pour down the fertilising showers.

Knots are used in India and Thibet as Talismans for Longevity and to avert the Evil Eye (see Illustration No. 27, Plate II), the Knot being considered potent to bind that which is good and precious, and to prove an obstacle or hindrance to that which is evil; for instance, at the time of marriage knots are lucky, and the ceremonies connected with a Chinese marriage include knotted red and green ribbons, which are held by the newly wedded pair, the bride holding the green ribbon whilst the bridegroom seizes the red; and in our own country the true-lover's knot is frequently used in the decoration of the wedding dress; but at childbirth and death, there must be no knots about the person to hamper the coming or going of the spirit.

Chinese Talismans. The origin of the ancient religion of China is unknown, and the faith has been handed down from generation to generation from periods many centuries B.C. It is based on the belief that the Universe was ruled by Divinities arranged in three groups, one ruling the heavens, the second the earth, (having dominion over mountains,) streams, and vegetation, and the third ruling the affairs of mankind. Illustration No. 21, Plate I is a Talisman that had its origin at this period, and was given to the Emperor Fu-hsi, the founder of the Chinese Empire, by a mystical dragon horse which rose from the waters of the Yellow River about 2800 B.C. These Trigrams, known as Pa-kwa, formed the basis of the written characters introduced by this wise Emperor. They are familiar to all Chinese, being worn as a Talisman for long life and to ward off evil influences. The Talisman is made of all sizes and shapes, from large ones on boards, one or two feet square, down to tiny medals for personal wear, no larger than a sixpence. It is also frequently used in circular form, as shown in the central part of the Bat Talisman (No. 20, Plate I), and is known as Tho, the symbol of longevity. The Pa-kwa Trigrams are based upon the ancient theory of the Yang Yin, or two first causes, indicated by the circular figure divided by a spiral line in the centre of the Talisman into two equal gadroons, which represent the Creative principle in its masculine and feminine manifestations; the active principle being Yang, and the passive Yin. This symbol also represents Heaven and Earth, Sun and Moon, Light and Darkness, and everything that is in contrast, or positive and negative.

The whole lines in the figures are described as strong in contrast to the short-divided lines, which are weak, the whole representing the two forms of subtle matter which forms the composition of all things. This Talisman is also a favourite in Japan and Thibet.

Confucianism, advocating the fulfilment of all duties to the utmost of one's power, in accordance with the position in life, socially and officially, ranging from the love of the child for his father to the Emperor's responsibility for his people's welfare, is still firmly believed in at the present time; and the Talisman of the five bats, the Weefuh, is for the five great happinesses that all men desire, Luck, Wealth, Longevity, Health, and Peace. The five bats are frequently used alone, but sometimes, as in Illustration No. 20, Plate I, the Trigrams, or some other symbol, is used in conjunction.

Two Bats signify good wishes; a Goose is depicted as a Talisman for domestic felicity, and a Deer for success and honour in study; a Stork, or Pine Tree, and a fabulous Peach which takes a thousand years in ripening, for longevity and good fortune. Another graceful way of wishing a guest good luck is to depict one of these symbols, or a lucky sentence, at the bottom of his tea-cup, such as "May your happiness know no bounds," enclosed by a border of the five bats.

The Phoenix, like the bird Feng, is a mystical bird said to live 500 or 600 years and then to build for itself in the desert a funeral pyre of dried grasses and sweet spices. To this it sets fire by fluttering its wings whilst hovering over it, is then consumed, but from the ashes it rises again renewed in youth and in its gorgeous plumage; an idea appropriated by old-established fire insurance offices, the symbol of which is familiar to all.

The Phoenix is believed by the Chinese to uphold their Empire and preside over its destiny; it is also worn as a Talisman for Longevity and Conjugal Happiness; whilst in the mystic sense it typifies the- whole world, its head the heavens, its eyes the Sun, its beak the Moon, its wings the wind, its feet the earth, and its tail the trees and plants.

To the Japanese the Phoenix, or ho-wo bird, is a Talisman for Rectitude, Obedience, Fidelity, Justice, and Benevolence, and they consider it a manifestation of the Sun, its appearance on earth being considered a portent of great events. The torii, a kind of gate elaborately carved and decorated at the entrances of Shinto temples, is erected for the Phoenix to perch upon should it visit the earth (see Illustration No. 40, Plate III). This fabled bird has also played a conspicuous part in British and foreign heraldry.

The Dragon is symbolical of everything imposing and terrible, and forms the Imperial coat-of-arms; the Emperor's throne being called the Dragon One.

There are three forms of Dragon—the "Lung," or sky dragon, the "Li," which lives in the sea, and the "Kiao," which inhabits the marshes. The dragon is worn for Longevity and Domestic Felicity (see Illustration No. 38, Plate III).

The type of the Dragon was thought to have been the boa-constrictor, until the researches of geology brought to light in the iguanodon such a near counterpart of the dragon that this is now regarded as more probably its prototype. The Lung is represented as a dragon-headed horse which carries on its back the book of the Law. It is very popular in Thibet, where it is known as the Wind Horse; but the Lamas have substituted for the book of the Law the emblems of the three gems (see Illustration No. 31, "Plate II"}), which include the Buddhist Law, and is thus worn by the Thibetans to bring material gain, wealth, and good luck; in this form it is painted on luck-bringing flags, which are hung from the ridges of the houses and in the vicinity of dwellings. The all-potent horse-shoe is not used by the Chinese, but the hoof of a horse has to them the same preservative virtue as the horse-shoe with us. Another charm extensively used in China amongst women, is a small gold or silver triangle bearing two swords suspended from the outer angles, and a trident from the centre of the base; on the triangles lucky characters frequently appear (see Illustration No. 39, Plate III). This is undoubtedly an imported Hindu Talisman of Siva, who is regarded as the Regenerator and Controller of reproductive power; and in addition to the acquirement of these qualities, this Talisman is worn for protection against Ghosts and Goblins who are under the control of Siva, and written charms of triangular shape are frequently made for this purpose.

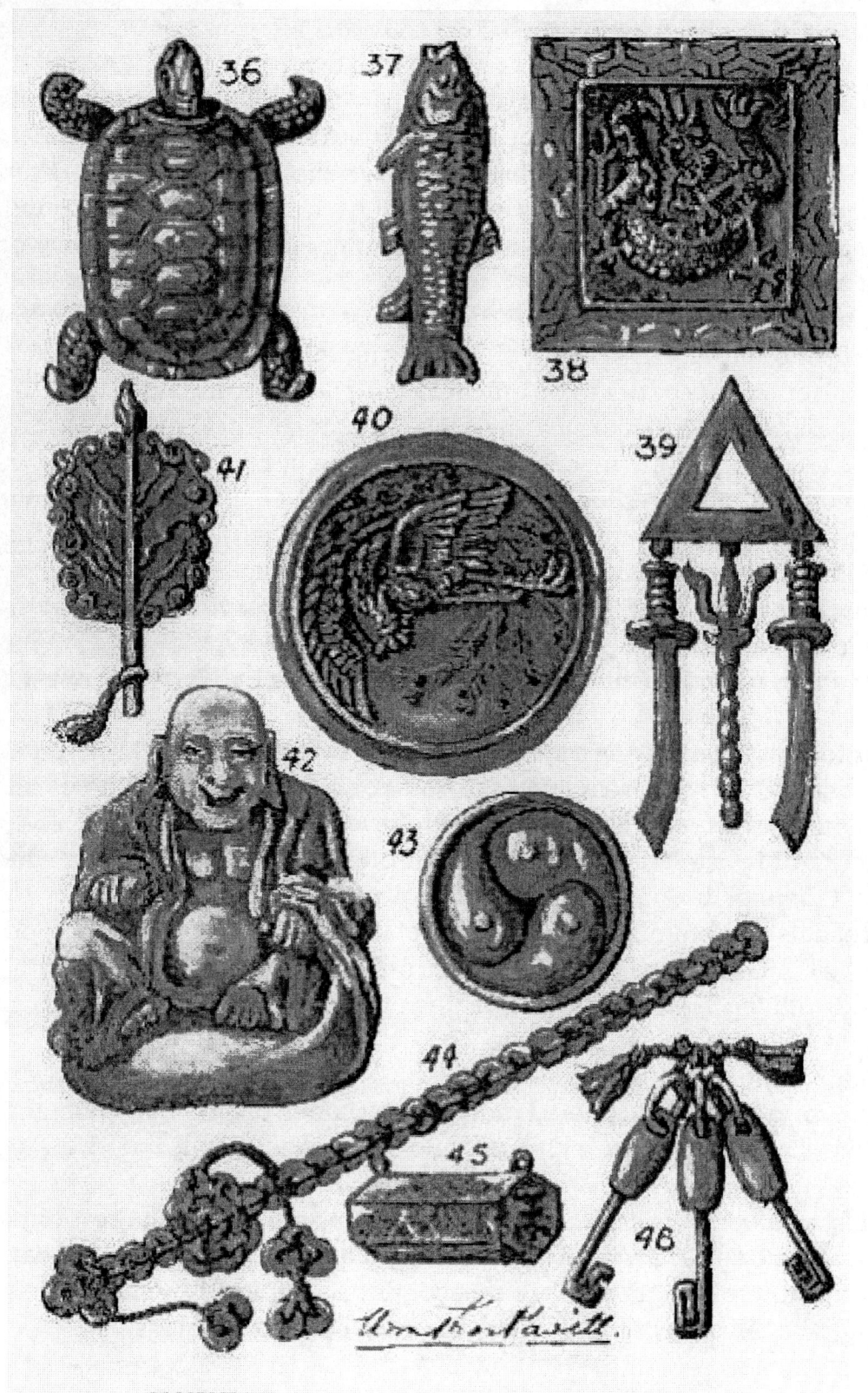

THE COMPLETE BOOK OF TALISMANS, AMULETS AND MAGIC GEMSTONES

CHINESE AND JAPANESE TALISMANS.

Plate 3.

PLATE 3. CHINESE AND JAPANESE TALISMANS

The Money Sword is regarded as all-powerful against ill-luck to the house and against the machinations of evil spirits, and it attracts cash to its fortunate possessor when suspended from right to left above the head of his bed. This Cash Sword is composed of two iron rods along which a quantity of coins, having holes in the centre, are tied with red silk, making a potent charm which is very popular (see Illustration No. 44, Plate III).

For talismanic purposes, Red is indispensable in China. It is interwoven with the pig-tail, and must form a part of children's clothing. Written charms must also be in red ink on yellow paper to be efficacious against the multitudinous ill-omens and evil spirits which seem to surround the Chinaman, and for this reason all Imperial decrees are written in vermilion. One of the commonest amulets worn by an only son is a small silver lock (see Illustration No. 45, Plate III). The father collects coins from about a hundred different heads of families and has them exchanged for silver, which is converted into a native padlock used to fasten a silver chain round the boy's neck; this it is believed will preserve him from evil spirits, lock him to life, and contribute to his health and longevity.

Bells are also worn by Chinese children to avert the Evil Eye and preserve the teeth.

The Tortoise is regarded as a symbol of the Universe in China, Japan, and India, its dome-shaped back representing the vault of the sky, its belly the earth which moves upon the waters, whilst the great age to which it attains and the endurance and strength of its shell make it a fitting emblem of the longevity for which it is worn as a Talisman. It also repels black magic.

It represents the feminine principle in Nature and, as such, it penetrated to the West, so that in Greek and Roman art Aphrodite and Venus are frequently found associated with the Tortoise, whose virtues or gifts were said by Pliny to number sixty-six (see Illustration No. 36, Plate III).

The Tiger is the god of the gambler in China, and a tiger's tooth is regarded as a Talisman for good luck in speculation and in games of chance; whilst the claws and whiskers are worn as love charms, and for success and good fortune generally.

Pigs are also considered lucky; and luck-bringers in the shape of little pigs made of gold and silk are worn to attract fortune's favours, but the black cat, which in our own country is regarded as a mascot, is not favoured by the Chinese, who believe it to be a harbinger of poverty, misfortune, and sickness.

CHAPTER V

The Pear Charm—"Show Fu"—Jade—The Blue Gown for Longevity—Japanese—The Tiger—Wolf—Fox—The Thunder, Fire, and Echo—The Fan of Power—Hotei, the God of Contentment—The Eagle—The Millet Dumpling—Carp—Sacred Dog—Stork—Tortoise—Crane—Child's Hand—Mitsu-Domoe—Hammer of Daikoku—The Keys—Anchor—Crystal Ball—Leaf Talisman—Ota-fu-ku—Bow—Temple at Ise.

A Personal charm, the efficacy of which depends entirely on the merits of its owner, consists of five thousand open dots arranged in the shape of a pear on a piece of paper; each dot being filled up when some good action is performed. There is a standard of value for each meritorious action; he who is able to claim credit for repairing a road, building a bridge, or digging a well, may fill up ten dots on his paper, whilst the cure of a disease, or to give enough money to purchase a grave counts thirty dots. To be the originator of a scheme of mutual benefit to all allows fifty dots to be filled up.

There is a debit as well as a credit side to this charm, and, therefore, he who reproves another unjustly has to fill up three extra dots; and the levelling of a tomb, which is a serious offence, adds fifty dots more to the account. At the end of the year the account is balanced, and all outstanding dots are settled by fasting and charitable deeds. When all the dots have been duly filled up the paper is burnt, so that the record may pass to the other world and be placed to its owner's credit.

All through life the Chinaman regards himself as surrounded by demons, to combat whom innumerable charms and amulets are necessary. A favourite charm to keep evil spirits from crossing the threshold is a leaf of the Sweet Flag (Acorus gramineus), or Artemisia, nailed on either side of the doorway; always providing that the leaf is placed in position early in the morning of the fifth Moon. The Chinese New Year starts when the Sun and Moon are in conjunction, in Aquarius, so that the fifth Moon would be at the time of the conjunction in Gemini.

Another household charm is to write "Show Fu" (long life and happiness) in red on a piece of paper and to fix it opposite, or upon the door, to ensure prosperity and good fortune.

THE COMPLETE BOOK OF TALISMANS, AMULETS AND MAGIC GEMSTONES

Jade has always been prized by the Chinese for its talismanic virtues, and is used extensively in various forms for personal adornment, particularly as a wristlet to give physical strength and protect from all ills.

Kwan Chung, writing in the seventh century B.C., relates that a piece of Jade symbolises to the Chinese nine of the highest attainments of Man—

"In its smoothness he recognises Benevolence,
 In its high polish—Knowledge Emblematic,
 In its unbending firmness—Righteousness,
 In its modest harmlessness—Virtuous Actions.
 In its rarity and spotlessness—Purity,
 In the way it exposes every flaw—Ingenuousness,
 In that it passes from hand to hand without being sullied—Moral Conduct,
 And in that when struck it gives forth a sweet note which floats sharply and distinctly to a distance—Music."

It is for these qualities that the Chinaman regards Jade as the most precious of his possessions, both as a diviner of judgments and as a valued charm of happy omen.

As a birthday gift to parents a long silken gown of the deepest blue is frequently presented as a Talisman for longevity. In reality it is the shroud which, sooner or later, will be worn by its owner to the grave; but, as a man is thought by the Chinese to lay in a large stock of renewed vital energy on his birthday, it is considered a fitting robe for that occasion, being made by young unmarried girls with a long life (it is presumed) before them. In a year which has an intercalary month, its capacity for prolonging life is considered to be of unusually high degree; moreover, it is embroidered all over with the word "longevity" in thread of gold, the influence of this word being, it is believed, absorbed into the being of its wearer, so that he may enjoy plenty of health and vigour and prolong his life. It is considered an act of the utmost piety to present one of these garments to an aged parent or relative who, decked in this gorgeous shroud, receives the congratulations of children and friends on festive occasions.

Japanese. Buddhism when it came to Japan about the sixth century was readily accepted and allowed to establish itself side by side with Shinto beliefs. A good many of its tenets and symbols having been adopted and being still in use at the present time, Buddhist Talismans similar to those worn in India and China are prevalent, the god Fulgen being regarded as an incarnation of Buddha. The Shintos believe their country was the birthplace of the Sun Goddess, whose descendants they are, being also predestined to rule the country for ever and ever; thus it is that ancestor-worship forms the basis of Shinto beliefs. The country, it is believed, was in the first place begotten by two gods, whose actions and impulses it is considered impossible for man with his limited intelligence to judge.

There are numerous deities of Heaven and Earth, typifying human beings of high degree, all brave men who are dead, or impressive formations of Nature, such as the Sea, Mountains, Trees; also, by reason of something strange, fearful, or wonderful in their nature, certain animals, the Tiger, the Wolf, and Fox; and all forces that manifest in the elements, such as Thunder, the Echo, Fire; in fact all things strange and wonderful are deified under the name Kami, and have shrines dedicated to their worship or are used in various forms as Talismans.

The Japanese believe that errors are the result of human weaknesses, and can be expiated, or forgiven, and that the steadfast following of the path of truth will win the approval of the gods, and bring them finally to eternal life and the companionship of their beloved dead. The female element is considered equal with the male, and occupies a very high rank in the Shinto system in contrast to China, where women have no status.

Fu-ku-ro-ku-jiu, the god of Fortune and Wisdom, Fu-ku, Luck and Happiness,
Ro-ku, Wealth and Prosperity,
Jiu, Longevity, represented by a long-headed man with a staff, attended by a Crane (sometimes he has the Fan of Power in one hand and a scroll in the other), and is valued as a Talisman for the qualities he represents;
Ebisu, the god of Plenty, the giver of daily food; and the household god
Daikoku, the god of Love,
Benzaiben, the god of Grace and Beauty,
Bishamon, the god of Glory, with the Spear of Power in his right hand, and in his left the Pagoda for Inspiration and Hope;
Benton, who gives fruitfulness to women, and
Hotei, the god of Contentment and Good Fortune

are all Talismans for the virtues which they express.

Hotei (Illustration No. 42, Plate III), the children's god, bringing happiness and good fortune, is found in every household; he is represented seated on his bag, which is well-filled with the good things he dispenses, his corpulent figure denoting his high attainment and personal importance.

The Eagle, because of his courage, fearlessness, tenacity, and aggressiveness, is worn as a Talisman for good fortune, and Captain Brinkley, in his book Japan and China, says:

"In November tens of thousands flock to the Eagle shrine to purchase harbingers of luck in the shape of big rakes, parent potatoes, and Millet dumplings. The Rake, as part of the paraphernalia of the pursuer of gain, explains itself; the parent potato denotes humble ambition, buried in the ground and grown in oblivion is at any rate the parent of a family. Millet dumplings are associated with the orthodox group of lucky articles by a play upon words—'to clutch Millet with wet hands' is a popular metaphor for greed; Mochi, which signifies a dumpling, therefore, signifies grasping largely and holding firmly."

The Dumpling is also regarded as a charm against the perils of wave and flood, it being the sacred bread of the Nation, and in its circular shape is the symbol of the Sun.

The Carp (Illustration No. 37, Plate III) is worn as a Talisman for endurance and pluck, because according to an old legend a Carp by the exercise of these virtues succeeded in leaping all cataracts, and in finally reaching the Chariot Cloud, which carried him to Heaven and eternal happiness. On all festival days, the Carp plays a very important part as a symbol of good fortune, and it is customary on these occasions to send up large fish-shaped kites, one for each son, the Carp being essentially a masculine Talisman.

As in China, Talismans frequently consist of inscriptions on paper, invocations to one or other of the gods for success and good fortune, the symbol of the god being used according to the purpose of the Talisman. The sacred dog of Mitsumine is used as a protection from robbers, the god Jurojin, the Stork, the Tortoise, or the Crane for health and longevity.

A very popular charm for the latter purpose is the impression of a child's hand made by inking the hand, which is then pressed on to a piece of paper. These paper Talismans are pasted up both inside and outside the house and are considered to avert all evil influences.

In Tokio a popular charm consists of a thin piece of wood on which is written the name of the famous shrine Narita; this is worn as a luck-bringer, and for protection from all dangers.

Symbols of the Houses of the Zodiac are also used as Talismans, worked in metal varying according to the House occupied by the Sun at the time of birth.

A very important Talisman is the symbol Mitsu-Domoe, the triple form of the source of life, representing the elements of Fire, Air, and Water. It is worn to protect the household and person from Fire, Flood, and Theft (see Illustration No. 43, Plate III). This diagram is considered to symbolise ceaseless change, and is said by some authorities to have had its. origin in a three-limbed Swastika Cross.

The Fan, which is regarded as an emblem of Power and Authority, is .a Talisman to ensure the safety of its wearers (Illustration No. 41, Plate III).

The Hammer of Daikoku, the god of Wealth, is worn for success and good fortune.

Illustration No. 46 represents the Keys of the Granary, or storehouse, which are worn for love, wealth, and happiness.

The Anchor is worn for security and safety.

Rock Crystal Balls, mounted as charms, are worn as a preventative of dropsy and other wasting diseases.

A charm popular with travellers is the leaf of the Teg-a-shiwa; the Japanese say that the movements of this leaf in the wind resemble the beckoning of a hand. When a relative is about to start on a journey he is served with a meal of fish on one of these leaves in lieu of a plate; when the meal is finished the leaf is hung over the door in the belief that it will ensure well-being on his journey and a safe return.

A Talisman for luck and good fortune is a representation of Ota-fu-ku, the joyful goddess, who is depicted with a chubby laughing face which is painted on purses and little gifts exchanged between friends, and it is thought that to look upon her face will bring prosperity, joy, and good fortune.

At the New Year it is customary to hang a rope before dwellings, in front of shrines, or to suspend it across the road to thwart evil spirits and avert ill-luck; it is called Shinenaka, and is made of rice-straw plucked up by the roots, the ends being allowed to dangle down at regular intervals.

To protect the house from demons, and to keep its occupants secure, a bow is fixed to the roof ridge, and if tiles are used impressed with an ornament like bubbles an efficient Talisman for protection against fire is obtained. The Japanese believe that the materials, principally wood, of which their temples are made become impregnated with favourable influences, as the result of the services that are held in them, and as these temples are entirely pulled down every twenty years there is a great demand for the old wood, from which Talismans are made.

One of the most ancient temples is at Ise, where a shrine has been in existence many hundreds of years B.C., and when this temple is broken up thousands of pilgrims assemble to secure fragments of its precious wood.

The temple is rebuilt of new wood exactly on the lines of the old one.

CHAPTER VI
Egyptian Beliefs—Crux Ansata—The Menat—The Two Plumes—The Single Plume—The Nefer—The Cartouche—The Angles and Plummet—The God Bes—Aper—The Tat—The Heart.

Of all civilisations known to us through history, that of ancient Egypt is the most marvellous, most fascinating, and most rich in occult significance; yet we have still much to discover, and although we have the assurance of Herodotus that the Egyptians were "beyond measure scrupulous in all matters appertaining to religion," the ancient religions—or such fragments as survive—appear at first glance confusing and even grotesque. It is necessary to remember that there was an inner as well as an outer theology, and that the occult mysteries were accessible only to those valiant and strenuous initiates who had successfully passed through a prolonged purification and course of preparation austere and difficult enough to discourage all save the most persistent and exalted spirits.

It is only available to us to wander on the outskirts of Egyptian mythology. The most familiar symbolic figures are those of Isis the Moon goddess, traditional Queen of Egypt, and Osiris her husband; and when we read that Isis was the sister, wife, and mother of Osiris we must seek the inner meaning of the strange and impossible relationship. It has been lucidly explained by Princess Karadja (in her King Solomon: a Mystic Drama, 1912, pp. 130-31):

"Originally the dual souls are part of the same Divine Ego. They are golden fruits upon the great Tree of Life: 'male and female He created them.'

Isis is the Sister of Osiris because she is of Divine origin like himself, and is a spirit of equal rank.

She is his Wife, because she alone can fill his highest cravings.

She is his Mother because it is the mission of Woman to restore Man unto spiritual life."

How Osiris was slain by his brother Typhon (or Set), the Spirit of Evil, and dismembered into fourteen fragments which were scattered and hidden by the destroyer; how Isis, widowed and broken-hearted, sought patiently until she found each fragment, and how Horus her son when he grew to manhood challenged and conquered Typhon,—all this is the figurative rendering of the eternal battle between light and darkness.

Typhon or Set symbolises autumn, decay, and destruction; Osiris springtime, light, and the fertilising and growing powers of nature. Isis is typified in many forms, but was especially revered as the goddess of procreation, Universal Mother of the living, and protectress of the spirits of the dead. Her symbol was the cow, and she is usually depicted wearing cow's horns, and between them the orb of the moon.

But more ancient and more exalted than Osiris was Ra, the Sun god, whose worship was blended with that of Isis and her husband and son. The priests of Ra established a famous temple at Heliopolis, and founded a special system of solar worship. Just as the Emperor Constantine subsequently fixed as saints' days in the Christian Church the days which had been dedicated to the ancient pagan gods, so the priests of Ra adapted their cult to the tastes and notions of the people, and a whole company of subordinate gods figured in the religions of Lower Egypt for many centuries. Sometimes divine virtues were portrayed in very material forms.

Between 4000 and 2000 B.C. the worship of Amen, or Amen Ra, as the greatest god of the Egyptians, was established at Thebes, which became the centre of religious teaching. The priests grew more and more powerful until finally the High Priest of Amen—whose name means the "hidden one"—became the King of Upper Egypt. Amen was regarded as the Creator, with all the power and attributes of Ra the Sun god, and as ruler of the lesser gods.

It has been asked why the Egyptians, who had no belief in a material resurrection, took such infinite trouble to preserve the bodies of their dead. They looked forward to a paradise in which eternal life would be the reward of the righteous, and their creed inculcated faith in the existence of a spiritual body to be inhabited by the soul which had ended its earthly pilgrimage; but such beliefs do not explain the care and attention bestowed upon the lifeless corpse. The explanation must be sought in the famous Book of the Dead, representing the convictions which prevailed throughout the whole of the Egyptian civilisation from pre-dynastic times. Briefly, the answer to our question is this: there was a Ka or double, in which the Heart-Soul was located; this Ka, equivalent to the astral body of modern occultists, was believed to be able to come into touch with material things through the preserved or mummified body. This theory accords with the axiom that each atom of physical substance has its relative equivalent on the astral plane. It will therefore be understood how, in the ancient religions, the image of a god was regarded as a medium through which his powers could be manifested. "As above, so below"; every living thing possessed some divine attribute.

Faith in prayer was an essential article of the Egyptian religion, and the spoken word of a priest was believed to have strong potency, because it had been the words of Ra uttered by Thoth which brought the universe into being. Amulets inscribed with words were consequently thought to ensure the fulfilment of the blessing expressed, or the granting of the bliss desired.

The Book of the Dead was not only a guide to the life hereafter, wherein they would join their friends in the realms of eternal bliss, but gave detailed particulars of the necessary knowledge, actions, and conduct during the earthly life to ensure a future existence in the spirit world, where everlasting life was the reward of the good and annihilation the fate of the wicked, thus showing that the belief in the existence of a future life was ever before them. Various qualities, though primarily considered a manifestation of the Almighty, were attributed each to a special god who controlled and typified one particular virtue. This partly accounts for the multiplied numbers of the Egyptian gods, and with the further complications that resulted from invasions and the adoption of alien beliefs, the religious philosophy of Egypt is not easy to follow, and is often seemingly contradictory; but when we take into consideration the vast period during which this Empire flourished it is natural that the external manifestations of faith should have varied as time went on.

A knowledge of the life, death, and resurrection of Osiris is assumed, and his worship in association with Isis and Horus, although not necessarily under these names, is continuous. Horus is frequently alluded to as the god of the ladder, and the mystic ladder seen by Jacob in his vision, and the ladder of seven steps known to the initiates of Egypt, Greece, Mexico, India, and Persia will be familiar to all students of occultism.

Throughout the whole of the Egyptian civilisation, which lasted for at least 6000 years, the influence and potency of Amulets, and Talismans, was recognised in the religious services, each Talisman and Amulet having a specified virtue.

Certain Amulets not only were worn during life, but were even attached to the dead body. They are described in the following notes:

The Crux Ansata, or Ankh (see Illustrations Nos. 47, 48, 49, Plate IV), was known as the symbol of life, the loop at the top of the Cross consisting of the hieroglyphic Ru (O) set in an upright form, meaning the gateway, or mouth, the creative power being signified by the loop which represents a fish's mouth giving birth to water as the life of the country, bringing the inundations and renewal of the fruitfulness of the earth to those who depended upon its increase to maintain life. It was regarded as the key of the Nile which overflowed periodically and so fertilised the land.

THE COMPLETE BOOK OF TALISMANS, AMULETS AND MAGIC GEMSTONES

EGYPTIAN TALISMANS.

PLATE 4.

THE COMPLETE BOOK OF TALISMANS, AMULETS AND MAGIC GEMSTONES

PLATE 4. EGYPTIAN TALISMANS.

It was also shown in the hands of the Egyptian kings, at whose coronations it played an important part, and the gods are invariably depicted holding this symbol of creative power; it was also worn to bring knowledge, power, and abundance. Again, it had reference to the spiritual life, for it was from the Crux Ansata, or Ankh, that the symbol of Venus originated, the Circle over the Cross being the triumph of Spirit, represented by the Circle, over matter, shown by the Cross.

The Menat (Illustrations Nos. 50, 53, Plate IV) were specially dedicated to Hathor, who was a type of Isis, and was worn for conjugal happiness, as it gave power and strength to the organs of reproduction, promoting health and fruitfulness. It frequently formed a part of a necklace, and was elaborately ornamented; No. 50, from the British Museum, is a good specimen, the Cow being an emblem of the maternal qualities which were the attributes of the goddess, who stood for all that is good and true in Wife, Mother, and Daughter.

The Two Plumes (Illustration No. 51, Plate IV) are Sun Amulets and the symbols of Ra and Thoth, the two feathers being typical of the two lives, spiritual and material. This was worn to promote Uprightness in dealing, Enlightenment, and Morality, being symbolical of the great gods of Light and Air.

The Single Plume (Illustration No. 52, Plate IV) was an emblem of Maat, the female counterpart of Thoth, who wears on her head the feather characteristic of the phonetic value of her name; she was the personification of Integrity, Righteousness, and Truth. Illustrations Nos. 54, 55, 56, Plate IV, show three forms of The Nefer, a symbol of Good Luck, worn to attract Success, Happiness, Vitality, and Friends.

The Cartouche, or Name Amulet (Illustration No. 61, Plate IV), was worn to secure Favour, Recognition, and Remembrance, and to prevent the name of its wearer being blotted out in the next world. This is a very important Amulet, as the name was believed to be an integral part of the man, without which his soul could not come before God, so that it was most essential that the name should be preserved, in order, as described in the Book of the Dead, "thou shalt never perish, thou shalt never, never come to an end," the loss of the name meaning the total annihilation of the individual.

The Amulets of The Angles (see Illustrations Nos. 58, 59, Plate IV) and The Plummet (No. 60 on the same Plate) were symbols of the god Thoth, and were worn for Moral Integrity, Wisdom, Knowledge, Order, and Truth.

Thoth was the personification of Law and Order, being the god who worked out the Creation as decreed by the god Ra. He knew all the words of power and the secrets of all hearts, and may be regarded as the chief recording angel; he was also the inventor of all arts and sciences.

Bes, shown in Illustration No. 57, Plate IV, was a very popular Talisman, being the god of Laughter, Merry-making, and Good Luck; by some authorities he is considered to be a foreign importation from pre-dynastic times, and he has been identified with Horus and regarded as the god who renewed youth. He was also the patron of beauty, the protector of children, and was undoubtedly the progenitor of the modern Billiken.

Illustrations Nos. 62, 66, Plate V, are examples of The Aper, which symbolised Providence and was worn for Steadfastness, Stability, and Alertness.

The Tat (Illustrations Nos. 63, 64, 65, Plate V) held a very important place in the religious services of the Egyptians, and formed the centre of the annual ceremony of the setting-up of the Tat, a service held to commemorate the death and resurrection of Osiris, this symbol representing the building-up of the backbone and reconstruction of the body of Osiris. In their services the Egyptians associated themselves with Osiris, through whose sufferings and death they hoped to rise glorified and immortal, and secure Everlasting Happiness. The four cross-bars symbolise the four cardinal points, and the four elements of Earth, Air, Fire, and Water, and were often very elaborately ornamented (see Illustration No. 64, Plate V, taken from an example at the British Museum). It was worn as a Talisman for Stability and Strength, and for Protection from enemies; also that all doors, (or opportunities,) might be open both in this life and the next. Moreover, a Tat of gold set in sycamore wood, which had been steeped in the water of Ankham flowers, was placed at the neck of the deceased on the day of interment, to protect him on his journey through the underworld and assist him in triumphing over his foes, that he might become perfect for ever and ever.

The Heart was believed to be the seat of the Soul, and Illustrations Nos. 67, 68, 69, Plate V, are examples of these Talismans worn to prevent black magicians from bewitching the Soul out of the body. The importance of these charms will be realised from the belief that if the Soul left the Heart, the Body would quickly fade away and die. According to Egyptian lore at the judgment of the dead the Heart is weighed, when if found perfect, it is returned to its owner, who immediately recovers his powers of locomotion and becomes his own master, with strength in his limbs and everlasting felicity in his soul.

THE COMPLETE BOOK OF TALISMANS, AMULETS AND MAGIC GEMSTONES

CHAPTER VII

The Buckle of the Girdle of Isis—The Scarab—The Eye of Osiris—The Two Fingers—The Collar—The Hawk—The Sma—The Ladder and Steps—The Snake's Head—The Serpent—The Sun's Disc—The Frog—The Fish—The Vulture—The Sa, or Tie.

The Buckle of the Girdle of Isis was worn to obtain the Good Will and Protection of this goddess, and symbolised "the blood of Isis" and her strength and power. Frequently made of Carnelian it was believed to protect its wearer from every kind of evil; also to secure the good will of Horus; and, when placed like the golden Tat at the neck of the dead on the day of the funeral in the soul's journey through the under-world it opened up all hidden places and procured the favour of Isis and her son, Horus, for ever and ever (see Illustrations Nos. 71, 72, 73, Plate V).

The Tie, or Sa (Illustration No. 70, Plate V) is the symbol of Ta-urt, the Hippopotamus-headed goddess, who was associated with the god Thoth, the personification of Divine Intelligence and Human Reason; it was worn for magical protection.

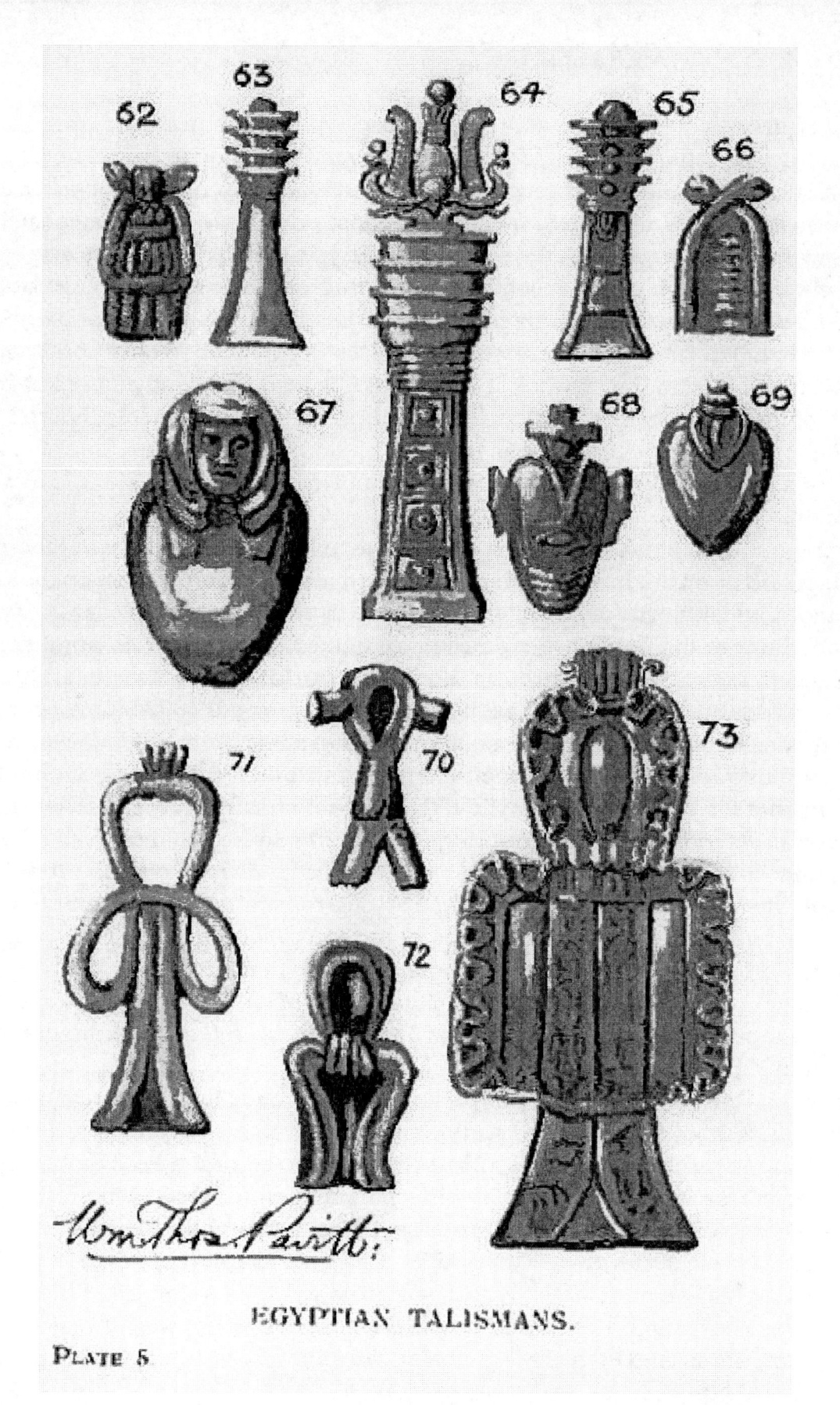

THE COMPLETE BOOK OF TALISMANS, AMULETS AND MAGIC GEMSTONES

EGYPTIAN TALISMANS.

PLATE 5

PLATE 5. EGYPTIAN TALISMANS.

The Scarab was the symbol of Khepera, a form of the Sun god who transforms inert matter into action, creates life, and typifies the glorified spiritual body that man shall possess at the resurrection. From the enormous number of Scarabs that have been found, this must have formed the most popular of the Talismans. The symbol was derived from a Beetle, common in Egypt, which deposits its eggs in a ball of clay, the action of the insect in rolling this ball along the ground being compared with the Sun itself in its progress across the sky; and as the ball contained the living germ which, (under the heat of the Sun,) hatched out into a Beetle, so the Scarab became the symbol of Creation. It is also frequently seen holding the disc of the Sun between its claws, with wings extended, and it is thought by some authorities that the Scarab was taken as an emblem of the Sun, because the burial of its ball was symbolic of the setting sun from which new life arises with each dawn.

Scarabs of green stones with rims of gold were buried in the heart of the deceased, or laid upon the breast, with a written prayer for his protection on the Day of Judgment, whilst words of power were frequently recited over the Scarab which was placed under the coffin as an emblem of immortality so that no fiend could harm the dead in his journey through the under-world. It is said the Scarab was associated with burial as far back as the IVth dynasty (about 4600 B.C.); it represented matter about to pass from a state of inertness into active life, so was considered a fitting emblem of resurrection and immortality, typifying not only the Sun's disc, but the evolutions of the Soul throughout eternity. It was also worn by the Egyptian warriors in their signet rings for Health, Strength, and Virility, it being thought that this species of Beetle was all males, so that it would attract all manly qualities, both of mind and body. For this reason it was very popular as presents between friends, many scarabs being found with good wishes or mottoes engraved on the under side, and some of the kings used the back of scarabs to commemorate historical events; one in the British Museum records the slaughter of 102 fierce lions by Amenhetep III, with his own hand (see Illustrations Nos. 74, 75, Plate VI).

Next to the Scarab, the ancient Egyptians attached much importance to the Eye Amulet, which, from the earliest Astral Mythology, was first represented by the point within the circle and was associated with the god of the Pole Star, which, from its fixity, was taken as a type of the Eternal, unchangeable as time rolled on, and thus a fitting emblem of Fixity of Purpose, Poise, and Stability. Later it was one of the hieroglyphic signs of the Sun god Ra, and represented the One Supreme Power casting his Eye over all the world, and instead of the point within the circle is sometimes represented as a widely open Eye. This symbol was also assigned to Osiris, Isis, Horus, and Ptah; the Amulet known as the Eye of Osiris being placed

THE COMPLETE BOOK OF TALISMANS, AMULETS AND MAGIC GEMSTONES

upon the incision made in the side of the body (for the purpose of embalming) to watch over and guard the soul of the deceased during its passing through the darkness of the tomb to the life beyond.

It was also worn by the living to ensure Health and Protection from the blighting influence of workers in black magic, and for the stability, strength, and courage of Horus, the wisdom and understanding of Ptah, and the foresight of Isis.

It was also extensively used in necklaces on account of the idea that representations of the Eye itself would watch over and guard its wearer from the malignant glances of the envious, it being universally believed that the fiery sparks of jealousy, hatred, and malice darting from the eyes of angry persons, envious of the good looks, health, and success of the fortunate ones, could so poison the surrounding atmosphere as even to cause sickness, decay, and death; horses were thought particularly liable to this injurious influence, and Talismans to avert such a misfortune to them were hung on their foreheads, or over the left eye.

Examples of Eye Amulets are illustrated on Plate VI, Nos. 79, 80, and 81.

'When two eyes are used together the right eye is symbolic of Ra, or Osiris and the Sun; whilst the left eye represents Isis, or the Moon, and is sometimes called the Amulet of the two Utchats: the word Utchat, signifying "strength," being applied to the Sun when he enters the summer solstice about June 22nd, his strength and power on earth being greatest at that time.

The Talisman of the Two Fingers (Illustration No. 82, Plate VI) was symbolical of Help, Assistance, and Benediction, typified by the two fingers extended by Horus to assist his father in mounting the ladder suspended between this world and the next. This Amulet was frequently placed in the interior of the mummified body to enable the departed to travel quickly to the regions of the blest. Amongst the ancient Egyptians the fingers were ever considered an emblem of Strength and Power, the raising of the first two fingers being regarded as a sign of Peace and Good Faith; the first finger being the indicator of divine will and justice and the only one that can stand erect by itself alone; the second representing the Holy Spirit, the Mediator, a symbolism handed down to us in the extension of the index and medius in the ecclesiastical benediction. It is also interesting to note that at the marriage ceremony in olden days the ring was first placed on the thumb, as typical of Man's allegiance to God, and lastly on the third finger of his bride to show that next to God in the Trinity, a man's life should be devoted to his wife.

The Collar Amulet (Illustrations Nos. 83, 84, Plate VI) was a symbol of Isis, and was worn to procure her protection and the strength of her son Horus. In both examples the head of the Hawk appears, this bird being attributed to Horus as well as to Ra. This collar, which was made of gold, was engraved with words of power and seems to have been chiefly used as a funeral amulet.

The Sma (Illustration No. 85, Plate VI) was a favourite Amulet from the dawn of Egyptian history, and is frequently used in various forms of decorated art. It was symbolical of Union and Stability of Affection, and was worn to strengthen love and friendship and ensure physical happiness and faithfulness.

The Ladder is a symbol of Horus, and was worn to secure his assistance in overcoming and surmounting difficulties in the material world, as well as to form a connection with the Heaven world, or Land of Light. The earliest traditions place this Heaven world above the earth, its floor being the sky, and to reach this a ladder was deemed necessary. From the Pyramid texts it seems there were two stages of ascent to the upper Paradise, represented by two ladders, one being the ladder of Sut, forming the ladder of ascent from the land of darkness, and the other the ladder of Horus reaching the Land of Light (Illustration No. 86, Plate VI).

The Steps (Illustrations Nos. 87, 88, Plate VI) are a symbol of Osiris, who is described as the god of the staircase, through whom it was hoped the deceased might reach the Heaven world and attain everlasting bliss.

The Snake's Head Talisman (Illustration No. 89, Plate VI) was worn to protect its wearer from the attacks of Rerek, or Apep, the servant of Set, who was typified as a terrible serpent, which when killed had the power of rising in new forms and who obstructed the passage to the Heaven world. The serpent, although sometimes assumed to be a form of evil, was generally regarded as a protecting influence, and for this reason was usually sculptured on either side of the doorways to the tombs of kings, temples, and other sacred buildings to guard the dead from enemies of every kind, and to prevent the entrance of evil in any shape or form. It was also placed round the heads of Divinities and round the crowns of their kings as a symbol of royal might and power, being one of the forms or types of Tern the son of Ptah, who is thought by some authorities to have been the first living man god of the Egyptians, and the god of the setting sun (in contrast to Horus, who was the god of the rising sun) Tern was typified by a huge snake, and it is curious to note in connection with this that amongst country folk at the present day there is a popular belief that a serpent will not die until the sun goes down.

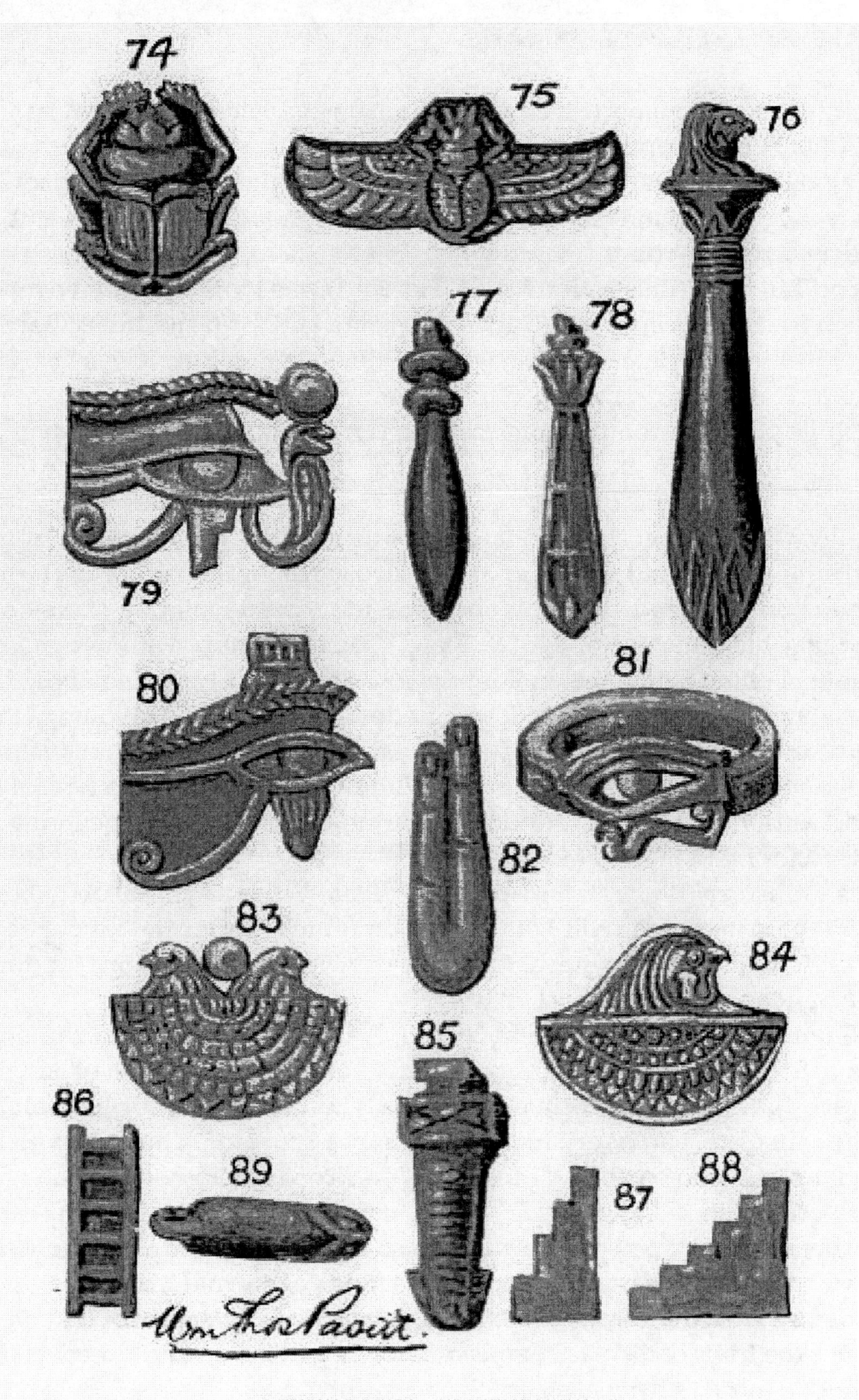

THE COMPLETE BOOK OF TALISMANS, AMULETS AND MAGIC GEMSTONES

EGYPTIAN TALISMANS.

PLATE 6.

PLATE 6. EGYPTIAN TALISMANS.

The Sun's Disc Talismans (Illustrations No. 90, 92, Plate VII) are symbols of the god Ra, No. 92 being appropriately placed upon the head of a Ram, the symbol of the Zodiacal house Aries, in which sign the sun is exalted. It was worn for Power and Renown, and to obtain the favours of the great ones, being also an emblem of new birth and resurrection.

The Frog Talisman (Illustration No. 91, Plate VII) was highly esteemed, and is an attribute of Isis, being worn to attract her favours and for fruitfulness. Because of its fertility its hieroglyphic meaning was an immense number. It was also used as a symbol of Ptah, as it represented life in embryo, and by the growth of its feet after birth it typified strength from weakness, and was worn for recovery from disease, also for Health and Long Life, taking the place sometimes of the Crux Ansata or Ankh, as a symbol of Life.

The Pillow (Illustration No. 93, Plate VII) was used for preservation from sickness and against pain and suffering; it was also worn for the favour of Horus, and was placed with the dead as a protection and to prevent violation of the Tomb.

The Lotus (Illustrations No. 94, 95, Plate VII) is a symbol with two meanings. Emblematical of the Sun in the ancient days of Egypt and typifying Light, Understanding, Fruitfulness, and Plenty, it was believed to bring the favours of the god Ra. Later it is described as "the pure Lily of the Celestial Ocean," the symbol of Isis, who is sometimes alluded to as "the White Virgin." It became typical of Virginity and Purity, and having the double virtue of chastity and fecundity it was alike prized for Maiden- and Motherhood.

The Fish Talisman (Illustrations Nos. 96, 97, Plate VII) is a symbol of Hathor (who controlled the rising of the Nile), as well as an Amulet under the influence of Isis and Horus. It typified the primeval Creative principle and was worn for domestic felicity, Abundance, and general Prosperity.

The Vulture Talisman (Illustration No. 98, Plate VII) was worn to protect from the bites of Scorpions, and to attract Motherly Love and Protection of Isis, who (it was believed) assumed the form of a vulture when searching for her son Horus, who, in her absence, had been stung to death by a Scorpion. Thoth, moved by her lamentations, came to earth and gave her "the Words of Power," which enabled her to restore Horus to life. For this reason, it was thought that this Amulet would endow its wearer with power and wisdom so that he might identify himself with Horus and partake of his good fortune in the fields of eternal bliss.

The Sceptre (Illustrations Nos. 76, 77, 78, Plate VI) is a symbol of Isis, typifying power over the fruits of the earth, and was worn to preserve and renew youth and vigour, and to attract physical strength and virility.

It is, of course, difficult and futile to speculate as to the extent of the influence these Egyptian Amulets and Talismans exercised over this ancient people, but in the light of our present knowledge we feel that the religious symbolism they represented, the conditions under which they were made, the faith in their efficacy, and the invocations and "words of power" which in every case were a most essential part of their mysterious composition makes them by far the most interesting of any yet dealt with.

THE COMPLETE BOOK OF TALISMANS, AMULETS AND MAGIC GEMSTONES

CHAPTER VIII

Gnosticism—Abraxas—Sacred Names—Khnoubis—The Seven Vowels—The Magic Symbols—The Archangels—Lion-headed Serpent—Aum—The Ineffable Name—Horus—Osiris—Isis—Etruscan, Greek, and Roman—The Crescent Symbol—The Horseshoe—Tusk, or Horn—Stable Keys—Amalthaea's Horn, or Cornucopia—Serapis—Bull's Head—Diana—Harpokrates—Anubis—Bellerophon—Salus Ring—Hygiea.

Gnosticism is the name given to a system of religion which carne into existence in the Roman Empire about the time Christianity was established; it was founded on a philosophy known in Asia Minor centuries previously and apparently based upon the Egyptian beliefs, the Zendavesta, Buddhism, and the Kabala, with their conception of the perpetual conflict between good and evil.

The name is derived from the Greek Gnosis, meaning knowledge, and, in brief, the Gnostics' belief was that the intellectual world, with its Spirits, Intelligences, and various Orders of Angels were created by the Almighty, and that the visible matter of creation was an emanation from these powers and forces.

The attributes of the Supreme Being were those of Kabala: Wisdom—Jeh, Prudence—Jehovah, Magnificence—El, Severity—Elohim, Victory and Glory—Zaboath, Empire—Adonai; the Gnostics also took from the Talmud the Planetary Princes and the Angels under them.

Basilides, the Gnostic Priest, taught that God first created (1) Nous, or mind, from this emanated (2) Logos, the Word, from this (3) Phronesis, Intelligence, and from this (4) Sophia, Wisdom, and from this last (5) Dynamis, Strength. The Almighty was known as Abraxas, which signifies in Coptic "the Blessed Name," and was symbolised by a figure, the head of which is that of a Cock, the body that of a man, with serpents forming the legs; in his right hand he holds a whip, and on his left arm is a shield. This Talisman (see Illustrations Nos. 102, 103, Plate VII) is a combination of the five emanations mentioned above: Nous and Logos are expressed by the two serpents, symbols of the inner sense and understanding, the head of the Cock representing Phronesis, for foresight and vigilance; the two arms hold the symbols of Sophia and Dynamis, the Shield of Wisdom and the Whip of

Power, worn for protection from moral and physical ill.

The Gnostics had great faith in the efficacy of sacred names and sigils when engraved on stones as Talismans; also in magical symbols derived principally from the Kabala.

One of the most popular inscriptions was IAW (Jehovah), and in Illustration No. 99, Plate VII, this is shown surrounded by the Serpent KHNOUBIS, taken from the Egyptian philosophy, representing the Creative principles, and was worn for Vitality, Understanding, and Protection. The Seven Greek Vowels (Illustration No. 100, Plate VII) symbolised the seven heavens, or Planets, whose harmony keeps the Universe in existence, each vowel having seven different methods of expression corresponding with a certain Force, the correct utterance of these letters and comprehension of the forces typified being believed to confer supreme power, bringing success in all enterprises and giving complete control over all the powers of darkness.

Illustration No. 101, Plate VII, is an example of the use of the Magic Symbols, the meaning of which has been lost. It is probably a composition of the initial letters of some mystical sigil, enclosed by a serpent and the names of the Archangels Gabriel, Paniel, Ragauel, Thureiel, Souriel, and Michael. It was worn for Health and Success; also for Protection from all evils, and it is cut in an agate and set in a gold mount.

A figure of a serpent with a lion's head, usually surrounded with a halo, was worn to protect its wearer from heart and chest complaints and to drive away demons.

THE COMPLETE BOOK OF TALISMANS, AMULETS AND MAGIC GEMSTONES

EGYPTIAN AND GNOSTIC TALISMANS.

PLATE 7.

PLATE 7. EGYPTIAN AND GNOSTIC TALISMANS.

The mystic Aum, already described in the chapter on Indian Talismans, was also a favourite with the Gnostics, and equally popular was a Talisman composed of the vowels I A U, repeated to make twelve, this number representing the Ineffable Name of God, which, according to the Talmud, was only communicated to the most pious of the priesthood. They also adopted from the Egyptians the following symbols: Horus, usually represented seated on a Lotus, for fertility; Osiris, usually in the form of a mummified figure, for spiritual attainment; and Isis for the qualities mentioned in the previous chapter.

Etruscan, Greek, and Roman. The Etruscans, Greeks, and Romans were all familiar with and great believers in the virtues of Talismans and Amulets, a belief based not only on the symbols of their own faith but largely influenced by the beliefs of the surrounding nations, that of the Egyptians being particularly noticeable. Amongst the earliest and most popular Talismans are many Scarab rings with inscriptions cut in the under sides; these were frequently used as seals.

In the course of the amalgamation of beliefs which took place under the Ptolemies, Isis and Osiris were associated with all kinds of Asiatic and Greek gods; but, as time went on, Isis became the most universal goddess, ruling heaven and earth and all Mankind, her worship quickly spreading throughout all the Roman dominions. Her name is usually understood to mean Wisdom, and upon the pavement of her temple was inscribed, "I am everything that has been, and is, and shall be, nor hath any mortal opened my veil."

The most common symbol of Isis was a Crescent Moon, which was worn by Roman women upon their shoes as a safeguard from witchcraft and to prevent the evil spirits of the moon from afflicting them with delusions, hysteria, or lunacy; also to attract the good-will of Isis that they might be successful in love, happy in motherhood, and fortunate in life. From this Crescent symbol (Illustration No. 113, Plate VIII) the Horseshoe undoubtedly became regarded as a Talisman, and as such was used by the Greeks and Romans, who nailed it with the horns upward as a charm against the Plague. In an old publication of 1618 we are instructed that the horseshoe should be nailed upon the threshold to keep Luck within the house and to keep out witches and nullify their evil powers; but in order to obtain the best results the horseshoe must be found by the owner of the house or by a member of the household. In the Middle Ages horseshoes were frequently buried amongst the roots of an Ash tree, which imparted such virtue to the Ash that a twig from it stroked upward over cattle that had been overlooked, charmed away the evil. In Suffolk the fishermen still believe that a horseshoe nailed to the mast of a smack will protect it against bad weather, and their Newfoundland brothers use the horseshoe as a specific against many dangers, especially as a charm to keep away the Devil. In this superstition they resemble the miners of Devon and Cornwall who fix a horseshoe to the mine with the horns upward, it being common knowledge that the Devil travels in a circle and is consequently frustrated in his evil course when he arrives at either of the horns and is obliged to take a retrograde course. To this day, it is still regarded by the country-folk as essential to the well-being of the finder of this charm to suspend it horns upward over the door of his dwelling to hold the luck in, it being thought to run out at each end of the horseshoe if reversed. In Gay's fable of the Old Woman and Her Cats the witch complains:

"Crowds of boys
Worry me with eternal noise.
Straws laid across my path retards,
The Horse shoes nailed each threshold guards.
The stunted broom the Wenches hide
In fear that I should up and ride."

The Single Horn, or Tusk, both singly, or as a pendant to another Talisman, as Illustration No. 106, Plate VIII, in all probability had its origin in the double horns, or Crescent, of Isis. It was worn to protect from harm, danger, and the evil influences of enemies, and also as a powerful charm to attract good fortune and success.

It is frequently mentioned in the Old and New Testaments, and in 2 Samuel xxii, 3, and Psalm xviii, 2 the Almighty is described as the "Horn of my Salvation"; and St. Luke in the first chapter, 69th and 71st verses, writes:

"Hath raised up an horn of Salvation." "That we should be saved from our enemies and from the hands of all that hate us."

The Horn, being a symbol of Isis, was considered a powerful charm to which to attach the keys of stables and cowsheds, ensuring the safety of the cattle and their protection from the evil spirits of the night, a practice that has been followed from remote ages to the present day, although its origin is not generally known amongst its modern users.

In India it is also a common belief amongst the natives that a Tiger's tooth will ensure protection from the ghosts of men and animals, making its wearer formidable to his foes and respected by his friends.

According to Pliny, the tooth of a Wolf was thought by the Romans to be a powerful Talisman for children, it being hung horizontally or suspended round the neck. It assisted them in cutting their teeth, and preserved them from maladies in connection with dentition.

The Cornucopia, or Amalthaea's Horn of Plenty, is the symbol of Abundance, Fruitfulness, and Prosperity, and is represented by a horn filled to overflowing with fruits and flowers, as Illustration No. 118, Plate VIII. Amalthaea was the daughter of Melissus (the King of Crete) who nursed the infant Jupiter, feeding him with the milk of a goat. Jupiter afterwards gave the goat's horn to his nurse, endowing it with magical properties, so that whosoever possessed it should immediately obtain in abundance all he desired and find it a veritable "horn of plenty." It is also a symbol of the goddess Fortuna, and was worn as an Amulet to attract good fortune in abundance.

With the introduction of Isis came also that of Osiris-Apis with whom the Greeks identified their god of the under-world Hades under the name of Serapis. His symbol is the Bull Apis, which was of divine origin and known by special markings, being black in colour and having a white triangle upon its forehead, the figure of a Vulture on its back, double hairs in its tail, and a scarab under its tongue.

The symbol of the Bull's Head (see Illustration No. 108, Plate VIII) was commonly worn as earrings, for success in love and friendship, and as the god of Hades could lengthen or shorten men's lives as he thought fit, the Bull's Head was also worn by men for Strength and Long Life.

To gain favour and protection small images of the Deities were worn as ornaments, such as Diana of Ephesus, Mithras, and especially Harpokrates and Anubis (Illustrations Nos. 104, 107, Plate VIII).

Harpokrates, the god of eternal youth and fecundity, was typified by the figure of a boy holding his tongue, representing all that is ever fresh and young; he is the type of the Vernal Sun, bringing fertility to the land, enabling it to produce both food and drink. He is also frequently represented seated on a Lotus, the symbol of the Sun and fecundity.

Anubis is symbolised as a Jackal-headed god who, in the Egyptian religion, is depicted in the Judgment as weighing the souls of the dead; he is the Guardian of Souls in the under-world.

Gems bearing the figure of Bellerophon mounted on the winged steed Pegasus were believed to confer courage and were much prized by the Greek and Roman soldiers, Bellerophon being reputed to have first taught the art of governing horses with a bridle; this service to mankind and the valour he displayed when he slew the Chimaera, made him a fitting prototype to adorn a warrior's device.

Another engraved Talisman in great favour was the figure of Andromeda, heroine of one of the most romantic and popular of ancient myths. The sea-nymphs, jealous of her beauty, chained her to a rock in mid-ocean, that she might be at the mercy of a vile monster of the deep. But the warrior Perseus slew the monster, and married Andromeda. Her image was thought to promote harmony between lovers and peace between man and wife.

The Salus Ring (Illustration No. 112, Plate VIII) was worn by the devotees of Salus, or Hygiea, daughter of Aesculapius, who was worshipped as the goddess of Health. Several holy days were appointed in her honour and worship, and she was publicly invoked for the welfare of the rulers and for the general peace and prosperity of the community; also for an abundant harvest. She is usually represented with a serpent as a tribute to her attainments in the art of medicine, and her symbol was worn for Health and Success in all undertakings, as well as for general Good Fortune.

THE COMPLETE BOOK OF TALISMANS, AMULETS AND MAGIC GEMSTONES

CHAPTER IX

The Bulla—The Tusk—Pine Cone—The Frog—Skull of an Ass—Key Talismans—Grylli, or Chimerae—Goat—The Ox—Lion—Eagle—The Caduceus—Mercury—Health Rings—Boar's Head—Clenched Hand—Open Hand—Figured Hands—The Lizard—The Spider—The Fish—Snails.

Bulla is the name given to a gold case, circular or heart-shaped, used in necklaces or worn separately as a pendant, sometimes attached as an ornament to a belt or badge which was placed over one shoulder and under the opposite arm. Macrobius says it was the special decoration of the victorious general in the triumphant processions, having enclosed within it such remedies as were esteemed most efficacious against the evil glance of envy.

Introduced into Rome by the Etruscans, it became very popular and was adopted as the badge of free-born boys; it usually contained an invocation to one or more of the gods. Among the poorer classes the golden case was replaced by a leathern pouch, with contents of similar virtue which added to its efficacy as a Talisman, and in particular averted the evil glance; to save its wearer from the Evil Eye a tusk in the form of a pendant was frequently added to accentuate its efficacy.

It was a common practice to wear on the Bulla some grotesque object (see Illustration No. 106, Plate VIII)

The Pine Cone, the symbol of Cybele the goddess of abundant benefits, was worn by her votaries for Health, Wealth, and Power, and all good and necessary things which flow in abundance without ceasing from her influence. She had many names, and was called by the Greeks, Pasithea, signifying Mother, as she was the great mother of all the gods. Her priests were famous for their magical powers, and it was customary to fix her symbol, the Pine Cone, on a pole in the vineyards, to protect them from blight and witchcraft, a practice still to be seen in Italy at the present time, and presumably this was the origin of the Pine Cones which surmount the gateways at the entrances of some of the carriage drives of old country seats (see Illustration No. 117, Plate VIII); it also survives as an ornament to the spikes of iron railings enclosing the grounds of old-fashioned houses on the outskirts of many of our provincial towns.

THE COMPLETE BOOK OF TALISMANS, AMULETS AND MAGIC GEMSTONES

The Frog (Illustration No. 119, Plate VIII) is a symbol of Aphrodite, the goddess of love born from the foam of the sea. In Rome a special temple was dedicated to her worship. Her symbol, the frog, was worn for fertility and abundance. Pliny attributes to it the power of keeping the affections true and constant, and of promoting harmonious relations between lovers and friends.

It is a very popular Talisman amongst the Italians, Greeks, and Turks at the present day and is worn not only against the Evil Eye but is particularly valued as a Health Amulet, especially when cut in Amber.

The Skull of an Ass, set up on a pole in the midst of a cornfield, was considered a potent charm against blight, and in Greece and Rome was placed in vineyards for the same purpose; it was sacred to Priapus, the god of the gardens, which he was thought to protect from thieves, wild beasts, and mischievous birds. There is a legend that the Ass was held in high estimation, as by gnawing the branches of the vine it taught the art of pruning.

The Key Talisman was a very important one with both Greeks and Romans. It is the joint symbol of Janus (or Apollo) and Jana, his wife (Diana, or the Moon), and was worn for Prudence, and for Remembrance of things past, and foresight of things to come, Janus being represented as the God with two faces, typifying the prudent man who with sagacity and ripe judgment observes things past and future possibilities, and so discerns the causes and effects of all happenings. Janus was also the inventor of locks, doors, and gates, and was the Janitor of the year, for which reason twelve cities were dedicated to him, according to the months; and he held the Key of the. Door through which the prayers of the faithful had access to the gods.

Diana, or Jana, his wife, presided over doors and thresholds and was the special protectress of childbirth, and as keeper of the Gate of Heaven held the key of light and life.

Some of these ancient key Amulets were made in silver (Diana's own metal) and have heart-shaped handles, implying, it is thought by some writers, that the affections must be prudently guarded. The key was also attributed to Hecate Proserpine, who was the guardian of the underworld and could release the spirits of the departed. The key (Illustration No. 110, Plate VIII) is shown attached to a finger ring, which was a very popular form of its use.

Grylli, or Chimerae, were grotesque figures belonging to an early period of Roman art, and not, as sometimes asserted, characteristic of Gnostic remains. They consist of strange combinations of various animal forms, representing some strange, ludicrous, impossible monster such as a Goat, Ox, Lion, and Eagle united into one. They were used as Talismans and Amulets according to the ideas they portrayed, being sometimes Astrological in their significance and at other times representative of some form of Grecian or Roman religion. Plutarch writes that these composite objects were fixed up to ward off witchcraft and the evil effects of

THE COMPLETE BOOK OF TALISMANS, AMULETS AND MAGIC GEMSTONES

the first glance of the Evil Eye, it being thought that if the mischief-working eye could be diverted from the object to be protected on to the strange and ridiculous figures represented by the "GRYLLI" the glance would be absorbed and its effects destroyed. "Grylli" is derived from the modern Italian word "grillo," meaning caprice. The Rev. C. W. King in his interesting book on engraved gems instances a Talisman of this kind intended to attract Sunshine and Abundance, also designed as a protection against dangers on land or sea. It was made up as follows:—

"A Ram with a Cornucopia on his head, holding a Rabbit by its tail (signifying fruitfulness and plenty) and a Cock bestride a Dolphin (the Cock being a symbol of the Sun, the Rabbit the Land, and the Dolphin the Sea). These Chimerae often encircled a portrait of the owner, thus unmistakably conveying to him their protective virtues."

The Caduceus, the wand of Mercury (Illustration No. 105, Plate VIII), was considered an extremely efficient Talisman, being worn to render its possessor wise and persuasive, to attract Health and Youthfulness, as well as to protect from the Evil Eye.

The Rod was given to Mercury by Apollo, and had the wonderful faculty of deciding all controversies and conferring irresistible eloquence on its owner. Its efficacy was proved, when one day whilst travelling Mercury came upon two serpents fighting, and by placing his rod between them and exercising his eloquence, he immediately reconciled the combatants. Mutually embracing they became attached to the rod, thus forming the Caduceus. Mercury received his name from his shrewd understanding of merchandise; he was the inventor of contracts, weights and measures, and of the arts of buying and selling; for this reason he was regarded as the patron of Merchants and Traders.

He invented letters, excelled in eloquence, and was so skilful in making peace, that he is said to have pacified not only men but the immortal gods of Heaven and Hell, whose quarrels he adjusted; for this reason he was known by the Greeks as Hermes. In its composition the Pine Cone, which surmounts the staff, was credited with great health-giving powers; is a symbol of Apollo, or the Sun; the wings are emblematic of the flight of thoughts in the minds of men, the two serpents in amity signifying love prototypes of Aesculapius and Hygiea who influence the health-giving attributes of the Sun and Moon respectively, both deities being associated with serpents because by their aid maladies are sloughed off and vigour renewed, just as serpents were believed to renew their lives each year by casting their skins.

With the Romans the Serpent was a household god, and Livy records that, by the advice of the Delphic Oracle, the bringing of a sacred serpent from the temple of Aesculapius to Rome immediately stayed the pestilence then raging. The wearing of a ring in the form of a serpent coiled round the finger, signified an invocation to the God of Health for preservation from sickness. Health rings were much in vogue amongst the Ancient Romans, who frequently presented their friends with such tokens on their birthdays, these anniversaries being considered the most important festivals. A favourite device was an intaglio cut in the ring itself, portraying the head of a youth, and the word "Vivas" (Mayst thou live). It was also believed that a Boar's Head engraved upon a ring conferred perpetual health and preservation from danger (the Boar being sacred to Demeter); whilst a ring engraved with three Ravens was worn for conjugal fidelity. Another device was that of a human head attached to an elephant's trunk, holding a trident (the symbol of Neptune), which was worn as a protective charm against peril by sea. Charmed rings have also been much in favour with many nations, the Greeks being very partial to enchanted rings, which were made according to the favourable positions of the planets, their power being strengthened when the head and neck of the owner was cut in green jasper and set in a ring engraved with the letters B.B.P.P.N.E.N.A., which signified "Wear this and thou shalt in no wise perish." Whether hallowed in the name of God or consecrated by the touch of the Pope, or of Royal personages, the ring has ever been the chosen Talisman through which Health, Wealth, and Love was transmitted to its wearer.

The Hand, aptly described by Aristotle as the "Tool of Tools," was used in many forms as a Talisman against fascination, and similar specimens to Illustration No. 109, Plate VIII have been found in early Etruscan tombs, dating back about 800 B.C. This particular form, the thumb placed between the first and second fingers with the hand clenched and pointing downwards, was considered an infallible protection against all evil influences, particularly against the Evil Eye. Another form was to close the second and third fingers with the thumb and to hold the hand pointing downward with the first and fourth fingers extended, a form which is known in Italy at the present time as making the Devil's Horns. The position of the hand in these ancient Amulets was very important; the open hand denoting Justice and Victory, and in this form sometimes surrounded by a wreath of laurel was used by the Romans as a finial to their standards, and carried in triumphal processions. In the British Museum may be seen a life-sized hand in bronze in the form assumed in the Benediction of the Christian Church, the third and fourth fingers being closed, with thumb and first two fingers extended; this form has its efficacy as a Talisman against the Evil Eye increased by numerous other symbols (already dealt with), a pine cone being balanced on the finger-tips, a serpent running along the whole length of the back of the hand and towering above the third finger; and, amongst others, the Asp, Lizard, Caduceus, Frog, and Scales may be seen, all probably connected with the worship of Isis and Serapis. This form, known as Mano Pantea, and the life-sized hands were kept in the house as Talismans to protect it against every evil influence of magic and of the Evil Eye, whilst small replicas were worn as Amulets for personal protection.

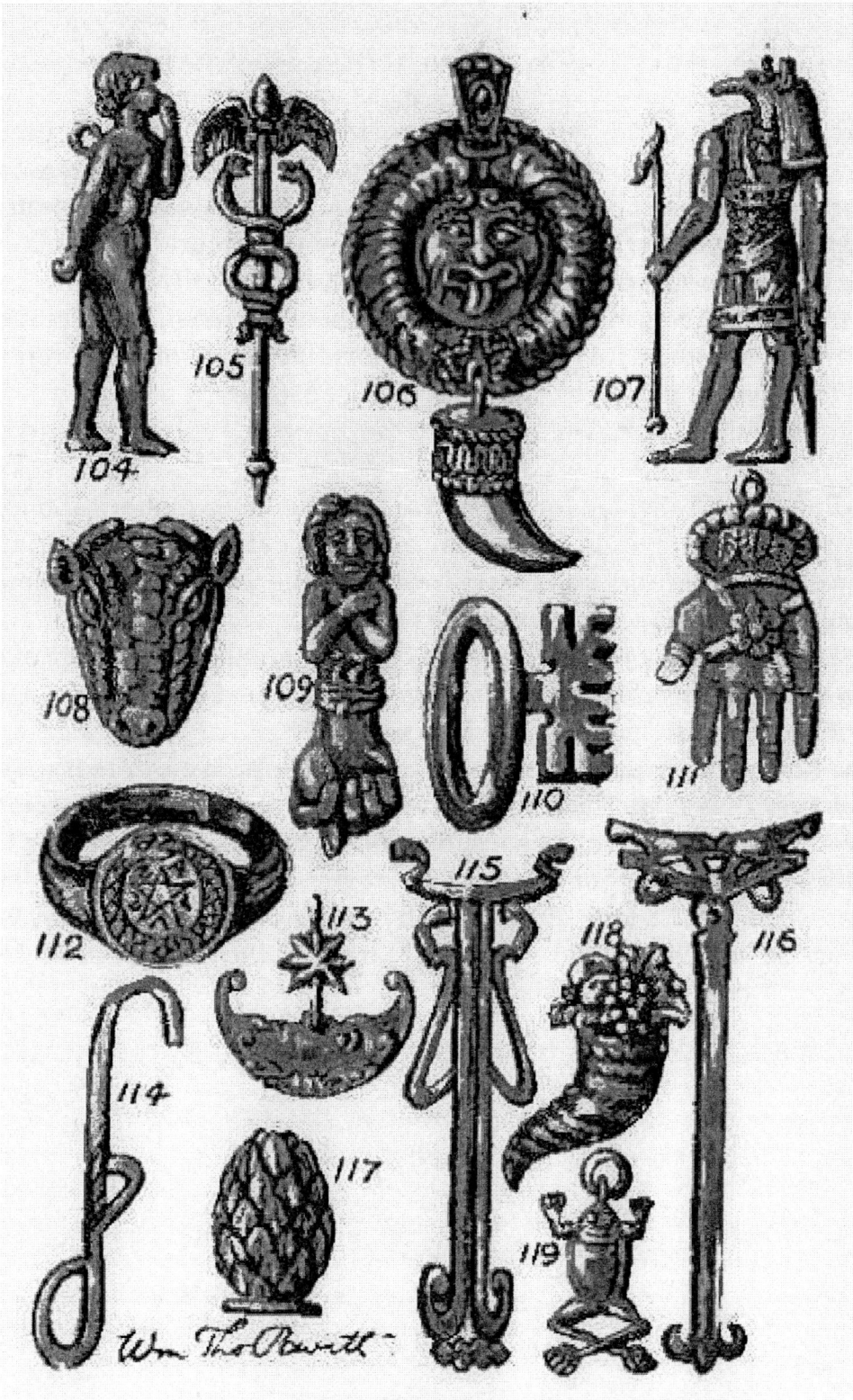

THE COMPLETE BOOK OF TALISMANS, AMULETS AND MAGIC GEMSTONES

ETRUSCAN, GREEK, ROMAN, AND ORIENTAL TALISMANS.

PLATE 8.

PLATE 8. ETRUSCAN, GREEK, ROMAN, AND ORIENTAL TALISMANS.

The Lizard and the Tortoise were symbols of Mercury, and the Caduceus is frequently depicted placed between them on ancient Talismans. The Lizard is also to be found engraved on many of the old Roman rings, and was used as charm against weak eyesight, the brilliant green of its body, like the Emerald, causing it to be held in high esteem, both spiritually and physically. It was a type of the Logos, or "Divine Wisdom," and was placed upon the breast of Minerva, as frequently seen on ancient engraved gems. It is also found in Portugal made of painted porcelain and affixed to the walls of houses to attract Good Fortune.

The Spider, like the Lizard, was sacred to Mercury and was considered a most fortunate symbol engraved on precious stones, its remarkable quickness of sight recommending it as a Talisman for shrewdness in business matters and foresight generally; and according to an old writer, prognostications were made from the manner of weaving spiders' webs, and it was deemed a sign that a man would receive money if a little spider fell upon his clothes.

The Eagle was typical of Jupiter because it predominates over birds of highest flight, and it was worn as a Talisman for Dignity, quickness of Perception, and the Favour of those who sit in high places.

Marcellus Empiricus prescribes the wearing of a ring as a preservative from Colic and Watery Diseases. This Talisman was made of gold thread melted down and engraved with the figure of a fish; such a ring exists in the Florentine Cabinet and may be seen at the present day.

Snails were also used in love divinations by the Ancient Romans; they were set to crawl upon the hearth and were thought to trace in the ashes the initials of the lover's name.

THE COMPLETE BOOK OF TALISMANS, AMULETS AND MAGIC GEMSTONES

CHAPTER X

The Orient—The Koran—Jochebed—Bead Necklaces—Mashallah—Hassan and Hussein—Hand of the Lady Fatima—Five Principal Commandments—Zufur Tukiah—Nasiree—Gadiri—Mohammed—Merzoum—The Diamond—Cube of Amber—Scorpion-charming—Early Christian and Mediaeval Talismans—Clement of Alexandria—The Fish—Dag—Palm Branch—The Ship—Sacred Monogram—Shen Constantine the Great—Thoth—The Cross—Household Cross—Yucatan—Hand and Cross—Wheel Cross.

A belief in Talismans and Charms of every kind is universal in the Orient; written prayers, verses from the Koran, the name of the Prophet, and even miniature editions of the Koran itself enclosed in leather or cloth cases, suspended from the neck or tied to the arm, being the most favoured. The belief in the power of the Evil Eye is also widespread, and charms of the kind above-recorded are frequently written on pieces of wood which are fixed to door-posts or trees in the gardens to prevent the harmful glance from resting on the house or plants; should the wood crack it is believed that the injury would have been done had not the glance been intercepted by the Talisman on guard.

Another charm of great potency is the name "Jochebed," being the name of the Mother of Moses. By its constant repetition it is believed to reveal hidden secrets, unfasten locked doors, and discover treachery and evil doings.

Whilst necklaces and armlets made of the beads of Kerbela are worn upon the person, or put into bales of goods to protect them from thieves, Amulets enclosed in leather are hung on the necks of horses to prevent them from stumbling. Other Talismans consist of discs of gold, or silver, with the word "Mashallah" (God is Great) engraved upon them. These are worn for protection from all calamities, whilst sentences such as "There is no God but God and Mohammed is his prophet" are also considered powerful charms. The names of the grandsons of Mohammed, Hassan and Hussein, engraved on beautifully polished Agate stones, are suspended from the neck or tied to the arms of children to protect them from falling. Blue beads are often sewn on the caps of poor children, and are frequently threaded on the hairs of the tails and manes of horses, being considered very

THE COMPLETE BOOK OF TALISMANS, AMULETS AND MAGIC GEMSTONES

efficacious in averting ill-wishing. A hand with one finger extended, not of coral as in the Levant, but of metal or of blue glass, is worn for the same reason; and at the present day small hands of blue glass made in this form are tied round the necks of children or attached to the part of the body to be protected from the Evil Eye. A hand with thumb and fingers outstretched, known as the Hand of the Lady Fatima (see Illustration No. 111, Plate VIII), is still regarded as a powerful charm amongst all Moslems, and is made in all metals, often very crude in execution, its material and detail varying according to the wealth and position of its wearer. This Hand is regarded as a sacred symbol representing Generosity, Hospitality, Power, and Divine Providence; as a whole it represents the Holy Family, the prophet Mohammed being typified by the thumb, the Lady Fatima by the first finger, Ali, her husband, by the second, and the third and fourth fingers respectively being allotted to Hassan and Hussein, the sons of Fatima and Mi. It also serves to keep the faithful in constant remembrance of the Five Principal Commandments, i.e. to keep the Fast of Ramadan, to accomplish the Pilgrimage to Mecca, to Give Alms, to Perform the necessary Ablutions, and to Oppose all Infidels.

Paintings of hands are to be met with throughout Italy, Syria, and Turkey, Asia, and India as symbols of good luck and for protection from witchcraft, showing how widespread and universal is the idea of the efficacy of the human emblem to push away and combat trouble and evil.

A form of Mussulman Talisman is The Zufur Tukiah, or sacred crutch, single and double, which is formed of a combination of letters making the name of a saint or holy man, of which three examples are shown on Plate VIII. Illustration No. 114 is formed in the shape of the letters that compose the name Nasiree, or the Preserver, one of the names of God; No. 115 is a double crutch forming the letters that compose the name Gadiri, or the Powerful, also one of the names of God and No. 116 is formed in the shape of the letters which comprise the name of MOHAMMED. The Talismans of the Shah of Persia are very numerous, and it is said exceed two hundred, the principal and most important being the following:

One called Merzoum, in the shape of a gold star, is said to have the power of making traitors confess; some years ago one of the Shah's brothers was suspected of treachery and this Talisman shown him, when terrified and overcome by remorse, he is said to have confessed his crime.

Another powerful Talisman is a diamond set in a scimitar which renders him invincible. He also possesses a cube of Amber, said to have fallen from Heaven in the time of Mohammed; the virtue of this is to render its wearer invulnerable if worn round the neck.

Another marvellous charm is a golden box set with emeralds and blessed by the prophet. This is said to render members of the Royal Family invisible as long as they remain unmarried; the Shah, however, had numerous wives before he became its possessor, so that its powers remain untested.

THE COMPLETE BOOK OF TALISMANS, AMULETS AND MAGIC GEMSTONES

Persians of high rank make use of Rubies, Emeralds, and other Gems, tied round the arm with pieces of red and green silk, as charms against the fascinations of the Devil whom they call "Deebs."

No journey is ever undertaken without first consulting a Book of Omens, each chapter of which begins with a particular letter of the alphabet, some fortunate and some inauspicious; should they unluckily pitch on one of the latter the journey is immediately postponed.

Persians have also a curious custom of charming Scorpions, of which, says Pinkerton, there are great numbers in that country, and they believe that by making use of a prayer, a person gifted with power of "binding" (as it is called) can deprive the Scorpion of its sting. To do this the charmer turns his face towards the sign Scorpio in the heavens, repeating a special prayer, and at the conclusion of each sentence claps his hands. After the ceremony his hearers do not scruple to handle scorpions, so great is their faith in the efficacy of the charm.

EARLY CHRISTIAN AND MEDIAeVAL TALISMANS.

At the time of the founding of the Christian religion and onwards through the Middle Ages the symbols used during the services, certain texts, mottoes, and prayers were very popular as Talismans. They are often found in combination with symbols used in preceding religions, and were worn for protection from temptation and all kinds of perils, dangers, and diseases.

In the earliest days when open avowal of faith meant peril and persecution, these Talismans were of great service in making fellow-believers known to each other, and when Christianity was established were extensively worn, with the approval of Clement of Alexandria.

One of the oldest Talismans of this kind is The Fish, said to have been adopted because its Greek name IKhThYS formed the initials of the sentence "Jesus Christ, Son of God, Saviour." The form of the Fish is very similar to that used by the Egyptians and is illustrated on Plate IX, No. 120.

Another explanation of its use is that in the Talmud the Messiah is often designated by the name "Dag," the Fish, and the sign of His second coming, it is said, would be the conjunction of Saturn and Jupiter in Pisces, which is the origin of the three fishes interlaced into a triangle, a very popular ornament in mediaeval architecture.

The Palm Branch was another popular Talisman used to symbolise triumph over sin and temptation; this undoubtedly was adapted from the pagan mythology, in which the Palm represented the Sun, and was also a token of victory and success. In Illustration No. 122, Plate IX, it is shown surrounding the Greek name for Fish.

Stones were also frequently used, and although valuable gems were in use, semi-precious stones such as the Carnelian, Sardonyx, and Jasper were the most general, the device illustrated on Plate IX, No. 126, being cut in a Sapphire, the usual method of treatment in those days being very seldom to cut in relief, as in more modern times.

A favourite gift was a ring with the name of the recipient cut in the stone with some appropriate motto, as in Illustration No. 124, Plate IX: "Rogate, Vivas in Deo" (Rogatus, Live in God). Bronze and silver rings were freely used for this purpose.

The Ship (Illustration No. 127, Plate IX) was a symbol universally used to represent the Church, and signified the belief of its wearers in their salvation and safety from temptations of the flesh. It was frequently used in combination with other symbols, as shown in Illustration No. 127, Plate IX, where the Sacred Monogram appears above the deck of the Ship. It is worthy of note, as the sign which encloses it is probably the Egyptian symbol of Eternity, Shen. This monogram is reputed to have been revealed in a vision to Constantine the Great, Emperor of Rome, on the evening of the battle in which he overcame Manentius. In consequence he adopted it as the device for the Imperial Standard. It was also commonly used as an abbreviation of the name of Christ. Nos. 126 and 131 are other examples of this symbol, and No. 126 is interesting as being in combination with the Tau Cross, which has been treated fully in a preceding chapter. This Cross when placed upon the top of a heart signified goodness, and was at the same time regarded as a Talisman for protection from evil. It was the monogram of Thoth, the Egyptian god of Wisdom, and when used with a circle at its base signified the eternal preserver of the world.

The Cross with four arms symbolises the four Cardinal Points, or Universe, the dominion of the Spirit. Making the sign of the Cross has always been considered efficacious in the treating of spells, the exorcising of the Devil, and also as a protection from evil spirits. For these reasons, in olden days kings and nobles used the sign of the Cross whether they could write or riot, regarding it as a symbol of good luck; even at the present time people ignorant of writing when called upon to sign a document mark it with a cross to show that it is their mark and deed. The primitive inhabitants of Yucatan prayed to the Cross as the god of Rain, and in Martin's Western Islands of Scotland we are told that "in the Island of Uist, one of the Outer Hebrides, opposite St. Mary's Church, there is a stone cross which was called by the natives the 'Water Cross,' and when they needed rain they set the cross up, and when sufficient had fallen, they laid it flat upon the ground."

THE COMPLETE BOOK OF TALISMANS, AMULETS AND MAGIC GEMSTONES

EARLY CHRISTIAN AND MEDIÆVAL TALISMANS.
PLATE 9.

THE COMPLETE BOOK OF TALISMANS, AMULETS AND MAGIC GEMSTONES

PLATE 9. EARLY CHRISTIAN AND MEDIAeVAL TALISMANS.

Illustrated on Plate IX (No. 121) is a Cross with Greek inscription for Life and Health, which is made in the form of a mould, or stamp; a household Talisman, in all probability used for making an impression upon bread, or cakes, its size being three and a half inches each way.

The combination of the Hand and the Cross as a Talisman is one of the most remarkable of all the composition charms of ancient times against the Evil Eye, and to break a Cross of this kind, or, in fact, any charm of this nature, was thought to be most unfortunate.

On ornaments belonging to the later Bronze Age, the Wheel Cross was symbolic of the Wheels of the Chariot which the Sun was supposed to drive through the sky; whilst the Golden Wheel Cross, so often placed behind the figure of the Saviour, is symbolic of His title as the "Sun of Righteousness." It was also used on the shields of ancient warriors as a symbol of the Sun and its worshippers. This same Wheel Cross, in the shape of a large Waggon Wheel, is said to be still used in Denmark and Holland, and is placed on the roofs of houses and stables to entice storks to build their nests thereon, the red legs of the bird suggesting to the inhabitants that it is a fire bird and will prevent the building from being destroyed by fire, whilst the wheel will bring good luck. Even in England the Wheel Cross, in the shape of a brass ornament, is still to be seen upon the foreheads of fine cart-horses; it was intended in olden days to ward off witchcraft and the Evil Eye and to attract Good Fortune.

The Irish Cross is also a type of the Wheel Cross.

CHAPTER XI

The Agnus Dei—The Coventry Ring—Ananizapta—Tau Cross—Cross of St. Benedict—Byzantine Ring—Simsum Ring—Abracadabra—Pentalpha, Pentacle, Pentagram, or Five-pointed Star—The Kabala—The Table of Jupiter—The Ten Divine Names—The Planetary Angels—The Agla—Dr. Dee.

The Talisman known as the Agnus Dei came into use after the Christian religion had become general; and it is in use at the present day. It consists of a Lamb carrying a flag and cross, as in Illustration No. 129, Plate IX, with the motto "Ecce Agnus Dei" (Behold the Lamb of God). It was made not only in various metals, but in wax, and is believed to possess the virtue of preserving its wearers from the danger of accidents, tempests, and pestilence.

The Coventry Ring is another good example of a religious Talisman of the fifteenth century, and is illustrated by No. 128, Plate IX. The outside is engraved with a scene representing Our Lord rising from the tomb, with the five wounds arranged on either side, and the following inscriptions:

"The Well of Everlasting Life,"
"The Well of Pitty,"
"The Well of Merci,"
"The Well of Comfort,"
"The Well of Gracy."

The Five Wounds symbolise the five senses through which we have the power of wounding Our Lord by yielding to the temptation of the Flesh and the Devil, and in themselves alone were regarded as an efficacious Talisman against all evil. Inside the ring is engraved the names of the Three Kings of Cologne (so named because their relics are preserved at Cologne), or the Magi—the Three Wise Kings—Caspar, signifying the White One; Melchior, King of Light; Baltasar the Lord of Treasures; also in Latin the verse Luke iv. 30, I.H.S.: "Autem transiens per medium illorum ibat" (Jesus passing through their midst went His way.) This text was worn as a charm against danger by sea and land, and especially against dangers from robbers; and to commemorate his escape in the great naval battle off Sluys in the year 1340 Edward III had this same verse struck upon his gold nobles.

The sigil Ananizapta is also engraved inside the ring and has been translated

THE COMPLETE BOOK OF TALISMANS, AMULETS AND MAGIC GEMSTONES

as meaning, "Have mercy on us, O Judge"; it was considered a powerful protection against disease, epilepsy, and intoxication, particularly when associated with the Tau Cross, as in Illustration No. 133, Plate X.

The Cross of St. Benedict was another popular charm, worn as a protection against disease and dangers. Each letter stands for a word, the four letters in the angles of the Cross, making the first line, then the upright of the Cross, next the horizontal bar, finally the lettering round the outside, as in Illustration No. 130, Plate IX.

The following is the Latin text and its translation:

1. Crux Sancti Patris Benedicte.
2. Crux Sancta sit mihi lux.
3. Ne daemon sit mini dux.
4. Vade retro Satana,
   Ne suade mihi vana;
   Sunt mala quae libas,
   Ipse venena bibas.

1. Cross of the Holy Father Benedict.
2. Holy Cross be my light.
3. Let no evil spirit be my guide.
4. Get thee behind me Satan,
   Suggest no vain delusions;
   What thou offerest is evil,
   Thou thyself drinkest poison.

The Ring illustrated on Plate X, No. 132, is Byzantine, and was worn as an Amulet for protection against disease and accident, the grotesque head being against the Evil Eye; the seven radiating spirits symbolise the seven gifts of the Spirit—Power, Wisdom, Honour, Glory, Blessing, Strength, and Riches. Round the hoop is engraved the inscription, "Lord preserve the wearer."

A popular astrological Talisman for good fortune was the formula in which the word Simsum was emphasised as containing the initial letters of each Planet and the Sun in their relative order, Saturni, Jovis, Martius, Solis, Veneris, Mercurii—the whole inscription reading:

"Post Simsvm sequitur septuna Luna subest," which has been translated as:

"After possibility follows certainty, the seventh moon is at hand." The seventh New Moon of our Calendar would fall in Cancer, the Moon's own Zodiacal house in which she is exalted, or at her strongest, and when there marks a very auspicious time for pushing public affairs or undertaking new business enterprises (see Illustration No. 137, Plate X).

The most famous Talisman, however, of the Middle Ages is the Abracadabra, which, says the Rev. C. W. King, was first mentioned by Serenus Sammonicus, the most learned Roman of his time, and physician to Caracalla. Serenus Alexander, a great admirer of Serenus Sammonicus, ordered the word to be written in the form of an inverted cone, and declares it to be of virtue against all diseases.

> "Thou shalt on paper write the spell divine
> ABRACADABRA called in many a line,
> Each under each in even order place,
> But the last letter in each line efface,
> As by degrees the elements grow few,
> Still take away but fix the residue,
> Till at the last one letter stands alone,
> And the whole dwindles to a tapering cone.
> Tie this about the neck with flaxen string,
> Mighty the good 'twill to the patient bring,
> Its wondrous potency shall guard his head
> And drive disease and death far from his bed."

The Illustration No. 136, Plate X, is from an example in the British Museum, and the probable origin of this Talisman is that it is a composition of the Hebrew words Ha—Brachab—Dabarah—"Speak or pronounce the Blessing"; "Blessing" standing for "The Blessed One," being equivalent to invoking the Holy Name of Jehovah.

Defoe mentions this Talisman as being worn written as described, for a safeguard against infection during the time of the Great Plague, the prescription being that the word Abracadabra be written on parchment and worn for nine days (nine being the number of the Planet Mars ruling fevers and infectious illnesses generally). It was then to be thrown backwards before sunrise into a stream running eastward (the East Wind being also under the influence of the Planet Mars). Another signification given to the word Abracadabra is said to be of Jewish origin, and means "God sends forth His lightning to scatter His enemies," which sentence occurs in a Psalm of David. It was also believed to have the power of curing the toothache, as an extract from an old MS. in the British Museum contains the following interesting information:

"Mr. Banester sayeth that he healed two hundred in one yer of an ague, by hanging Abracadbra about their necks, it would stanch blood or heal the toothache although the parties were ten miles off."

Other writers affirm that in order to cure mild attacks of ague it is only necessary to repeat the word Abracadabra, dropping each time one letter, but in severe cases the word was to be written as prescribed and eaten by the patient!

The Pentalpha, Pentacle, Pentagram, or Five-pointed Star, has always had very mysterious powers ascribed to it, and Rennet, Bishop of Peterborough, says: "When it is delineated on the body of a man it points out the five places wherein the Saviour was wounded, and, therefore, the devils are afraid of it." No evil spirit could pass where it was displayed, and for this reason it was always used in magic ceremonies to "bind with," as the spirits of darkness can have no power over the magician who stands within this Pentacle or is provided with this symbol. Audrey says: "It was used by the Christian Greeks (as the sign of the Cross was later), at the heading of MS. and at the beginning of books for 'good luck's sake.'"

In the Middle Ages it was looked upon as a symbol of immense power, and was worn for health and safety, both in the spiritual as well as in the physical sense; and the magical Pentacle in the western window of the southern aisle of Westminster Abbey is one of the emblems still existing to prove that the worshippers of old were deeply read in Occult lore. Eliphas Levi describes it "as the seal of the Microcosm through which Man can command the powers and beings of the Elements and restrain Elementals from evil." In Illustration No. 134, Plate X, it is shown with the symbols of the Planets and the Sacred Names of God which give it added power and efficacy. Scott, in Marmion, describing a wizard, also alludes to this Talisman as follows:

"His shoon were marked with cross and spell,
  Upon his breast a pentacle";

and in Germany it is still considered a Talisman against the powers of witchcraft.

The Kabala, the source and inspiration of numerous Talismans, came into being very soon after the establishment of the Christian Religion, when the Jewish Rabbis developed a complete science of Divine things, received, as the name implies, by direct revelation, according to which all created things from the highest to the lowest are ruled, through the ten principal names of God, acting first through the nine orders of the Angelic Hosts and blessed souls, and through them to the Celestial Spheres, Planets, and Mankind. Lower degrees of Angels and celestial influences, known as Intelligences, ruling each element, nation, language, animal and vegetable life, atmospheric conditions, emotions and aspirations. The early Christians had great faith and belief in the power of numbers, and their magical formulas were largely composed of letters having numerical values, usually expressed in Hebrew. Sometimes Greek letters were used, which, combined with astrological formulas, attracted the good influences of the Angels and Intelligences ruling through the Planets, the houses of the Zodiac, their triplicities and degrees.

One form described as the Table of Jupiter, which is illustrated on Plate X, Illustration No. 139, contains sixteen numbers which total up to thirty-four whichever way they are added. This, with the Divine names around it, is to be made in a plate of silver when Jupiter is strong, and was worn for riches, favour, peace, and concord, to appease enemies, and to confer honours and dignities.

The Good Spirits were always working to preserve mankind from the machinations of Evil Spirits; the Jupiterian Spirits working especially to preserve Justice and Mercy on Earth. This Talisman may be seen reproduced in Albrecht Durer's picture of "Melancholy." The complete set of the Planetary Tables with their Angels and Intelligences, together with full instructions for their making, may be found in the Magus by Francis Barrett.

The Ten Names of God were used to attract the virtues and powers they represent, or to accomplish some desire signified.

The first is the name Eheia, the essence of Divinity, influencing the angelic order of Seraphim through whom the gift of being is bestowed on all things.

The second is Jod, signifying wisdom, ruling through the order of Cherubim.

The third is Elohim, signifying providence and understanding, ruling through the order of Thrones.

The fourth is El, signifying clemency and goodness, grace, piety, and magnificence, ruling through the order of Dominions.

The fifth name is Elohim Gibor, signifying power and judgment, ruling through the Seraphim.

The sixth name is Eloha, meaning Beauty and Glory, and has power through the order of Virtues.

The seventh name is Adonai Sabaoth, the God of Hosts, triumph and victory, justice and eternity, ruling through the order of Principalities.

The eighth is Elohim Sabaoth, signifying Piety and Agreement, ruling through the Archangels.

The ninth is called Sadai, that is, Omnipotent, and has influence through the Cherubim, ruling the increase and decrease of all things.

The tenth name is Adonai Melech, signifying Kingdom and Empire, and has rule through the Blessed Souls giving knowledge and understanding.

Very powerful in Talismans were the names of the Angels ruling the Planets, as follows:

Saturn ruled by Zaphiel.
Jupiter ruled by Zadkiel.
Mars ruled by Camael.
Sun ruled by Raphael.
Venus ruled by Haniel.
Mercury ruled by Michael.
Moon ruled by Gabriel.

Names of power were compounded from letters taken from verses of Scripture: for example, the Agla is formed from the initial letters of the words Ate Gebir

Leilam Adonai—"Thou art mighty for ever, O Lord"; a popular charm during the fourteenth century against Fever, frequently found on rings and brooches of this period. It was used by Dr. Dee, as illustrated on Plate X, Illustration No. 138.

THE COMPLETE BOOK OF TALISMANS, AMULETS AND MAGIC GEMSTONES

CHAPTER XII

Tetragrammaton—Phylactery—Talismans against all mischiefs, the Magus—Venus Talisman—Totaphoth—Abraxas—Eye of a Cock—Bells—Gargoyles—Cramp Rings—Blessing of Rings—Musseltaub—Posie Rings—Gemmel Rings—Zodiacal Rings—The Signs of the Zodiac in Rhyme—General Talismans—The Lee Penny—Crystal—The Moon Talismans—Peacock—Juno—Fire Talismans—Gold Nugget—Coins—Card Talismans—Badger's Tooth—Four-leaved Clover.

Tetragrammaton, or mystic name, had its derivation in a Hebrew word, "Yod-he-vau-he," which signified the unutterable name of Jehovah, its meaning being "He that is and shall be." The sigil is composed of letters formed from the following four texts: Exodus xiii. 2nd and 10th verses, also verses 11 and 16; and Deuteronomy vi. 4th and 9th verses. It was very popular as a Talisman in the Middle Ages for protection from enemies, also to bring peace, harmony, and long life, and was usually made in the form of a pentacle with the five syllables engraved in each corner (see Illustration No. 142, Plate X) with the Hebrew letter Yod, or Shin, in the centre.

It was also worn by the Jews in the form of a Phylactery, which was a strip of cowhide parchment inscribed with verses from the Talmud, or with the Tetragrammaton and the sigil formed from the four passages of Scripture already referred to. It was enclosed in a black calfskin case which had thongs attached to it for binding on the forehead, or round the left arm. Worn when attending worship in their synagogues, it was considered to have great potency as a Talisman.

The illustration of the Tetragrammaton is taken from Barrett's Magus, as are also Nos. 140 and 141, Plate X, which are described as containing "the beginnings and ends of the first five verses of Genesis, and representation of the creation of the world; and by this ligature they say that a man shall be free from all mischiefs if that he firmly believes in God, the Creator of all things."

No. 135, Plate X, is a Talisman of Venus which is in the British Museum, and is also described in the Magus as worn for success and good fortune in love, joyfulness, and to make travellers fortunate. The written inscription is an addition probably made personally, and reads:

"Accipe my petitione, O domine, keep me as apple of an eye, hide me under the shadow of thy wings from all evel, up Lord and help us for thou art my strong rock and my castle. Amen."

The Totaphoth was another species of Talisman worn by the Hebrews as a frontlet, consisting of a plate slightly curved, inscribed with passages from the Talmud, which covered the forehead from ear to ear and was bound with a fillet of gold or silver by those who could afford it, and with strips of coloured cloth by the poor. Scapulars, or pieces of brown cloth, in which were stitched certain verses from the Gospel of St. John written on paper, or parchment, guarded against perils by flood or field, and a Dove with a branch of Olive in its mouth engraved in pyrites, ensured for the pilgrim the utmost hospitality wheresoever he journeyed.

The Gnostic god Abraxas is frequently depicted with the head of a Cock, this bird being considered a powerful Talisman for vigilance, and also a symbol of the Sun, as well as of Mercury. It is sometimes represented with an ear of corn in its beak, denoting that "vigilance produces plenty."

The Eye of a Cock was considered a potent Talisman against witchcraft and the wiles of the Devil, even the lion being afraid of its hypnotic glance; and as Christ was thought by the early Christians to have arisen from the tomb at cockcrow, the Cock was from an early period used as a symbol of the Resurrection, and its image was engraved on many of the ancient tombs. Placed as it still is, on the highest point of the church tower or spire, it is singularly appropriate as a church Talisman.

THE COMPLETE BOOK OF TALISMANS, AMULETS AND MAGIC GEMSTONES

MEDIÆVAL TALISMANS.

PLATE 10.

PLATE 10. MEDIAeVAL TALISMANS.

Bells were another form of Talisman used in olden days, the traditional idea being that any great noise would terrify the Devil and all evil spirits, so that bells were attached to the heads of. horses and to the playthings of children to protect them from harm; and were also hung in church towers to scare the ears of demons, whilst the Gargoyles struck terror to the eyes of the evil ones.

Cramp Rings were another form of Talisman worn for the prevention or cure of cramp. These rings were at one time hallowed by the Kings and Queens of England, but the custom was discontinued in the reign of Edward VI. An old MS., emblazoned with the arms of Philip and Mary, gives the prayers used in the consecration of these rings. The rings were placed in a dish and the ceremony commenced with the reading of a Psalm and a prayer for the communication of the divine gift of healing, after which the sovereign hallowed the rings by saying:

"O God of Abraham, Isaac and Jacob, hear mercifully our prayers, Spare those who feare thee, and be propitious to thy suppliants, and graciously be pleased to send down from heaven, thy holy angel, that he may sanctify and bless these rings to the end that they may prove a healthy remedy to such as implore thy name with humilitie. Amen." After the blessing of the rings, the King rubbed them between the palms of his hands, saying:

"Sanctify, O Lord, these rings and graciously bedew them with the dew of thine benediction and consecration, and hallow them by the rubbing of our hands which thou hast been pleased according to our ministry, to the end that what the nature of the metal is not able to perform may be wrought by the greatness of thy grace."

Then holy water was sprinkled on the rings:

"In the name of the Father, Son, and Holy Ghost."

These rings were considered most efficacious if formed out of the screws and nails taken from old coffins, and were frequently considered most beneficial in the cure of epileptic fits if hallowed on Good Friday. This custom, according to Hospinian, took its rise from a famous ring long preserved in Westminster Abbey; this ring had been brought from Jerusalem by Edward the Confessor, and was believed to be efficacious against cramp and epilepsy when touched by those afflicted. Another Talisman ring of the sixteenth century was of Jewish origin, engraved with a Hebrew word "Musseltaub," meaning "We wish you good luck," inscribed inside.

Within the hoop of the betrothal or wedding ring it was customary to inscribe sentences, or poesies (posies), and this custom appears to have lasted into the latter part of the eighteenth century, when it fell into disuse. It has been revived of late years, devices, mottoes, and hieroglyphics being once more inscribed in engagement rings, to express the sentiment of the giver and to act as a mutual token of love and friendship. Some of these ancient posies may be found interest-

THE COMPLETE BOOK OF TALISMANS, AMULETS AND MAGIC GEMSTONES

ing, such as:

"The eye did find, the heart did chuse, the hand doth bind, till death doth loose."

"Let Love Encrease."

"God did decree the Unitie."

"Where Hearts agree there love will be."

"Hearts united live contented."

"Keep fayth till deth."

"I seek to be, not thine, but thee."

"Let lyking laste."

"Hearts truly tied none can divide."

"Joye sans cesse."

"Let us be one till we are none."

"Fear the Lord and rest content, so shall we live and not repent."

"This and the giver are thine for ever."

A very old ring (says the author of Ring Lore) is in the collection of J. Evans, Esq.; it is of gold set with a small sapphire, inscribed:

JE, SVI, ICI, EN, LI'V, D'AMI.

(I am here in place of a friend.)

Other devices express the sentiment of the giver in the setting of the gems of the ring, as, for instance, the word "Regard" is represented by a

Ruby
Emerald
Garnet
Amethyst
Ruby
Diamond

placed in sequence round the ring.

The Gemmel, Or Gemmow, rings were frequently double or even triply made, the word "Gemmel" denoting jointed hinges, or jimmers. At the time of the betrothal the parties concerned broke away the upper and lower rings over an open Bible, each wearing the respective ring severed (the third ring being held by the witness of their betrothal) until the marriage took place, when the rings were reunited and became the Wedding Ring. It was considered most unlucky for a ring to hurt its wearer, or fall to the ground during the betrothal or marriage, and it is said to be a curious fact that when this has happened the incident has been followed by disappointment or misfortune to one or both of the persons concerned.

The Ancients had great faith in Zodiacal Rings, in the construction of which the aspects and positions of the planets were of the utmost importance. They were worn for the gift of eloquence and were in great favour with lawyers, poets, and orators, being worn on the fourth finger (Mercury ruling speech and the tongue).

These Zodiacal rings, engraved with the representation of the twelve signs of the Zodiac in their order, are aptly described in the following rhyme, for which we are indebted to the Rev. C. W. King's book, The Natural History of Precious Stones and Gems, although it is not from that author's pen, but merely quoted by him:

"THE SIGNS OF THE ZODIAC IN RHYME
"Hear how each sign the body's portion sways,
 How every part its proper lord obeys
 And what the members of the human frame
 Wherein to rule, their several forces claim.
 First to the Ram, the Head hath been assigned;
 Lord of the sinews, Neck, the Bull we find;
 The arms and shoulders joined in union fair
 Possess the Twins, each one an equal share.
 The Crab, as sovereign o'er the Breast presides;
 The Lion, the shoulder blades and sides.
 Down to the flank, 'the Virgin's' lot descends,
 And with the buttock Libra's influence ends;
 The fiery Scorpion in the groin delights,
 The Centaur in the thighs exerts his rights,
 While either knee doth Capricornus rule,
 The legs the province of Aquarius cool;
 Last, the twain Fishes as their region meet,
 Hold jurisdiction on the pairs of feet."

General Talismans

An historic Talisman of Oriental origin which was famous during the fourteenth century, is the

Lee Penny, which is described as a small red stone of triangular or heart shape, and of unknown origin, set in a groat of Edward IV.

According to tradition, it was brought from the Holy Land by Sir Simon Locard of Lee, who accompanied Sir James Douglas to Palestine bearing the heart of Robert Bruce enclosed in a golden casket, and, for his services in connection with this, was given the name of Lockhart, and for armorial bearings, a lock and a heart. Fighting in the Holy Land, Sir Simon captured a Saracen Emir whom he held to ransom. The Emir's lady willingly paid the ransom; but while handing out a goodly supply of golden bezants, she dropped a small jewel. So marked was her anxiety to recover it, that the canny Sir Simon, with a true Caledonian instinct for a bargain, conjectured the apparently valueless stone must be a potent Talisman. Consequently he refused to set his prisoner at liberty unless the stone was included in the ransom.

Amongst its many merits it cures hydrophobia, takes away disease from horned cattle, and counteracts the poison of infectious complaints if it is soaked in water and the water is used as a cordial.

For its use during an epidemic of the plague Newcastle is reputed to have granted a bond of L6000 for its safe return.

Another Scottish Talisman is a Crystal set in silver, which is worn hung round the back for diseases of the kidneys; it is also directed to be steeped in water seven times, the water to be drunk by the patient.

The Moon is another symbol of importance in connection with the talismanic properties of water, upon which it has a vitalising influence. In Oudh a silver basin is filled with water by the people, who hold it so that the orb of the full moon is reflected therein, their doctors recommending this as a remedy for nervous hysteria and palpitation, patients being directed to look steadfastly for a while at the reflection, then to shut their eyes and drink the water at a gulp.

Many and various are the ways in which lunar sympathy and influence were turned to account in olden days, warts being considered particularly susceptible to its influence, and a charm repeated over them at the junction of four cross roads as the moon waned in light was believed to be most efficacious in removing the blemishes. The formula prescribed:

"As the moon decreases
 So may these warts disappear,"

is still in vogue in certain remote country villages in England. Christians and Moslems alike turn silver money in their pockets that their goods and money may increase when the moon is new and gaining in light, and their ills decrease as it wanes. The Moon's image in crescent shape was also considered a fortunate Talisman for expectant mothers.

The Peacock was regarded in very ancient times a symbol of triumph over the grave; its flesh was believed to be incorruptible, which probably accounts for its presence in church decoration; and because it renews its plumage yearly it was taken as the symbol of immortality.

It was the bird of Juno, the goddess and protectress of Malta; and on one of the old gateways her statue is still in existence bearing her symbolic bird. The supposition that the feathers of a Peacock are unlucky is said to have had its origin in the anger of the goddess Juno, having been aroused by the plucking of the feathers of her favourite bird; in her wrath she decreed that no suitors should come for the daughters of any house wherein should be found Peacocks' feathers, that the children should never be well, nor the occupants of a house healthy where these feathers were used as ornaments. It is believed the Egyptians also considered the feathers a perpetual emblem of the Evil Eye.

In many parts of the country old houses are still to be seen with one, or even two pieces of iron in the shape of the letter S attached to the outer walls. These are

THE COMPLETE BOOK OF TALISMANS, AMULETS AND MAGIC GEMSTONES

intended to protect the building from being destroyed by fire, and are not, as is generally supposed, employed as a support; sometimes the S will have a bar across its centre; another form is shaped like two crescents, placed back to back, also with a bar across the centre; but in each case they are only bolted at one point, and their meaning is the same—a charm against destruction by fire, and in all probability. it was intended as a form of the Swastika Cross.

Gold Nuggets are considered lucky charms for speculators in mines, and miners; and Leap Year Pennies should always be kept in the kitchen to bring unexpected windfalls to the house.

To card players the Deuce of Clubs is said to be the Talisman of the pack, and is generally the sign of four or five trumps in the dealer's hand; whilst the Four of Clubs is the most unlucky card, the holder of it seldom if ever winning the game; in old writings this card is known as "the devil's bedstead."

A Badger's Tooth sewn inside the right-hand pocket of the waistcoat is also a well-known Talisman for luck at cards.

The Four-Leaved Clover is another well-known charm for good luck, generally, for—

"One leaf is for fame,
And one leaf is for wealth
And one for a faithful lover,
And one to bring you glorious health
Are all in the four-leaved clover."

THE COMPLETE BOOK OF TALISMANS, AMULETS AND MAGIC GEMSTONES

PART II
THE GEMS OF THE ZODIAC
CHAPTER I
ARIES—THE RAM

The Zodiac—Zodiacal and Calendar Months—The New Year—The Constellation—Hamal—The Passover—Characteristics of Aries People—Gems of Aries—The Bloodstone and Heliotrope—Mars the Ruling Planet—Marbodeus Gallus—The Diamond—The Qualities of the Diamond—Tavernier—The Regent—The Koh-i-Noor—The Hope Diamond.

The Sun enters the Zodiacal House of Aries on March 21st of each year, and remains in occupation until April 10th, his entrance to this House marking the commencement of the Zodiacal year, with days and nights of equal length, and also signifying the advent of Spring.

The Zodiac is an imaginary belt in the heavens which extends for several degrees on either side of the apparent path of the Sun, called the Ecliptic, which is divided into twelve sections of thirty degrees each, known as the Houses of the Zodiac; and it is in this belt that the planets move and form aspects.

The Sun takes a year to travel through the twelve houses, remaining a month in each; the months are not, however, the familiar ones of the Calendar, but are for periods from the 21st of one Calendar month to the 10th of the next approximately. The time of the Sun's entry into Aries marks the Zodiacal beginning of the year, as from this time the days are longer than the nights, and are still increasing in length; the fact remains, however, that the First of January was fixed by Act of Parliament as the beginning of the New Year, although our law-makers in 1752, when re-forming the Calendar, would have been wiser and more accurate had they fixed the New Year at the Vernal Equinox instead of adopting the System of the Romans which was originally formed out of compliment to Julius Caesar.

The Constellation of Aries is situated in the Northern Celestial Hemisphere near the Pleiades, between the Constellations of Pisces and Taurus. In its group it has three very bright stars visible to the naked eye, the brightest of which is known as Hamal, or the Sheep, and was much more poetically described in the Akkadian tongue as "Dilkur," the dawn proclaimer. The Chinese have a tradition giving the greatest prominence to Aries from the fact that it was believed to have occupied the centre of the heavens at the Creation of the World, a belief that was also held by the Babylonians.

The Symbol of this House is the Ram (see Frontispiece, No. 1), which in the early religions was considered symbolic of sacrifice, and in connection with this may be noted the fact that the Jewish Passover was commenced in this sign when Moses was commanded to sacrifice a young Ram, a sacrifice which was the forecast of our Easter Services. Chemical evidence reveals the fact that the human body is composed of separate elements, common to all physical formations, and that the differences between individuals is caused by different and varying combinations of these elements, portions of which are vivified to a greater or lesser degree by the Planets of our Solar System. The influence of this force should be taken into account when the relative effect of one person's mind qualities, or magnetic emanations, on any other person is under consideration. Aries rules the Head and Face, and brain-workers are consequently typical of this sign, Reason being their ruler, and this the most positive of the twelve houses. Those born under the influence of Aries must be leaders, the brain being the most active part of their bodies. Having unbounded confidence in their own abilities when working out their plans, difficulties are scorned, or even welcomed, for they have the true Martian spirit—the love of conquest.

Pioneers in thought and action, ever exploring and originating, they bring unflagging energy and fearlessness in emergency to their pursuits, seeming specially gifted by Nature to tread the thorny paths of life, making the ways smoother for their weaker brethren. Their methods must, however, be their own. If required to work on conventional lines they are never happy, and seldom successful; understanding what they require, they must be left to accomplish it according to their own ideas. Optimistic in regard to their enterprises, difficulties are underrated; but where any matter requires to be dealt with quickly and promptly, they are at their best.

Aries people are very enthusiastic, brave, venturesome, generous, and impulsive, self-willed and opinionated, fond of change, romance, and adventure, ever ready to champion the cause of the weak and suffering, this tendency frequently leading them to acts of indiscriminate charity often wasted on undeserving subjects. They have great ideality, are highly strung, often hypersensitive, with remarkably keen perceptions in which they are rarely deceived. They are naturally ambitious, and often lacking in caution; but, as they are ruled by their reasoning powers, it is in this direction they are open to control and should find their Zodiacal and Planetary Stones of great benefit to them. In matters of business, friendship, and the affections this type will harmonise best with those between April 21st and May 21st, July 22nd and August 21st, also November 22nd and December

10th.

The gems of this House are the Bloodstone and Diamond, which, as a rule, will not be good for people born between June 21st and July 21st, unless Mars was very favourable at their birth.

The Bloodstone is a variety of green Jasper which derives its distinctive name from a number of blood-red specks formed by iron oxide with which it is impregnated. It is an opaque stone, but as its surface is capable of taking a very high polish, and in consistency being very suitable to the graver, it has from time immemorial been a great favourite for the cutting of seals and cameos. It exists in large quantities and is, in consequence, inexpensive, and is found in India, Bokhara, Siberia, Tartary, and in the Hebrides.

There is much disagreement between ancient writers with regard to the Heliotrope and Bloodstone, some asserting there is no difference, the name Heliotrope having been conferred upon this variety from the idea that when plunged in water it presents a red reflection of the image of the Sun; others maintain that the Heliotrope is a translucent green Chalcedony with crimson spots, and the Bloodstone a green Jasper flecked with red.

An old tradition records that the Bloodstone had its origin at the Crucifixion, being formed by drops of blood which, following the thrust of the Roman soldier's spear, fell upon some green jasper on which the cross was erected, the stains penetrating the stones and thus originating this particular variety. From this time onwards the stone seems to have been endowed with magical and divine powers in arresting hemorrhage from wounds, and was worn by Roman soldiers for this reason; among the natives of India it is customary to place the Bloodstone itself upon wounds and injuries after dipping it in cold water. Its curative properties in this respect have been explained in modern times by the fact that the iron oxide in this stone is an active and effective astringent even now used in surgery.

Rings of dark green Jasper flecked with red were favourite ornaments amongst the Egyptians, who frequently wore them upon the thumb, probably because the thumb is under Martian influence, Mars being the ruling planet of the House of Aries.

One of these talismanic stones was worn by Nechepsos, an Egyptian king, to strengthen the digestive organs, and was engraved in the form of a dragon surrounded by rays. The Gnostics wore the Bloodstone as an Amulet to prolong life, and to make its wearer courageous and wealthy, as well as to strengthen the stomach and dispel melancholy; and in the Middle Ages it was considered good for those engaged in husbandry and the breeding of cattle.

Amongst the ancient Greeks and Romans, the Bloodstone was worn to bring renown and the favour of the great; to inspire constancy and endurance, and as a charm against the bites of scorpions and all venomous creatures. It was also a great favourite with their athletes, who wore it as a Talisman for success in the games.

In an essay written by a certain Thomas Boyle on "The Origine and Virtues of Gems," dated 1675, we read that a gentleman of sanguine habit having been long troubled with excessive bleeding from the nose, was unable to find a cure until "an ancient gentleman presented him with a Bloodstone the size of a pigeon's egg, to be worn round the neck, and upon the use of this stone he not only cured himself, but stopped hemorrhage in a neighbour."

Marbodeus Gallus, writing in verse on this stone, after mentioning its virtue against the Ague and Dropsy, says:

"Againe it is believed to be a safeguard frank and free
 To such as ware and beare the same; and if it hallowed bee,
 It makes the parties gratious and mightier too that have it
 And noysome fancies as they write who ment not to deprave it
 It doth dispel out of the mind. The force thereof is stronger
 In silver, if this stone be set, it doth endure the longer."

The Chinese advise its being set in gold to obtain the best results; and the Rev. C. W. King tells us that a Bloodstone, engraved with the figure of a scorpion when the Sun was entering the sign of Scorpio, was believed by the Ancients to be a sure preservation against the formation of stone in the bladder.

The Diamond.—Amongst the many precious crystallised stones the diamond stands pre-eminent for beauty, brilliancy, and strength. It is the hardest stone known, hence the name of Adamas, meaning "the Indomitable," given it by its ancient discoverers, as with it every known substance can be cut, although it cannot be cut, nor be scratched by other stones; nor have acids nor solvents any effect upon it. It also resists the action of the file.

When found, the diamond is covered with a thick crust, so hard that there is no substance known that will remove it but that of itself, and it is only by grinding and polishing with diamond dust and minute diamonds that it is shaped and its wonderful brilliancy developed.

It was believed by the old writers to be the most powerful of all precious stones in its influence and effect upon humanity both spiritually and physically, and it is connected with marvellous records of adventure and enterprise, as well as representing Purity, Innocence, and protection from witchcraft and evil. To this day in India, amongst natives sufficiently wealthy, tiny diamonds are sprinkled from a white cloth over the heads of infants during the ceremony of naming the child, to keep it pure and virtuous.

The Romans also regarded the diamond with much reverence, fastening it upon the left arm so that the gem should touch the flesh, believing it powerful in making its wearer brave and daring, giving him the victory over his enemies; and when set in fine steel, was considered a charm against insanity.

It was thought by the old astrologers to be particularly powerful when worn by a subject born under a strong aspect of the planet Mars, bestowing fortitude, strength of mind, and constancy in wedded love; it repelled sorcery, poison, and nightmares, calmed anger, and strengthened friendship. It is often referred to as the Stone of Reconciliation; and was worn to promote love and harmony between man and wife.

Sir John Mandeville writes the following:

"A diamond should be worn on the left side of the body for it is of greater value there than on the right, for the strength of their growing is towards the North, that is, the left side of the world, and the left part of a man is when he turns his face to the East."

Another old writer says:

"He who carries a diamond on the left side shall be hardy and manly; it will guard him from accidents to the limbs; but nevertheless a good diamond will lose its power and virtue if worn by one who is incontinent, or drunken."

In the Middle Ages the diamond was thought to protect its wearer from the plague, and for this reason Queen Elizabeth was given a diamond to guard her against infection, which she is said to have worn in her bosom. It was a diamond worn in the girdle of Queen Donna Isabel II of Spain that saved her on the day when the murderous attempt was made upon her life. The point of the assassin's dagger struck the stone and glanced off, so the wound, which might otherwise have proved fatal, resulted in a flesh wound only. Napoleon, too, attached great value to the qualities of the diamond, and wore the famous Regent diamond in the hilt of his sword. The history of this remarkable stone is so curious that a brief account of its discovery and subsequent owners may be interesting. It was found at Parteal, south of Golconda, by a slave who concealed it by making a gash in the calf of his leg and hiding the stone in the folds of the bandage until he could escape to Madras. Deceived by the promises made to him by a sailor in whom he had confided, he consented, when a purchaser had been found for the stone, to share profits, but was thrown overboard by the seaman, who disposed of the diamond to a dealer named Jamchund for L1000, which he quickly spent, afterwards hanging himself.

The stone was next purchased by Thomas Pitt, grandfather to the Earl of Chatham, who purchased it after much bargaining for L20,400; but the jewel brought him no happiness. So fearful was he of losing it, it is said that he never slept twice at the same house whilst it was in his possession; also serious reflections were made on his character as to when and under what conditions he had obtained it. About the year 1717, having offered the gem to several sovereigns, the Regent of France was persuaded that his country should possess the most beautiful and perfect diamond known, so the purchase was effected for L135,000.

In its natural state it weighed 410 carats, but after its cutting, which took two years to complete, it was reduced to 137 carats, and was the size of a large plum, perfectly white, without spot or flaw, and of admirable water.

In the disorder attendant on the French Revolution the Regent diamond was stolen from the public treasury. Twelve years afterwards it was recovered, and subsequently was amongst the stones set in the Imperial diadem of France.

Another celebrated diamond is the Koh-i-Noor, or "Mountain of Light." Its history, according to Tavernier, the French traveller, can be traced back to half a century B.C. This stone is reported by Baber, the founder of the Mogul Empire, to have come into the treasury at Delhi from the conquest of Malwa in 1304, since when it has passed through the hands of many Indian rulers, who believed that the safety of their dynasty depended on the possession of this fateful jewel.

After many vicissitudes it came into the possession of Runjeet Singh King of Lahore, who wore it on his arm set between two smaller diamonds. So convinced was he of its mystical powers, that he bequeathed it to the Shrine of Juggernaut so that he might obtain benefits for his soul after death. His successors, however, would not allow the treasure to be disposed of in this manner, and it was subsequently presented to the late Queen Victoria by Lord Dalhousie on the annexation of the Punjaub, and was brought to London in 1850. The Brahmins believe that the Crimean War and Sepoy Mutiny, which occurred seven years afterwards, were due to its influence, and they say that misfortune will follow the possessor until it is restored to the line of Vikramaditya; but we are justified in the hope that as England is under the influence of the Zodiacal House of Aries, the house of the diamond, our Empire may still flourish and prosper.

Since the Koh-i-Noor came into our possession it has been recut, an operation which has decreased its size but greatly improved its brilliancy.

According to ancient lore, very large diamonds should never be worn as ornaments, as they bring disaster and anxiety; nor should they be used as sleeve-links or buttons or they will bring misfortune and sudden death. The losing of a diamond was considered (and still is), apart from its material value, an omen of mishaps. To be efficacious as a Talisman the diamond should be given freely, never sold, never lent, never coveted, and never taken by fraud or force. It is a curious fact that large diamonds have ever brought anxiety and often death to those who have taken them by violence and sold them; and the strange fatality which, for so many years, seems to have surrounded the famous HOPE diamond is an example.

The Hope Diamond was originally owned by Tavernier, the French traveller, already mentioned. Born in Paris in 1605, he spent some years in the East, traded extensively in precious stones, and accumulated a vast fortune. In the year 1668 the gem, subsequently known as "the Hope Diamond," was sold by Tavernier in a parcel of fine diamonds to Louis XIV, the Grand Monarque. Tavernier was soon after robbed by his son of an immense sum of money; left destitute, at the age of eighty-one he died in exile. The King's haughty and arrogant favourite, the

Duchesse de Montespan, prevailed upon her Royal lover to allow her to wear the dazzling gem at a Court Ball. From that hour she lost her fascination for the fickle monarch, and the circumstances of her fall confirmed the sinister superstition as to the fateful nature of the blue diamond. Most beautiful and most unhappy of all its wearers was Marie Antoinette. She not only wore it herself, but lent it to her dearest friend the Princesse de Lamballe. When Madame de Lamballe's head was paraded on a pike by the revolutionary mob, and shown to the King and Queen—then practically prisoners—and when subsequently the ill-fated Louis XVI perished on the guillotine, and finally was followed by his Queen, who was driven slowly to the scaffold so that she should be made to "drink long of death," the superstitious remembered the reputed curse which the blue diamond was said to bring upon its possessors. For thirty years after this the ill-fated diamond was lost to the public gaze, until it was found in the possession of a lapidary of Amsterdam, whose son stole it from his father and disappeared, Fals, the gem-cutter, dying in absolute want. The son gave the jewel to a Frenchman named Beaulieu, and after disposing of it committed suicide. Francois Beaulieu brought the gem to London and sold it to a dealer named Daniel Eliason, Beaulieu himself dying the next day mysteriously.

Mr. Henry Thomas Hope was the next purchaser, paying Eliason the sum of L18,000 for it. The stone remained in the Hope family until 1901, when Lord Francis Hope (who had married and divorced an actress) sold it to a diamond merchant, who resold it to an American, who, becoming financially embarrassed, disposed of it to M. Jacques Colot. He in his turn disposed of it to a Russian Prince who was stabbed; and the French dealer from whom he purchased it ended his own life. Next a Greek merchant met with a violent death after selling the diamond to Abdul Hamid, the ex-Sultan of Turkey, who narrowly escaped with his life after losing his throne. A firm of New York jewellers next bought the sinister gem, and although a story was circulated that they had disposed of it to a gentleman who had gone down in the ill-fated Titanic, it is believed to be, at present, in the possession of Mr. McLean, an American millionaire, to whom so far nothing untoward has happened.

The preceding paragraph was written in 1914, and in May, 1919, further proof was given of the strange fatality that accompanies this stone in the announcement in all European papers of the death of Vincent Walsh McLean, aged eleven years, who was accidentally killed by a motor-car whilst playing in the road (having escaped from his nurse) near his father's estate.

Great importance was attached by the Hindus to the original shape of a diamond, a triangular stone being thought to cause quarrels, a square diamond terrors; but a six-cornered stone was thought to bring the best of good fortune and to renew the strength in old age.

CHAPTER II
TAURUS—THE BULL

The Constellation—Aldebaran—The Chaldeans—The Temples—Apis Bull—Aphrodite—Characteristics of Taurus—Training—Gems of Taurus—The Sapphire—Bishop's Ring—St. Jerome Qualities of the Sapphire—Star Sapphire—Solomon's Seal—Charlemagne's Talisman—The Turquoise—Boetius de Boot—Horseman's Talisman—Qualities of the Stone.

The Sun enters the Celestial House of Taurus, the second sign of the Zodiac, on April 21st, and remains in occupation until May 22nd. Taurus is situated between the constellations of Aries and Gemini, and its position is marked by a beautiful cluster of stars named Hyades, from a Greek word meaning rain, because the influence of these stars was considered to be conducive to rainfalls. Its most brilliant star is Aldebaran, a star of the first magnitude; Taurus also contains the Pleiades, and it is a generally accepted theory amongst astronomers that the motion of the Sun, probably in a circle, has its centre in one of these stars. According to ancient mythology, the Pleiades were the seven daughters of Atlas and Pheione, who, because of their great virtue and purity, were rewarded by a place in the heavens as a constellation of stars.

The symbol of this House is the Bull (as illustrated Frontispiece, No. 2), which was selected by the early Chaldean astrologers as typifying the nature of those born under this sign, and not from any fancied resemblance of its stars to a Bull. Undoubtedly the Zodiac had a prehistoric origin, and one of the ancient names given to this sign was Te, meaning foundation, which is interesting from the fact that it was in this sign period that the foundations of the two Jewish temples were laid.

As Taurus is the first of the earthly signs it typifies the creative forces of Nature; Apis, the sacred Bull of the Egyptians, was used as its symbol and was adopted by the Greeks as typical of fecundity, and is mentioned in Part I, Chapter VIII, on Greek Talismans. In Ancient Greece, Venus, the ruling planet of this House, was represented by the goddess Aphrodite, usually shown with horns on her head (not intended to represent the goddess Isis as has been sometimes imagined, but the planet Venus, which occasionally in the course of her revolution round the Sun is seen in crescent form)

The dominating characteristic of Taurus subjects is their tenacity of purpose, which makes them staunch friends but determined enemies; and although this may to some extent cause difficulty in adapting their opinions to those of others, on the other hand it enables them, when once they have grasped existing conditions, to reap the benefit of their industry and application.

They possess strong mental and physical powers, and are persistent students, their qualities of concentration making them capable of high educational attainments. They are determined, fearless, enthusiastic, and unyielding in carrying out their schemes; and, when not irritated, are generous. The temper is, under normal circumstances, even, if at times sullen, not easily provoked, but very hot and tempestuous when aroused. They can be influenced through their enthusiasm, but will resent to the utmost with dogged obstinacy any attempt to drive them against their inclinations. Their memories are, as a rule, good, and their tenacity of purpose is usually accompanied by a great deal of patience, so that they usually accomplish aims, although not always with a due regard to cost. Their outlook is practical, but not miserly, and money is valued as a medium of power, and for the use that can be made of it. Owing to their strong vitality, they generate life forces very rapidly, which gives them the power of healing, making them very helpful to people of nervous temperament lacking in vitality which this type possesses in excess. When attracted their friendship is sincere and trustworthy; and, although they are undoubtedly shrewd in business matters, they are also sensitive to psychic and emotional influences, being apt to allow their feelings and emotions to rule, laying themselves open to deception, and the unscrupulous, by working upon their sympathies, can prejudice their judgment, so that as a rule it will be best for this type to make all important decisions when alone, either in the early morning or after retiring at night.

They do not usually suffer from lack of appetite, and their tastes are of an epicurean nature, the masculine subjects being critical and not easily satisfied; the gentler sex are apt to be hypercritical and with a strong bias in favour of their own culinary theories or methods over those of others.

Their success in life comes, as a rule, after thirty, when they have their dispositions well in hand and are able to benefit by their experiences.

In this sign the Moon is in exaltation, and subjects born when she is so placed have their characters strengthened, and have more reserve and self-control. Their ambitions become practical and successful; the constitution is stronger, and there is less liability to disease.

With Taurean subjects, the early impressions of life are vivid and lasting, and their future career and welfare depend very largely on their training and influences through childhood and youth, surrounding conditions and early attachments

THE COMPLETE BOOK OF TALISMANS, AMULETS AND MAGIC GEMSTONES

being never forgotten.

Although producing practical business people, this sign has also its artistic side natural to the planet Venus. Many talented musicians and singers are born during this period, and the type as a whole, even when personally unaccomplished, is greatly influenced by music and singing which make a strong appeal to their emotional tendencies.

Unless following a very active vocation, their abundant vitality predisposes them to put on flesh, and it is through this tendency that disease attacks them and they become liable to stomach troubles, dropsy, affections of the heart, kidneys, and generative system; they are also prone to complaints affecting the throat, such as quinsies, diphtheria, and laryngitis.

They will harmonise best with people whose birthdays come between August 22nd and September 22nd; December 21st and January 20th; and June 21st and July 22nd.

The Gems of this House are the Sapphire and Turquoise, which are especially suitable for the expression of the Taurean qualities.

The Sapphire.—The Sapphire, one of the earliest gems known to man, is found in riverbeds and torrents, the force of the water washing the stones from their matrix; and to this day are still found under these conditions. In its finest quality the sapphire is of a deep blue colour, and the more it resembles the dark velvety blue of the Pansy the greater is its value.

Of coloured gems, the Sapphire has been the most venerated amongst all nations, and particularly in the East it is the stone most frequently consecrated to the various deities. Amongst Buddhists it is believed to produce a desire for prayer, and is regarded as the Stone of Stones to give Spiritual Light, and to bring Peace and Happiness as long as its wearer leads a moral life.

In the early days of the Christian Church, the stones and metal used in making the ring of a Bishop was left very much to the taste of the individual, but in the twelfth century Innocent III decreed that these rings should be made of pure gold, set with an unengraved stone, the Sapphire being the gem selected, as possessing the virtues and qualities essential to its dignified position as the badge of Pontifical rank and "a seal of secrets," for there be many things "that a priest conceals from the senses of the vulgar and less intelligent; which he keeps locked up as it were under seal."

Of this gem St. Jerome writes that "it procures favours with princes, pacifies enemies, frees from enchantment, and obtains freedom from captivity."

The Jews also held this stone in high veneration, the seal-stone in the ring of King Solomon being said to be a Sapphire, and in Exodus xxiv. 10, we read in the description of a manifestation of Jehovah:

"There was under his feet as it were a paved work of a sapphire stone, and as it were the body of heaven in his clearness."

This description of clearness, if taken as meaning transparency, would indicate a familiarity with the qualities of the stone as we know it, although in most of the ancient writings all blue stones are loosely described as Sapphires, including the Tables of the Law, which it is practically certain could not have been of Sapphire and in all probability were of Lapis Lazuli.

During the Middle Ages the qualities attributed to the Sapphire were that it preserved Chastity, discovered Fraud and Treachery, protected from Poison, Plague, Fever, and Skin Diseases, and had great power in resisting black magic and ill-wishing; in smallpox it preserved the eyes from injury if rubbed on them. It also gave concentration; but if worn by an intemperate or impious person, it lost its lustre, thus indicating the presence of vice and impurity. It is recorded that in the Church of Old St. Paul's, London, there was a famous Sapphire given by "Richard de Preston, Citizen and Grocer of that city, for the cure of infirmities in the eyes of those thus afflicted who might resort to it."

Cloudy Sapphires are sometimes found which owing to a peculiarity in their composition show six rays of light running from the top of the stone. These are known as Asteria, or Star Stones, and this Star Sapphire was much valued by the Ancients as a love charm; they considered it peculiarly powerful for the procuring of favours, for bringing good fortune and averting witchcraft. Six is the number given to Venus, and is also the number of the true Solomon's Seal, whose virtues and qualities (treated of under Talismans, Part I, Chapter II) this stone represents.

The wife of the Emperor Charlemagne is reputed to have possessed a very powerful Talisman composed of two rough Sapphires and a portion of the Holy Cross, made by the Magi in the train of Haaroon Al Raschid, Emperor of the East. This Talisman was made for the purpose of keeping Charlemagne's affections constant to his wife, and it was so efficacious that his love endured after her death. He would not allow the body, on which the Talisman hung, to be interred, even when decomposition had set in; and burial was only permitted when Charlemagne's confessor, who knew of the Talisman and its virtue, removed it from the body. The confessor kept the Talisman and was raised to high honours by Charlemagne, becoming Archbishop of Mainz and Chancellor of the Empire. It was, however, restored to the monarch on his death-bed when he was suffering great agony, and it enabled him to pass peacefully away.

The Turquoise.—The Turquoise is universally recognised as a Venus stone, though sometimes erroneously attributed to the Zodiacal House of Capricorn, which is ruled by the planet Saturn. It responds to the vibrations of both Venus Houses, but seems strongest in Taurus.

This stone was, in ancient times, known as the Turkis, or Turkeystone, as most of the specimens found in Europe in those days came from Persia through the hands of Constantinople merchants. The best specimens still come from Persia, although Turquoises are also mined in Arizona, U.S.A.; in China and Thibet and Russia; and in the Crown Jewels of Spain are many Turquoises brought from New Mexico over two hundred years ago.

The Turquoise is more frequently used for Amulets than any other stone, as much for its mystic virtues as for its beauty, particularly in the East, where sentences from the Koran are engraved upon it and the characters gilded.

Amongst its many virtues it was believed to warn of poison by becoming moist and changing colour; and it is said that King John, by these indications, detected the poison that caused his death. This gem has always been regarded as a pledge of true affections, and is also credited with the power of drawing upon itself the evil that threatens its wearer; but this quality belongs only to the Turquoise that has been given, and not purchased. Boetius de Boot tells of a stone that had been in the possession of a Spanish gentleman living near his father; the stone was of exceptional beauty, but at the time of its owner's death it had entirely lost its colour and was said to resemble Malachite more than Turquoise. Because of this de Boot's father bought it for a very small sum, but not liking to wear so shabby-looking a gem, he gave it to his son, saying, "Son, as the virtues of the Turkois are said to exist only when the stone has been received as a gift, I will try its efficacy by bestowing it upon thee." De Boot, although he did not much appreciate the gift, had his crest engraved upon it, but had not worn it a month before it regained its original beauty. Shortly after this the stone gave evidence of its power, for as de Boot was riding home in the dark his horse stumbled and fell from a bank to the road ten feet below, neither horse nor rider being any the worse for the fall; in the morning the stone was found to be split in two.

It is for qualities such as these that it is prized by the Turks as a horseman's Talisman, they believing that it makes a horse sure-footed and protects its rider from injury by falls; and Camillus Leonardus says: "So long as a rider hath the Turquoise with him his horse will never tire him and will preserve him from any accident, and defend him that carries it from untoward and evil casualties."

In the Middle Ages the Turquoise was believed to appease hatred, relieve and prevent headaches, and to change colour when its owner was in peril or ill-health. The change of colour must not be permanent, and the stone should recover its real hue when the illness or danger is passed.

A gentleman who is a practical business man, holding an important position in the City, to whom I supplied a Turquoise, assured me that on two occasions when he was in personal danger the stone paled, but afterwards recovered its natural colour. It is not, however, sensitive to the changes in his states of health.

THE COMPLETE BOOK OF TALISMANS, AMULETS AND MAGIC GEMSTONES

CHAPTER III
GEMINI—THE HOUSE OF THE TWINS

Period—The Twins, Castor and Pollux—The Argonauts—King Solomon's Pillars—Maia—Ovid and Wedding of Mary Queen of Scots—Gemini Number—Characteristics—Agates and their Virtues—Orpheus—Chrysoprase—Alexander the Great—Virtues of the Stone.

Gemini, the Zodiacal House of the Twins, is occupied by the Sun from the 22nd of May until the 21st of June approximately, and is ruled by the planet Mercury. In the earliest Zodiacs this House was symbolised by two kids, for which the Greeks substituted twin children, the sons of Jupiter, represented by two bright stars, Castor and Pollux.

Gemini is also symbolised by two Pillars joined at the top and base (gemini), which is a diagrammatic representation of the Twins seated side by side with embracing arms. Castor was killed in battle, and Pollux, overwhelmed at his loss, entreated Jupiter to restore his brother to life, or make them both immortal. As a reward for this great affection, and in recognition of their noble deeds when on earth, Jupiter translated the two brothers, thus forming the Constellation Gemini in the heavens. It was believed that among other achievements they cleared the neighbouring seas of pirates, and when the Argonauts were in distress from a violent tempest, two lambent flames descended from the clouds and settled upon the heads of Castor and Pollux, a calm immediately ensuing.

From these circumstances they were regarded as protectors of navigation, it being inferred that whenever both stars were visible it was a harbinger of fine weather, the appearance of one star only signifying storms and tempests.

It may be noted that as a rule the seas are calm when the Sun is in Gemini, and it was at this period of the year that the forty days' rain of the Deluge ceased.

The symbol of the two Pillars joined at the top and base, already referred to, were also believed to typify the two pillars set up by King Solomon in the porch of the Temple, which were quite distinct and apart from the building itself and were not for any structural purpose, their use being entirely symbolical.

One was named "Jachin," meaning "He will establish," and the other "Boaz," signifying "In Him is strength"; also they denoted the union of Intellect and Intuition.

The symbols of the Twins and Pillars are shown in No. 3 of the coloured Frontispiece.

Amongst the Romans the month of May was sacred to Maia the goddess of Sterility, and this month was, therefore, considered by them a most unfavourable time for marriages. Ovid in his Fasti tells us that—

"Neither are the times suitable for the marriage of the widow nor the virgin. She who was married was not so for long. Also for this cause (if proverbs affect you) they commonly say evil things for marrying in the month of Mai."

This last sentence (in its original Latin) was affixed to the gates of Holyrood Palace after the wedding of Mary Queen of Scots to Bothwell on the 15th of May, 1567. Another old writer says that the day of the week on which the 14th of May falls is not only unlucky for marriage in this unfortunate month, but that throughout the remainder of the year that particular day will bring ill-luck to those who marry on it; and another old proverb runs: "May never was ye month of love." Even now it is stated fewer marriages take place in this month than in any other.

The fortunate number of the Gemini type is 5, which was considered to have peculiar virtues as a Talisman by the Ancient Egyptians and Greeks because it unites the first even and odd numbers 2 and 3. It was often inscribed over doors to keep out evil spirits. In connection with this, it is interesting to note that in Roman ceremonies of marriage it was usual to light five tapers and to admit the guests by five; Jewish history records a frequent use of this number, five gifts to the priests, five things only to be eaten in camp. Joseph gave five suits of raiment to Benjamin, and presented only five of his brothers to Pharaoh. David took five pebbles when he went to fight Goliath, and Joshua hanged five kings on five trees; further, every important measurement of the Tabernacle was five or a multiple of five; also there were five wise and five foolish virgins. In the Mohammedan religion there are five articles of belief, namely in Allah, in the Prophets, in Angels, the Day of Judgment, and Predestination.

In Astrology there are five principal aspects of the planets which rule the good, or bad fortunes of the subject; also in Masonry the grand scheme is five points of fellowship, also five brethren can hold a fellow-craft's lodge. The fifth son of Jacob, Issachar, represents Gemini, and, in naming him, Leah expresses the leading qualities of the symbol—that is, reward and recompense which its mental qualities bring.

The subjects born during this period are invariably of an intellectual disposition, and when well-educated their ideals and aspirations are high, with an intense desire to do useful work. When inclined to religion they favour the intellectual and idealistic. In family life they are very loyal and faithful, helping their relations however undeserving. Though generous to their families or when prompted

THE COMPLETE BOOK OF TALISMANS, AMULETS AND MAGIC GEMSTONES

by personal influence, these subjects are not lavish in their expenditure. Being fond of money and ingenious in their schemes and methods of making it, they like to secure a good return for money spent and their natural shrewdness enables them to get the better of their fellows. They have a quick comprehension of human nature which assists them in their schemes, enabling them to weigh up any one they may be dealing with, and consequently to get the best of a bargain. Their success, or otherwise, will depend to a great extent on the positions occupied and the aspects in relation to each other of the Moon and planets at the time of their birth.

Under harmonious circumstances they possess keen judgment, quick wit, ability in artistic directions, and the faculty of acquiring knowledge without much apparent effort, their capabilities carrying them to the highest mental attainments but, when ill-balanced, they sink to the extreme of clever trickery and fraud.

Their characteristics are often contradictory. Being peculiarly undecided in their dispositions and invariably of two minds, the constant influx of new ideas causes much innate restlessness, the realisation of their plans seldom coming up to anticipations. Owing to the antagonism between their feelings and their reason, they are seldom able to concentrate on any one thing for any length of time, thus they start many schemes and enterprises which they abandon before completion. In consequence, Intuition and its forces, (as opposed to Impulse and individual inclination,) strain and perplex the versatile mind of this type, making them capricious and irritable, although their anger is easily appeased. They are highly strung, vivacious, restless, and fond of change and variety in their friends and associates, having great dislike to monotonous work and ever seeking fresh outlets for their effervescence.

In argument, from their facility of expression and dual nature, they are the most difficult of opponents to overcome. Many of our most clever advocates and solicitors have been born during this period, and as illustrative of the duality of this House, it produces, when favourably aspected, the best physicians, authors, orators, actors, schoolmasters, journalists, merchants, accountants, secretaries, and linguists; also our smartest detectives; but when the worst side of their character is developed, the subjects of this House become the craftiest of law-breakers. The cleverest of criminals come from this type, ranging from fraudulent company promoters to thieves and pickpockets.

Gemini rules the arms, shoulders, and hands; and ailments such as sprains and displacements attack Gemini subjects in their limbs. The lungs, too, are sometimes afflicted, generally through defections in breathing; also a tendency to rheumatic and gouty pains in those portions of the body ruled by this sign, and when Mercury, the ruling planet, is badly aspected, digestive trouble, nervous ailments, and imperfect action of the liver are indicated.

In marriage and business relations those born during the Gemini period will agree best with Aries, Leo, Libra, and Aquarius characters, and it is a curious fact that in the lives of those born whilst the Sun occupies the House of the Twins, nearly all important events, fortunate or unfortunate, happen twice, and incidents in the career are repeated in a similar way.

The fortunate stones of this House are all varieties of Agates and the Chrysoprase.

The Agate.—The Agate is a variety of quartz found in different colours, often with alternate layers of red and white known as "ribbon" Agate, also of a milky white. The latter can be artificially coloured and, in consequence, is obtainable in bright greens and blues as well as in various tones of greyish purple.

The Moss or Tree Agate is a variety ornamented by Nature in a most remarkable manner with lines, spots, and frequently with natural objects taking the distinct forms of ferns, trees, clouds, and moss, giving a very mysterious effect to the stone. In the days of the Romans this variety was held in high repute as possessing both medicinal and talismanic virtues, it being claimed that the wonderful markings formed in this stone indicated that it had been specially singled out by the Creator to receive wondrous occult power. According to Orpheus, "If thou wear a piece of Tree Agate upon thine hand the Immortal Gods shall be well pleased with thee; if the same be tied to the harness of thy oxen when ploughing, or about the ploughman's sturdy arm, wheat-crowned Ceres shall descend from heaven with full lap upon thy furrows."

The Moss Agate was also considered good for the sight and was used by physicians for palettes on which they ground down the ingredients used in making up lotions and ointments.

The vegetable representations in the Tree Agates are supposed to have been produced by particles of metallic substances, such as iron and magnesium; the name Mocha Stone, sometimes used to indicate this variety, is derived from Mocha in Arabia, where it was found.

In the British Museum there is a striking specimen of Moss Agate representing a likeness of the poet Chaucer; and the Strawberry Hill Collection has another with a portrait of Voltaire, and a third showing the profile of a woman. There are also numerous varieties of Agate dependent upon the arrangement of the layers; sometimes the stone shows parallel lines of light and dark tints, when it is called banded or ribbon Agate. When the colours are very sharp and defined it becomes Onyx Agate, and when the stripes converge towards the centre of the stone it is known as Eye Agate; whilst another variety showing many colours becomes Rainbow or Iris Agate.

According to Mr. Streeter, Agates in their natural state are formed in the cavities of rocks, and it is conjectured that when the rocks were in a fluid state the Agates were formed by the escape of gas or steam. These cavities were afterwards filled with some mineral substance, such as silica, held in solution and deposited on the interior walls of these receptacles, forming a kind of geode.

In addition to the Moss or Tree Agate, the Greeks and Romans had great faith in the talismanic and medicinal virtues of all other Agates, wearing them to avert sickness, regarding them particularly as an antidote to the bite of an Asp, if taken powdered in wine, or as an infallible cure for the sting of a Scorpion if tied over the wound. They also brought success in love and friendship, great gain, and the favours of the great, if strung on a hair taken from a lion's mane.

Pliny was a great believer in the virtues of the Agate, and writes that storms may be averted by burning these stones; whilst Camillo Leonardo, in addition to their power to avert lightning and tempest, says they bring strength, vigour, and great success to their wearers. Marbodus, Bishop of Rennes, ascribes the escape of Aeneas from all his perils to the virtue of an Agate Talisman which he always carried with him.

Although these stones eventually ceased to be in much demand for signets amongst the Romans, they never lost their popularity as Talismans, and were in great request, not only amongst the Latin races, but also among the Persians and peoples of the Orient, amongst whom it was universally believed to confer eloquence, to enlighten the mind, to allay fevers, also to bring luck in connection with wills and legacies, to sharpen the sight, aid in the discovery of treasure, and make its wearer amiable and agreeable.

Amongst Mohammedans it was believed to cure insanity if taken powdered in apple juice. In Elizabethan days our forefathers had great faith in its talismanic virtues, the Queen having amongst her jewels a large oval Agate engraved with scenes representing Vulcan at his forge with Venus looking on. This jewel was presented to her by Archbishop Parker, and was accompanied by a parchment giving in Latin a long list of its properties, concluding to the effect that as long as Her Majesty possessed this jewel she would ever have a trusty friend.

Agates of all kinds were much esteemed by the Greeks, particularly those specimens in which could be traced resemblances to natural objects. The following verse poetically describes its many qualities:

"Who comes with summer to this earth
And owes to June her day of birth,
With ring of Agate on her hand
Can Health, Wealth and long life command."

The Chrysoprase.—The Chrysoprase, like the Agate, is a variety of quartz and takes its name from two Greek words meaning "golden leek," in reference to its colour, which varies from an opaque yellowish green to a very light dirty white-green. The colour has a tendency to fade from long exposure to the light and sun, but can be restored if the stone is dipped in a solution of nitrate of nickel.

The finest specimens come from Silesia, and when the stone was in demand it used to be customary to close the mines for every two years out of three.

According to Albertus Magnus, a Chrysoprase formed the Amulet of Alexander the Great, and Chrysoprase was much used by the ancient Greeks and Romans for signet rings and cameos; and also by the Egyptians, who set it with lapis lazuli.

The virtues attributed to the Chrysoprase were that it imparted cheerfulness, making the heart glad by removing uneasiness, protecting its wearers from evil dreams and the assaults of demons.

It also bestowed all kinds of blessings on its owner, giving assiduity in good works, and taking away all greedy and covetous desires, bringing success in new enterprises, and true and faithful friends: and it was also worn as an Amulet against rheumatism and gout.

The Agates and Chrysoprase stones will not, however, be fortunate for those born during the time that the Sun occupies the Houses of Virgo and Pisces.

CHAPTER IV
CANCER—THE HOUSE OF THE CRAB

The Dark Sign—Its Duration—Origins—Summer Solstice—Hercules and the Crab—Characteristics—Goddess Esmeralda and the Ancient Peruvians—The Emerald Isle—Moonstones—Blue Moon—Pearls—Cat's Eyes—Rock Crystals—Crystal-gazing—Virtues of the Crystal.

Cancer, the fourth sign of the Zodiac, is situated in the northern celestial hemisphere; being composed of small stars, the brightest of which are only of the third magnitude, and very few visible to the naked eye, it was known in olden times as the dark sign, and is shown with its symbols in No. 4 of the coloured Frontispiece.

The Sun enters this sign on June 22nd, remaining in occupation up to and including July 23rd, being in that part of the Ecliptic highest above the Equator, marking midsummer.

Its name Cancer, meaning a Crab, is popularly supposed to have originated in the resemblance of its constellation to this crustacean, but the likeness is not at all obvious, even if it may once have existed, so that the name probably had its origin from some other cause.

The earliest known illustration of this symbol is very like the Egyptian Scarab, many antiquarians favouring this as the real symbol, it having been used as an emblem of resurrection for over 3000 years B.C., and as this sign marked the resurrection of the earth from the Flood which ended in the preceding Zodiacal sign Gemini, the Beetle or Scarab is sometimes shown placed in the centre of the Crab's back. The significance of this, the new world bearing its symbol of eternity, is not so very surprising when we remember that the Zodiac characterised highly developed religious ideas.

The beginning of the sign cancer is called the Tropic of Cancer, and when the Sun arrives within this sign it has reached its utmost limit of north declination and seems to remain stationary a few days before it begins to decline again to the south. This stationary altitude is called the Summer Solstice, or "Sun standing still"; and the Hindus, having derived their knowledge of the stars principally from the Chaldeans, used the Crab as symbolic of this House, as in order to move forward it is compelled, as it were, to walk backwards, which illustrates the apparent motion of the Sun when it commences to move backwards towards the Equator.

In Ancient Mythology we are told that this constellation was formed by a Crab placed in the heavens by the goddess Juno as a reward for the sacrifice of its life which it lost in an attack on Hercules in her service, and so earned its translation to the celestial domains.

Cancer, being the Zodiacal House of the Moon, is much under her influence. It is the first of the watery signs and presides over the Ocean; subjects born during this period, because of their receptive and plastic natures, may be said to reflect the influences of their surroundings like the sea. Impressionable, yet tenacious, they are well symbolised by the Crab, as their tenacity when roused is remarkable, requiring little prompting to move them to determined action; but owing to the changeability of their moods, alternately hopeful and depressed, they often surprise their friends by suddenly letting opportunities slip just when success is within their grasp. They appreciate congenial society, but can be quite happy alone, and most intensely do they object to having their plans or arrangements made for them.

They are keenly interested in the domestic side of life, this sign representing the principles of home life; family ties and duties are in consequence more keenly felt by this type than by any other, and old friendships or associations are held sacred.

Children born during this period are very sensitive to the physical and mental conditions of others, and if forced to live with natures that are inharmonious and not in sympathy with them, their vitality is readily depleted and they become nervous, listless, and morbid. For this reason children should never sleep with the elderly or ailing.

Strongly imaginative and reserved, they are at times mistrustful, over-anxious, and exacting; and so great is their tendency to experience every kind of sensation, that when badly aspected by the planets of their horoscope their feelings amount to an obsession, and from the overdevelopment of their intuitional faculties they become the subjects of presentiments and delusions. When their characters are well developed and their erratic tenacity made consistent, they become firm-willed and reliant, with clear keen intellects and strong intuitions capable of high accomplishments. Although generally quiet and reserved, brilliant conversationalists are sometimes found among them. Where clans and sects meet they will be found, and they form no small portion of the intellectual members of secret societies and mystic and occult communities. They greatly appreciate old customs, curios, books, and relics of the past, their faculty of imagination placing them pre-eminently above all other types in the realms of poesy and fancy. They are keen observers of Nature in all her changing moods, and in the solitude of woods, or by shady lane, stream, and hedgerow they can best recover their balance when out of conceit with a practical and unsympathetic world.

This sign has given us some of our greatest composers and writers of romance. As a rule their work is spasmodic, but energetic whilst the fit lasts or when spurred by approbation, but slackens when the mood has passed or the incentive is removed.

They succeed best in professions or employments affecting the public, as authors, artists, musicians, politicians, and clairvoyants. They also make good naval officers and sailors, and do well in professions connected with the sea and liquids.

They will be most in harmony with people born during the periods of Taurus, Virgo, Scorpio, and Pisces.

The fortunate gems for this House are the Emerald, Moonstone, Pearl, Cat's Eye, and Crystal.

The Emerald held a very high place in the esteem of the Ancients, and no other precious stone has probably been the subject of so much regard and admiration, one of its principal charms being its brilliant green colour. Very curious are some of the traditions connected with it.

In the first place, it is interesting to note that this gem being the Zodiacal stone of Cancer, the Crab was thought to have the same healing powers as the Oculi Cancrorum, or Crab's Eye ointment, prescribed in olden days as a cure for ulcerous sores.

Emeralds are found in Siberia, India, the United States, and Mexico, and the belief that demons and griffins guarded the mines is said to be as strong amongst the Peruvians of the present time as in the days of the Romans.

The origin of the word Emerald is from a Sanskrit word meaning green, it being thought that there was nothing in Nature to equal its colour and brilliancy, and it was an old Hebrew belief that if a serpent fixed its eye upon the lustre of this stone it would become blind.

The cause of its beautiful green tint has been attributed by some scientists to the presence of oxide of chromium, by others to copper, whilst in 1848 an experimenter believed it to be derived from an organic matter called chlorophyl, similar to the colouring substance of the leaves of plants.

Pizarro, in his conquest of Mexico, found numerous Emeralds of surpassing beauty; but d'Acosta, a contemporary writer, states that many of the finest stones were ruined by the Spanish soldiers, who, being informed by a priest that to test their genuineness they should be placed upon an anvil and struck with a hammer, followed these instructions with most disastrous results.

The Incas possessed some wonderful Emeralds; one (described by de la Viga) as large as the egg of an ostrich, was believed to be inhabited by Esmeralda, the chief goddess of Peru. When sacking her temples the Spaniards discovered immense quantities of Emeralds, it being customary for her priests to obtain them

THE COMPLETE BOOK OF TALISMANS, AMULETS AND MAGIC GEMSTONES

by representing to the worshippers that these gems were esteemed by the goddess above all else, Emeralds being her own daughters.

Emeralds were known and esteemed in most remote times of the world's history, and are to be met with amongst even Egyptian and Etruscan remains. Faith in its virtues and qualities exist amongst the Orientals to the present time, representing to them hope in immortality, courage and exalted faith, and protection from pestilence, as well as a preserver of eyesight, its efficacy being increased by a verse from the Koran engraved upon it.

In India it is believed to confer the gift of memory and a knowledge of secrets and future events. Frequently used in the decorations of sacred images, and is endowed by the Indians with very high attributes.

The Romans believed that nothing evil could remain in the presence of this gem which discovered falsehood and treachery by changing colour and turning pale, and when powerless to avert misfortune would fall from its setting, giving rise to the belief that the falling of this gem is a bad omen.

This stone was also considered very beneficial to the eyes, on which account it was worn as a seal ring; in connection with this Pliny states: "If the sight hath been dimmed and wearied by intense poring upon anything, the beholding of this stone doth refresh and restore it again." It is also recorded that Nero, who was very shortsighted, used an emerald eye-glass to watch the gladiatorial contests. Probably from its connection with the Moon, which rules the House of Cancer (and was the goddess of midwives), it was considered particularly fortunate for women at childbirth, and was held to promote constancy and domestic felicity.

Worn in a ring it strengthens the memory and protects from giddiness; it was also said to guard sailors and fishermen from perils and mishaps at sea if suspended round the neck so as to lie upon the breast (the part of the body ruled by Cancer). It taught unknown secrets, and bestowed eloquence and renown, and, in the words of Miss Landon, an English poetess:

"It is a gem which hath the power to show
 If plighted lovers keep their faith or no.
 If faithful, it is like the leaves of Spring.
 If faithless, like those leaves when withering."

It should, however (being a very sensitive gem), be only worn by those whose birthdays fall between the 22nd of June and July 23rd, or by those with the Moon in good aspect.

The Moonstone.—The Moonstone is a variety of Feldspar and, as its name suggests, is considered to be in close affinity with the Moon, because its pale lustrous blue colour resembles moonlight, which is believed by the natives of India to give the stone its colour. Indians believe that the best variety of the blue Moonstones are washed up by the tides when the Sun and Moon are in very harmonious relation, at intervals of twenty-one years (three periods of the Moon whose number is seven), and from this has arisen the saying of "Once in a blue moon"—to express a lengthy period.

It was known to the Ancients as Selenite, and Camillus Leonardus says it is powerful in reconciling lovers, and helpful to consumptives when the Moon is increasing in light, but when the Moon is waning, its stone will only enable its wearer to foretell future happenings; he also tells us that if the Moonstone be held in the mouth it will decide which affair should be taken in hand and which left alone; if to be undertaken, the matter is firmly fixed on the mind; if not, it passes out and is soon forgotten.

Pliny asserted that this stone contained an image of the Moon which waxed or waned according to the state of that luminary.

The virtues attributed to this stone were to protect from harm and danger in travelling by sea and land; to give mental inspiration, and to bring success and good fortune in love; also to preserve its wearer against dropsy and other watery diseases to which the Cancer type is liable.

Pearls.—Amongst all nations Pearls have ever been considered the most beautiful products of Nature, but having their origin in a living organism cannot be called a precious stone. Most scientists are agreed that Pearls are formed in the endeavour of certain bivalves to obtain relief from the irritation caused by some foreign substance which has penetrated the shell and which the Oyster, by covering with a pearly secretion, forms into a beautiful gem.

The idea that Pearls are symbolic of tears arose from this fact, and illustrates the old adage that the most noble achievements have their origin in painful and enduring effort. Nowadays in the Pearl Fisheries, particularly in the Bay of Ago, (Japan,) foreign matter is intentionally introduced into the shell, but the results do not equal the Pearls found as the outcome of natural influences, a considerable time being required to bring them to perfection.

Pearls are extremely hard, and the well-known story of Cleopatra's Pearl cannot be believed, unless the Pearl was first ground to powder, as any acid sufficiently strong to dissolve a Pearl would be fatal to human life.

Among Eastern nations this gem is credited with the power of preserving the purity of their wearers, and as an emblem of maidenly purity. The Romans also set a high value on Pearls, consecrating them to Isis, and wearing them for her favours. Pearls were also made into a decoction with distilled water and given to lunatics to restore their reason. In China Pearls are powdered and taken as medicine for syncope and stomachic ailments.

The occult properties of the Pearl in olden times caused them to be worn as Amulets by divers as a protection against sharks.

This gem is, however, considered unfortunate for those in love, and if worn by the married signified "torrents of tears," and for this reason is seldom used in engagement rings, even at the present day.

The Cat's Eye.—The Cat's Eye, a semi-transparent stone of the Chrysoberyl family, has a distinct ray of light running across it, which ray has been compared to a drop of water enclosing a beam of light. It is most commonly translucent, of a milky-white colour, but is also found in shades of yellow, red, and brown. It has always been greatly valued in India, where it is regarded not only as a bringer of wealth, but a Talisman to prevent its owner's gain diminishing. The Cat's Eye is also considered powerful against the terrors of the night; it will relieve asthma if hung round the neck, also helps babies suffering from croup, and it is also worn for mental balance, foresight, and general attractiveness. As a popular charm for success in speculation, gambling, and games of chance, it is said to have no equal.

The Crystal.—Rock Crystal is a form of quartz, clear and transparent, the name Crystal coming from a Greek word signifying "frozen water" or "clear ice." The magical powers of revealing the hidden secrets of the future supposed to exist in the ball of Crystal is of very ancient origin; and it is said that Saint Augustine believed that Crystal-gazing, as it is called, originated in Persia.

The Moon, the ruler of the House of Cancer, has direct influence upon the intuitive faculties of the brain, through which seers visualise events foreshadowed in the Crystal; making it peculiarly appropriate and sympathetic to subjects of this type, so that it is not surprising that this sign produces some of the best seers. Pliny states that Roman physicians also used the ball of Crystal for cauterising purposes, holding it against the rays of the Sun; they also used them applied externally as a remedy for diseases of the kidneys.

Those whose birthdays fall within the periods of Aries or Libra, however, should not wear the Emerald, Moonstones, Pearls, Cat's Eyes, or Crystal, as they would not be in harmony with these gems.

CHAPTER V
LEO—THE HOUSE OF THE LION

Period—Constellation—The Fiery Sign—Hercules and the Lion—Characteristics—Personal Magnetism of the Type—Disposition—Money-makers—Entertainers—Health Defects—Marriage and Love Affairs—Artistic Tendencies—Gems of the House—The Sardonyx—Qualities of the Stone—The Chrysolite and the Romans—The Tourmaline—Peculiarities of the Stone—Amber—Virtues and Medicinal Uses—The Topaz.

The Sun enters the Zodiacal House of Leo on the 23rd of July and remains in occupation until the 23rd of August. Leo is the fifth sign in the order of the Zodiac, and is marked by the constellation of stars bearing this name, situated in the Northern Celestial Hemisphere, just below the Great Bear or Plough, and contains over seventy stars visible to the naked eye, the principal star of which being designated Cor Leonis, or the Lion's Heart. This star is also known as Regulus, and is useful to navigators for ascertaining their longitude at sea. The constellation is easily identified by a group of stars forming a well-shaped sickle on the west side of the cluster. Leo and Cancer, being the most northerly of the twelve signs, are the nearest to the zenith of the earth, causing the greatest warmth and heat, and are consequently assigned to the Houses of the two luminaries, Cancer, as being feminine, to the Moon, and Leo, as masculine, to the Sun. Leo, coming in the centre of the fiery signs, is specially suited for the Sun's manifestations, and it is said that the symbol of this house, the Lion, was given because, when the Sun, the Ruler of this House, is in occupation, his heat resembles that of a raging lion; and it is a well-known fact that the Sun was worshipped as a Lion by the Ancients, the Egyptians keeping the month of July sacred to him and holding the Ludi Apollinares in his honour.

In Greek Mythology the Lion is said to represent the monster who was the terror of travellers in the forests of Nemaea; it was slain by Hercules in battle, and to commemorate the great combat Jupiter gave it a place amongst the stars.

As a symbol of this sign it is, however, much older than the Greeks, being represented in both the Egyptian and Indian Zodiacs.

(The symbols of the House of Leo are illustrated in No. 5 of the coloured Frontispiece.)

Astrologically, Leo is known as a fixed sign, and fixity of aims and ideas is a marked characteristic of this type, for when they believe themselves right in their views or opinions on any subject in which they are interested, they are immovable although never aggressive, deeming it not worth while to argue or explain unless their hearers are sympathetic or reasonable.

In religious matters they have unbounded zeal and enthusiasm, often believing they have a special mission in life which they are persistent in fulfilling, no matter at what cost, personal sacrifice, or inconvenience. They formulate ideas quickly, possessing a marvellous faculty of presenting well-known facts in a new light and also of adapting a thought or suggestion from a sermon or lecture and enlarging and developing its meaning and purpose without reference to the literal words of the speaker, astonishing their listeners by their apparent mastery of the subject under discussion. Possessing a clear brain, they invariably consider matters from a practical point of view, scorning petty actions, and, for this reason, those with whom they come in contact are more often ready to forward their interests than to oppose them, so that they succeed from force of circumstances, and are often helped by these means into advantageous positions. It is not, therefore, surprising that in the majority of cases where phenomenal good fortune has elevated the ordinary tradesman into the wealthy magnate they have belonged to the Leo type. Under ordinary circumstances these subjects are of bright sunny disposition, high-spirited and large-hearted, with a pleasant, affable temperament free from envy or malice. Although liable to quick flashes of temper they harbour no grudge, having the ability to win even their worst enemy into seeming friendliness. They are frequently great money-makers, although not being economical by nature they do not save, yet, luxurious and inclined to be extravagant in their tastes, their proverbial good luck seems to carry them ever on the crest of the wave, no matter how profuse their expenditure, In social entertainments they come to the fore, and are good raconteurs, able to tell a story well, the point (although always in good taste) losing nothing in their hands, making them often the objects of envy among their less-favoured fellows.

The constitution is usually healthy and vigorous, but they are subject to affections of the heart which is apt from overstrain to become irregular in its action, and the cause of palpitation and fainting fits; they are also liable to sunstroke and diseases of the eye, and in every case that has come under the writer's notice, where the Sun in Leo was in opposition to the Moon at the time of birth, the subject has been afflicted with a squint.

In marriage and love affairs they are often unfortunate, their high standard of excellence with their idealistic emotional natures causing them to endow the objects of their affections with attributes of their own imagining. In consequence they are frequently disappointed and mistaken in their judgments; but fortunately great sympathy, tolerance, and forbearance to the feelings of others is so natural to this type that, in many cases of inharmonious marriage they have adapted themselves to circumstances and conditions almost impossible of endurance. When undeveloped, or badly aspected by other planets, however, Leo subjects will degenerate greatly, becoming empty-headed boasters and reckless investors, stopping at no folly in their efforts to become popular and conspicuous; taking risky chances, and through careless speculation losing heavily, yet even so they are often successful in escaping the consequences of their imprudence. Being versatile and brilliant, subjects of the Leo type succeed best as Artists, Actors, Authors, Commanders, Officers, Stockbrokers, Inventors, Goldsmiths, Jewellers, Fancy Dealers, etc. It is usual to attribute artistic talent to this type, but this is not always correct, for although they invariably possess a keen appreciation of Art and are fond of beautiful and harmonious surroundings, the executive ability is not frequently noticeable, although when present the artist excels in producing pictures of golden sunlight effects of late afternoon and sunset colourings.

In matters of friendship, partnership, or marriage they will be most in harmony with those born during the Aries, Sagittarius, Libra, and Gemini periods.

The gems of the House are the Sardonyx, Chrysolite, Tourmaline, and Amber.

The Sardonyx.—The Sardonyx is a rich red-brown stone, the top part of which is formed of a layer of white Chalcedony, or Sard, through which the lower part of the stone shows as a pale flesh colour; when found without the Sard the stone becomes the Cornelian.

The Sard derives its name from a Greek word meaning flesh, and is the Sardius of the Ancients.

The finest Sardonyx come from India and Arabia, but it is also found in Germany and the Tyrol. It is especially good for engraving upon, having a hard smooth surface capable of taking a high polish, and in ancient cameos the under-stone is generally used to form the ground, the lighter top layer being carved into figures, the different depths of the carving affording variety to the effect. These qualities made it a favourite with the Romans, who believed that the virtue of stones could be increased if suitably engraved, so that the Sardonyx was frequently carved with a figure representing Mars or Hercules to render its wearer fearless and courageous.

It was also believed that in common with Agates this stone had the property of preserving its wearers from infectious complaints and the bites of venomous creatures, particularly from the sting of the scorpion; and that if hung round the neck it would allay pain, give self-control, attract friends, ensure conjugal happiness, and success in legal matters. Also, Camillus Leonardus says, it puts restraint upon those inclined to dissipation and makes a man agreeable as a companion.

The Chrysolite.—The Chrysolite is a very beautiful yellow-green gem which derives its name from two Greek words meaning "golden stone," by which name it is referred to by Pliny. It varies in colour, and although exactly the same stone it bears different names; when of a deep bright green, it is known as Peridot, and when of an olive-green it is called the Olivine. It is one of the softest of the hard stones, being easily scratched by quartz.

The stones are found in Egypt, Ceylon, and Brazil, and specimens have been found in meteorites and the lava of Vesuvius.

The Peridot was much valued by the Ancients, the name signifying in Arabic precious stone, and it was at one time considered of more value than the diamond. These were the only gems set in transparent form by the Romans who wore them for protection from enchantment and against melancholy and illusion. Marbodus says they should be set in gold (gold being the metal of the Sun) to dispel the vague terrors of the night.

During the Middle Ages these stones were worn for foresight with regard to future events, and for Divine inspiration and eloquence.

The Tourmaline.—The Tourmaline is of comparatively modern origin in Europe as far as its use as a precious stone is concerned. It is very remarkable because of its electrical qualities, for when heated one end will become positive and attract straws or ashes, whilst the other end will be negative and non-attractive.

It is transparent in one direction, but if looked at from another it may be found quite opaque.

It is found in India, Siberia, Brazil, and America, and of all colours and shadings of red, pink, yellow, green, and white; two colours may also exist on the same crystal, which may be green at one end and red at the other. This is probably the stone Pliny describes as the Lychnis, which, being very susceptible to solar influences, attracted small particles of chaff when heated by the sun, and had the power of "dispersing fears and melancholic passions." It was also worn to procure inspiration, to attract favours, and to secure friends.

Amber.—Amber has from the most remote ages been familiar to humanity, ornaments in this material having come down to us, shaped by men of the Stone Age, thus proving its antiquity. Many fanciful theories were given in bygone days with regard to its origin, amongst others the historian Nicias stating that the heat of the Sun was so great in some regions as to set up intense perspiration in the earth, from which Amber resulted; whilst among the Greeks a legend existed that it originated in the tears of the sisters of Phaethon, who, in their sorrow at his death, were turned into poplar trees, and whose perpetual tears congealed into Amber. Pliny asserted it to be the overflowing sap of certain trees, hence the name Succinum, from a word signifying "juice"; and modern research confirms this idea of a vegetable origin, for Amber is now known to be the fossil resin of an extinct species of pine of the Tertiary Period.

Amber is found in large quantities on the coast of the Baltic, washed up after storms, and the German Government exercises a strict monopoly over the trade. It is also found round the coasts of Denmark, Norway, Sweden, and parts of Asia and the United States; and in Essex, Suffolk, and Norfolk. It is very light and soft, possessing remarkable electric properties when heated. That it was once in a liquid state is shown by the insects and plants sometimes found in it, a good many of the insects belonging to species that no longer exist. These specimens specially attracted the attention of the Romans and doubtless gave Pliny his idea of its origin.

Great quantities were introduced into Rome during the reign of the Emperor Nero, who in verse described the hair of his wife as amber-coloured, causing much emulation amongst the ladies of his court in their endeavours to secure the fashionable colour. The name Amuletum was given to Amber as well as to the flower Cyclamen (see Chapter I, Part I), both having the power to protect from poisonous drugs, necklaces being worn specially by children for this purpose, and also as a counter-charm against witchcraft and sorcery.

Its range of medicinal virtues is very extensive, Callistratus asserting it to be of great service at any period of life against insanity, either taken as a powder, or worn round the neck; the golden-yellow variety known as the Chryselutum being specially used to ward off ague. The Rev. C. W. King says that "the wearing of an Amber necklace has been known to prevent the attacks of erysipelas in a person subject to them, which has been proved by repeated experiments beyond all possibility of doubt. Its action here cannot be explained, but its efficacy as a defender of the throat against chills is evidently due to its extreme warmth when in contact with the skin, and the circle of electricity so maintained, which latter may account for its remedial agency in the instance quoted above." He also says: "In Pliny's time Amber was universally worn as necklaces by the Transpadane females of Lombardy and Piedmont, partly as an ornament and partly as a prophylactic against goitres, to which they were subject in consequence of the hard quality of the water they drank."

Amber was also worn to protect from deafness, digestive troubles, catarrh, jaundice, loss of teeth from looseness, and as a child's Amulet against convulsions when teething.

Its popularity as mouth-pieces to pipes, cigar-and cigarette-holders arose from a belief in the East that Amber will not transmit infection. It has ever been in vogue throughout China, Japan, India, and the East, and retains its favour to the present day.

The Chinese use it extensively in incense, and it is also used in the manufacture of various perfumes and medical compounds.

Topaz.—The Yellow Topaz is also a stone of this House, but being more particularly a stone of Sagittarius it will be found dealt with under that sign.

All yellow stones are, more or less, under the influence of the Sun, who, as already mentioned, rules the House of the Lion.

Those whose birthdays fall in the Taurus or Scorpio periods should not, however, wear the Sardonyx, Chrysolite, Tourmaline, Amber, or Yellow Topaz.

CHAPTER VI
VIRGO—THE HOUSE OF THE VIRGIN

Period—Constellation—Mythology—Symbols—Paris under Virgo—Reflecting Qualities of the Sign—Characteristics—Marriage—Professions—Ailments—Harmonious Types—Gems of the House—Cornelian—Virtues of the Cornelian—Napoleon's Seal Talisman—Clairvoyant Properties of the Stone—Jade—New Zealanders' Faith—The Tiki—Jade as Racing Talisman.

The Sun enters the Zodiacal House of Virgo, which is ruled by the planet Mercury, on the 24th August, remaining there until the 22nd of September approximately. The Constellation of stars marking the position of Virgo was known to the Babylonians as the Ear of Corn, and has been symbolised by three ears of corn and also by the figure of a Virgin holding some wheat in her hand, representing a gleaner, the principal star of this group, Spica, being very near the place of the Sun at gleaning time in the warmer parts of the Temperate Zone.

In Ancient Mythology Virgo is represented by Ceres or Isis, typified as a tall majestic lady with golden hair crowned with corn, holding wheat and poppies in her right hand, and in her left a sickle, a torch, or a caduceus. In modern representations, Virgo being also the symbol of the Virgin Mary, the Lily takes the place of the corn and poppies.

Ceres was the goddess of the harvest and fruits, deriving her name from the care she exercised in producing and preserving them. She is said to have invented the arts of husbandry (previous to which humanity existed on a diet of acorns,) and for her services was crowned with wheat. The poppies were given her by Jupiter to cause sleep and forgetfulness, when through the loss of her daughter, Proserpine, she was unable to rest, the torch being kindled from the flames of Aetna, by the aid of which she sought the lost one throughout the world.

In very Ancient Zodiacs, ten Houses only are shown, the House of the Scorpion including the positions now occupied by Virgo and Libra; it was first divided into two, Scorpio and Virgo, and finally, more adequately to express its influence, it was again divided, Libra being inserted between, making the Zodiac of twelve Houses as we now know it.

It is believed by some authorities that the symbol of Virgo (see Plate No. 6 of the coloured Frontispiece) was adapted from the symbol of Scorpio (shown in No. 8 of same Plate) and their resemblance is noticeable by comparison of the two. It is believed that when the Hebrew language was formed, the Virgo symbol was taken to form the name Jehovah. yhwh Yod-he-vau-he, reading from right to left.

Virgo is also typified by the Virgin Mary as already referred to, and it is worthy of note that the founder of the ancient city of Paris believed in the power and influence of the heavenly bodies, it being named by an old astrologer, Para-Isis, meaning in Phoenician, the Star of Being, or Existence. Corroboration of this can be seen at the present day in Notre Dame Cathedral, where, amongst the twelve signs of the Zodiac engraved on the outside when entering from the North, the sixth sign has been represented by a figure of the Virgin elevated above all the rest. The birth of the Virgin Mary is said to have taken place when the Sun was in the sixth sign, and characteristics attributed to her correspond in many instances to those of the Virgo type.

This House has been found to be well suited to be the significator of virgins, because as a rule those born under the influence of this sign are cool, patient, and self-respecting, and do not usually fall into error through unrestrained affections; whilst Mercury is the ruling planet of this House as well as that of Gemini, both signs being typical of youth and purity as represented by the Twin Children and the Maiden.

One of the most interesting features of the Virgo sign is that it gives to those born under its influence the qualities of any planet which is in the strongest position of the horoscope at birth, without in any way detracting from its own: for instance, if the Sun is strongest in its aspects than its natural ruler Mercury, it will brighten the financial and social standing, as well as energise and give added power to the Virgo qualities. In the same way, if there is a detrimental aspect from a malefic planet, it will accentuate the misfortune and disappointments indicated. The effect of these complex blends of influence is very far-reaching, so that it is impossible to judge accurately of this type without seeing the individual horoscope, although many of their general characteristics can be recognised in the following brief outline of the Sun's influence on those born during the time of his passing through Virgo.

When the planet Mercury is strong in the horoscope it will give great versatility and natural aptitude for figures and business generally, increasing the critical and observant faculties and qualifying them for serious study, making them capable and efficient in professional as well as financial transactions. They will also be very curious and interested in new ideas and inventions, also in hobbies of all kinds, and many collectors of coins, etc., are under the influence of Virgo. Mars present in this House gives a restless activity to these impressionable subjects, and there will be many changes of friends and occupations; it will also bring resource in emergencies, ready repartee, and an inclination to biting wit, sarcasm, and promptness and ingenuity in plans and methods.

The influence of Saturn will render the mind more tenacious and less impressionable; there will be less inclination for social life, but the seclusion of monastic life or a studious career will be preferred, many priests being born under the Saturnian influence.

Those born during the Virgo period will have a marked individuality, being ingenious, orderly, and methodical; also capable of great proficiency in whatever they undertake, Having the power of combining the practical with the ideal, possessing a keen perception, they have the faculty of at once grasping the salient points of an object or action, making them admirable mimics; but they are at the same time very sensitive to the opinions of others, and very disappointed if their efforts to please or entertain are unrecognised. In contrast to the Gemini type who begin much and finish little, they hate to leave their work uncompleted, or for others to finish what they have commenced; and one of their most noticeable characteristics is their disapproval and condemnation of the methods or suggestions of others, finding many reasons for doing things their own way, which is always different to that of other people. Because of this trait in their character they often lose their friends, for, although critical themselves, they are super-sensitive to a remarkable degree, interpreting any remark or comment to its extremest significance.

In whatever direction the activities of this type may be carried on they will ever seek mental freedom, so that although they may pursue one idea or habit for some time, they are always liable to make sudden changes and completely alter their former views, often with undesirable results, but always with apparent reason to themselves.

There is also a lack of responsiveness to enthusiasm or plans formed by their family and friends which is very damping in its effect on those born under fiery signs.

In temper they are difficult to understand, being annoyed and irritated at trifles, yet slow to anger and slow to forgive, remaining apart chilly and repellent until an advance is made from the other side.

In marriage, as a rule, they are constant and true, and although undemonstrative, their affection is deep, for they will do, endure, and spend much for the sake of those they love, but will be least in harmony with the Sagittarian and Gemini types.

The subjects of Virgo like to be on good terms with those who are prosperous and in good position, and they are suited both by temperament and ability to succeed as Government Officials, Secretaries, Lawyers, Cashiers, Doctors, Authors, Philosophers, Proof-readers, Actors, Chemists, Agents, Schoolmasters, also as Hospital Nurses, Watch- and Clock-makers, etc., and often do their best work when alone.

As may be expected from the mental activity of this House, the ailments are chiefly those of the nervous system, worry or anxiety developing indigestion, general debility, and neuralgia; they are also liable to stomachic complaints and weakness of the bladder, feeling atmospheric changes very acutely. Their recuperative powers, however, are very marked and they soon recover, without recourse to doctors, drugs, or patent medicines, although the latter possess a great attraction for them. Fortunately they are usually most fastidious as to the purity and wholesomeness of their diet, many vegetarians coming under this sign. Children of this type should be encouraged and never repressed, particular care being given to their feet which are naturally tender and easily deformed by ill-fitting boots and shoes, often causing lameness. Virgo being in opposition to Pisces which rules the feet, these subjects are peculiarly sensitive in this respect.

This type has a great sympathy with and a liking for Nature, and is fond of watching the habits of birds and insects, particularly bees, (which seem to be closely associated with this sign). They are also intensely interested in anything that travels or moves quickly.

In partnerships, business or marriage, they will harmonise best with Capricorn, Cancer, and Scorpio subjects, and their fortunate gems will be the Cornelian and Jade.

The Cornelian.—Cornelians are a variety of Chalcedony, and are found of a bright red, yellow, and white colour, in varying tones, and frequently with two or all the colours combined in one stone. On exposure to the Sun the colour becomes brighter and deeper, although artificial light and heat fail to produce the same effect. This stone is capable of taking a very high polish, and for this reason and for its hardness Pliny extols it above all other stones when used as a seal. The best specimens come from India; but Cornelians are also found in New Zealand, and in various parts of Europe. The range of its popularity extended throughout the Old and the New Worlds, and it was extensively used by the Egyptians who devote a chapter of their Book of the Dead to the Cornelian Buckle of Isis, which is described in the chapters on Egyptian Talismans; and is also frequently found in necklaces and hair ornaments.

In Arabia and throughout Turkey Cornelians are considered to be the best of all stones for talismanic purposes, and it is a curious fact that in certain districts of Europe under Turkish rule, it was common for Moslems to take their stones to the Christian priest whose blessing was considered to add greatly to their efficacy. The deep red stones were the ones most prized, and they were frequently to be seen engraved with verses from the Koran; of these, there are several examples in the British Museum in the galleries devoted to comparative religions.

The Rev. C. W. King, in his work on Antique Gems, describes a Cornelian picked up by Napoleon Buonaparte during the campaign in Egypt, and which he wore on his watch-chain as a seal, always carrying it about with him. It is octagonal in shape, and has an inscription in Arabic, as follows:

"The slave Abraham relying upon the merciful (God)."

engraved upon it. Amongst Oriental nations the Cornelian was believed to protect from witchcraft, and, by warding off the glance of the envious, to avert the Evil Eye; it also preserved its wearers from ill-health, and particularly from the plague, a belief also shared by the Hebrews.

Marbodus, writing in the eleventh century, declares that if worn on the neck or finger it has a soothing effect, cooling the blood and "stilling angry passions," preserving concord and driving away evil thoughts; whilst Camillus Leonardus adds to its virtues the powers of preservation from lightning and tempest, from vice and enchantment, blood-posioning and fever, and that it was good for the staunching of bleeding. Marcellus Empiricus calls it the "Scythian Jaspis" in his prescription for the making of an Amulet against Pleurisy.

In Spain it was specially worn to give courage and fluency of speech, and to strengthen the voice; and in China it was highly prized as being beneficial to the stomach, which is frequently weak in the Virgo type.

White Cornelians were very popular with the ladies of Ancient Greece, who wore them as hair ornaments, frequently elaborately carved, and as Talismans against Rheumatism and Neuralgia.

In Volume II of Isis Unveiled, Madame Blavatsky mentions a Cornelian possessed by a Shaman, a native of Tartary, who was acting as her guide whilst travelling. By the aid of this stone the Shaman's astral body was not only able to travel wherever Madame Blavatsky's thought directed, but was able to bring the astral form of a Roumanian lady to her presence; also to bring to their rescue in the desert a party from the Khutchi of Lhassa.

Jade.—Jade, or Nephrite, is a very hard stone which varies from white to a rich green, some specimens being translucent and some (particularly the New Zealand variety) being opaque. It is very highly esteemed by the Chinese, who wear it carved in the form of the Bat, Pear, Stork, etc., as Talismans for longevity. (Its qualities and attributes being fully described in Chapter V, Part I.)

The finest Jade comes from China, and Jade is also found in New Zealand, Mexico, and Turkestan.

It has always been popular among Asiatics, who wear it for protection from accidents and injuries and against witchcraft.

Among the Greeks and Romans it was worn to avert Ophthalmia and Epilepsy, besides being universally regarded as peculiarly efficacious against stomach and kidney trouble, its name Nephrite being derived from a Greek word meaning kidney. Galen records that a necklace which he wore relieved him of stomach trouble, and its efficacy in this direction extended to South America, for when Pizzaro conquered Mexico he found the natives believed Jade beneficial for diseases of the kidneys; and Sir Walter Raleigh, in his discovery of Guiana, describes the inhabitants as using it both for stomach trouble and stone in the bladder. Humboldt also mentions it as being used for the same purpose by natives on both sides of the Orinoco.

It was also known to the Egyptians, and a Talisman of Jade in the form of an axehead may be seen in the Egyptian Galleries at the British Museum, both sides being engraved with Gnostic symbols.

Jade is essentially the stone of New Zealand, the Maoris regarding it as sacred, their famous Talisman, the Tiki, being invariably carved in Jade. The Tiki is worn round the neck as a protection from witchcraft, and consists of a grotesque representation of the human figure with the head bent either to the left or right, in a listening attitude, resting on the shoulder; it was regarded as a precious heirloom to be religiously handed down from father to son, elaborate precautions being taken to prevent the Tiki from falling into the hands of strangers, as it was believed to embody all the qualities and virtues of their ancestors, its burial with the last male member of a family being always insisted upon.

Several very fine specimens may be seen in the Ethnographical Gallery at the British Museum.

Jade is also very popular amongst modern sportsmen as a Talisman for success in racing; but neither Jade nor Cornelian stones should be worn by those born during the Sagittarius or Gemini periods.

CHAPTER VII
LIBRA—THE HOUSE OF THE BALANCE

Period—Constellation—Origin of, the Sign—The Yoke—The Altar—Characteristics of the Type—Influence of Saturn—Inclination for Companionship—Marriage—Moods—Partnership—Professions—Health Defects of the Type—Gems of the House—The Opal—Coral—Lapis Lazuli—The Modern Ill-luck of the Opal—Its Ancient Virtues—Sensitiveness of the Opal—Its Virtues as a Libra Gem—Coral—Virtues—As Infant's Talisman—Lapis Lazuli—Egyptian Talisman—Qualities of the Stone.

The Sun enters Libra, the Seventh House of the Zodiac, about September 23rd, marking the commencement of the autumnal equinox, and completes its stay on October 24th approximately.

This House is ruled by the planet Venus and is symbolised by a pair of Scales, as illustrated in No. 7 of the coloured Frontispiece. As a Constellation it is very difficult to distinguish, appearing on the meridian about midnight in June, and is situated between the constellation of Virgo on the West and Scorpio on the East.

It is the first of the Autumnal signs, and, as with the Sun's entry into Libra the balance is reached, the days and nights then being of equal length, this would afford a practical reason for its name, although there exists no authority for this assumption.

As mentioned in the previous chapter, Libra the Balance was not included in the earliest Zodiacs, and how its predecessor was named and when it was lost does not seem ascertainable, although in some Archaic records a seventh month is indicated as occupying that part of the heavens marked by the claws of the Scorpion.

It is believed to have been known to the Egyptians as Zugon, or the Yoke, the beam only of the scales being represented, typifying the Nileometer, the instrument by which the inundations of the Nile were measured. According to some Akkadian writings the name of the seventh month was Tul-ku, meaning Holy Altar, and it is interesting to note that both the Altars of the first and second temples were dedicated in the seventh month, which has afforded ground for the assumption that the symbol for this period originally took the form of an Altar. It is also remarkable that this is the only Zodiacal House the symbol of which is not based on some living prototype.

Those born under the influence of Libra are remarkable for their powers of comparison, being able to mentally weigh and balance all things in a way that none of the other types seem capable of doing; and owing to extraordinary intuitive and perceptive qualities, Libra subjects are very susceptible to the thoughts of others, often unconsciously sensing their feelings and intentions before a word is spoken.

In matters appertaining to religion they claim an individual liberty of thought and are the least exclusive and most tolerant of all classes and creeds, seeming to act as connecting links between the various sects and faiths which without their mediation would be constantly at variance, drawing men together in the bond of brotherhood, although never forcing their convictions or opinions upon others unasked.

Although apt in all intellectual pursuits and having many interests, subjects of this type seldom make a success of their lives until after middle age, seeming constantly retarded by indecision, a failing to which they are inclined, living on from day to day, contemplating changes but submitting to the yoke of circumstances and environment for years, until some event occurs to break up the groove and force them into new conditions.

The planet Saturn, which has its exaltation in this House, and curiously enough is often afflicted in the horoscope of this type, diminishes the influence of its natural ruler Venus, giving a tinge of moodiness and dissatisfaction detrimental to advancement. When unhampered by adverse Saturnian influences, and armed with an education adapted to the development of the profession or calling they are best suited for, they attain to the front rank and, having once made up their minds, do not change easily.

They are impartial and painstaking, but, although they can and do labour strenuously for others, they rarely distinguish themselves when their efforts are merely on their own behalf or to their own personal advantage; and there is an inclination to accept fate as it comes.

Having a strong inclination for companionship and congenial sympathy, the Librans above all the Zodiacal Houses are best suited to run in double harness, the selflessness of these subjects taking the form of being happiest when confirmed in their habits and tastes by those of whom they are fond. They are the least suited of any to live alone, although they enjoy themselves best in quiet surroundings far from the noise and conflict of towns, being partial to hillsides and sunny heaths, with ample leisure at command for study and reading when inclined. They are also interested in Botany and the growing of old-world flowers and plants. Even in old age they never lose their interests although disliking social conventionalities and emotional excitement at all times.

In love and marriage relations they are attached and devoted, those born during this period being able to live amicably with any other sign, although most in harmony with those born in Gemini, Leo, and Sagittarius periods, Cancer and Capricorn being the least harmonious. As a rule this type is courteous and affable in disposition, always granting a favour gracefully although keenly resenting any attempt to impose upon their good nature, and in connection with this trait we may mention that China and Japan, the two countries so typical of courtesy, come under the sign of Libra.

The temper of this type is as a rule even, and they are usually lenient to the faults of others, but when aggravated they are cutting and sharp in speech, leaving nothing they feel unexpressed, although never malicious.

Inclined to be fastidious over small things, yet they have a tendency to lose and mislay their belongings; but having much adaptability and' resource in emergency, they seldom feel any inconvenience from this failing.

To be successful they should be in partnership, or engaged in a profession or business that is neither monotonous nor arduous, as they work best in accordance with their moods; and when in harmony with their associates and surroundings, make good Musicians, Artists, Singers, Poets, Lawyers, Composers, Designers, Botanists, Librarians, Landscape Gardeners and Florists; they are also adapted for mechanical and commercial business, and to deal in goods that can be purchased and sold again quickly; and it is interesting to note that as a general rule this type is unfortunate in gambling and affairs of chance, although lucky in speculation, and as long as they follow their natural foresight will rarely be cheated.

The health defects of these subjects are kidney trouble, pains in the back, afflictions of the reproductive organs, varicose veins, indigestion, headaches, and depression of spirits; also loin trouble.

Quiet and plenty of fresh air are their best medicines.

The gems of this House are the Opal, Coral, and Lapis Lazuli.

The Opal.—The Opal is the most beautiful and mysterious of all gems, containing as it does all the colours of the rainbow, which flash and glow in sparks and minute flames as the light plays over the surface, causing it to be aptly described as combining in itself the beauties of all the other stones. It is a species of soft quartz, and the wonderful play of colour is believed to be caused by extremely minute particles of air enclosed in its fissures.

The finest variety is known as Harlequin Opal, in which the colourings are distributed in numerous very small flakes throughout the stone. Mexican Opals are more transparent, with the colouring less definite, and arranged in much larger patches; from Mexico we also get fire Opals which are of one colour, the deep red "fire-like" stones being the best, though they vary in colour to a warm yellow.

Opals are very soft when first taken from the mine, but harden by exposure.

THE COMPLETE BOOK OF TALISMANS, AMULETS AND MAGIC GEMSTONES

Great care is necessary in cutting and also in setting them, as they are very brittle and liable to chip.

In the fourteenth century the Opal was known as the Ophthalmius, or Eye Stone, because it was believed to sharpen and strengthen the eyesight; also that its flashes of coloured fire were especially efficacious in arresting the glance of envy. In India, the passing of an Opal across the brow is believed to clear the brain and strengthen the memory.

The idea of its being an unlucky stone had its origin in the misfortunes that befell Anne of Geierstein in Sir Walter Scott's novel, her principal jewel consisting of a large Opal; they are not, in reality, more unlucky than other stones, though being a Libra gem and essentially a pledge of friendship, they are not fortunate for any one having Venus afflicted in their horoscope. In the East it is regarded as a sacred stone which contains the Spirit of Truth, and in Ancient Greece the Opal was supposed to possess the power of giving foresight and the light of prophecy to its owner, provided it was not used for selfish ends; its misuse bringing ill-luck in love (which probably accounts for its being unlucky when used in an engagement ring) and disappointment and misfortune in all enterprises.

Pliny tells, as an illustration of its high value, that Nonnius, a Roman Senator, endured outlawry and exile at the hands of Marcus Antonius rather than part with an Opal he possessed.

All Opals are very sensitive to atmospheric conditions, varying in brilliancy according to the temperature, their colouring being at its best when worn and kept warm and dry. This sensitiveness was believed by the ancients to make them susceptible to influences of an occult nature, so that when the colour of an Opal was bright and lively it indicated success and good fortune to enterprises or travel, and when dull and lifeless it warned of failure and disappointments. It also indicated to its wearer whether it was favourable or otherwise, being full of colour and brilliancy when in sympathy with its owner's interests and lacking in colour and lustre when adverse in its influence.

Coral.—Coral has been classed amongst gems from time immemorial by all nations, although, as is well known, it is the product of a marine insect.

It is found in various colours, the pink, red, and white, however, being the only kinds generally used as gems. It is produced in enormous quantities in the Southern Seas, where it forms huge reefs and even islands; but practically the whole of the Coral used for ornamental purposes is obtained in the Mediterranean off the African coasts, the Greeks maintaining an extensive fleet solely engaged in this trade. It is exported in very large quantities to China, Japan, India, and Persia, where it is used not only for its talismanic virtues, but also for its medicinal qualities. Amongst the Ancient Greeks and Romans it was highly valued, being used in many ways for various ailments. Orpheus recommended that it should be powdered and scattered amongst growing crops to safeguard them from locusts, blight, caterpillars, and thunderstorms. Dioscorides considered it efficacious against the delusions of the devil; and the Romans believed it specially favourable for the prevention of childish ailments, Coral in various forms being worn as charms against Whooping-cough, Colic, and Teething troubles; also for the prevention of fits. The Coral rattle of bells used in modern nurseries is a survival from this period when Coral was worn for health purposes, and the bells to drive away evil spirits. They also used powdered Coral, taking it internally in water for pains in the stomach; and, after burning the powder, used it as an important ingredient in ointments for ulcers and sore eyes because of its soothing and healing qualities. The Roman ladies wore small branches of Coral suspended from the neck as charms against sterility.

In India, China, and Japan, it is extensively used in Rosaries, and is very popular, being regarded as a sovereign remedy against cholera and all epidemics, and invaluable in indicating to its wearer the presence of poison, or the danger of illness, by changing colour. In Southern Europe necklaces of Coral beads are worn to avert the Evil Eye.

Camillus Leonardus recommends it to keep evil spirits from the house, prevent mental delusions and nightmare, give relief in intestinal trouble, and to avert diseases of the spleen. It is still extensively used in Italy for the numerous carved charms worn to avert the Evil Eye.

Lapis Lazuli.—Lapis Lazuli is a deep blue stone well known to all ancient nations, and is most probably the stone mentioned in early writings as the Sapphire, the Tables of the Law stated in the Bible as being of the latter, although there is not much doubt that Lapis Lazuli is the stone meant.

It is an opaque stone, and is frequently flecked with gold owing to the presence of iron pyrites in its composition.

The best qualities come from China, Persia, and Siberia; whilst the lighter-coloured and less valuable is found in Germany and South America. Its name is derived from Lapis, meaning "a stone," and the Arabic word Azul, meaning "blue."

It was very popular with the Egyptians, several of their Talismans being made of this gem, particularly the Eye and Heart, specimens of which may be seen in the fourth Egyptian Room at the British Museum. On account of its beautiful deep blue colour it has always been dedicated to Venus, and in Christian religions is regarded as the stone of the Virgin Mary. It was freely used by the Greeks and Romans both for ornamental purposes and for the cure of Apoplexy, Epilepsy, diseases of the Spleen, and all skin ailments and blood disorders. Also a necklace of Lapis Lazuli beads was considered beneficial to inspire courage in timid children, cure depression of spirits and melancholia, whilst it strengthened the affections, ensured fidelity in friends, and brought success in love.

The Opal, Coral, and Lapis Lazuli should not, however, be worn by those whose birthdays fall in the Cancer or Capricorn periods.

CHAPTER VIII
SCORPIO—THE HOUSE OF THE SCORPION

Period—Ruling Planet—Mythology—Symbology—Characteristics of the Type—Effect of the Malefic Aspects—Health Defects—Professions—Religion—Marriage—The Gems of the House—The Beryl and Aquamarine differing only in Colour—Qualities of the Beryl—Clairvoyant Properties—The Carbuncle as Transmitter of Light—Noah's Lamp—Talisman against Infection—The Lodestone—Magnetic Qualities as an Amulet against Shipwreck and Gout.

Scorpio forms the eighth sign of the Zodiac and is situated very low down on the Southern horizon, being seen at its best late at night during the months of July and August, and it is occupied by the Sun from the 24th October until November 23rd.

The House of the Scorpion is ruled by the planet Mars, and its largest star is Antares, so named by the Greeks to signify that it was equal in brilliancy to Mars, which, however, does not coincide with modern observation, as Mars when at his nearest to the Earth far exceeds in splendour and ruddiness the star Antares.

In very ancient records this sign has been called "The Oldest"; but no reason can be found for this, although it has been suggested that the title refers to "that old serpent" originally responsible for the Fall of Mankind, which, according to ancient writers, is visible in the heavens and may be followed by taking diagrammatic representation of the constellations, where Hercules is shown trampling on the head of the Serpent, or Scorpion. As the Serpent, it typifies the temptation of Eve, who won wisdom and knowledge at the price of bitter sorrow and suffering. According to Greek Mythology the Scorpion was placed in the heavens by Juno the Queen of Gods (and wife of Jupiter), because it carried out her wishes by stinging Orion, who had offended the goddess by boasting that he could outrun and subdue the wildest and fiercest of beasts. Orion died from the effects of the sting and, with the Scorpion, was translated to the heavens, forming different constellations so placed that as one sets the other rises; and amongst mariners, when Orion is obscured it is considered to indicate storm and tempest, or when he is visible, fair weather.

THE COMPLETE BOOK OF TALISMANS, AMULETS AND MAGIC GEMSTONES

The symbol and stone of the House are shown in No. 8 of the Frontispiece.

Scorpio has been described as the sign accursed, because during this period unfavourable weather is usually experienced, bringing gales and storms, the wind being stinging and bitterly cold, whilst diseases such as cholera and digestive disorders incidental to the fruit season are rife, aptly expressed by the symbol of this House.

The leading characteristics of those born under the influence of Scorpio are intensity of purpose, indomitable will, and unflinching determination, as shown by the thoroughness and persistency with which they carry out their plans and desires, whether for good or evil. Although this type includes many extremes of temperament, from the highest and best natures down to the lowest and most degraded, whatever their stage of development may be, weak natures are seldom if ever found amongst them, all possessing the same positive methodical mentality with unflagging and powerful energy, in whichever sphere they are found. Having naturally a strong magnetic personality and dominant will-power, they exercise a strange psychological influence over others, and, although most convincing and powerful speakers, can frequently make themselves felt and understood without a word being spoken. They are invaluable when in positions of authority, which enables them to exercise this force, being persistent in seeing that those working under their direction shall carry out duties with precision, and although affable to those of an inferior social status they are always ready to resent familiarity and stand upon their dignity when necessary, which enables them to insist on the observance of rules and laws even by the most refractory. These Scorpio subjects are also endowed with a strong perception of right and wrong, their sense of justice making them endeavour as far as possible to give due reward or otherwise for value received, even, to the extent of observing the ancient doctrine of an eye for an eye and a tooth for a tooth. Although apparently matter-of-fact they are more or less psychic according to the stage of their development, but often fail to realise this power, attributing their experiences in this direction to keen perception and quick and accurate deduction, for they always discredit all they cannot personally feel or understand, looking upon the limits of their understanding as the limit of nature. One of their strongest traits of character is their wonderful power of resistance, for even when the chances of success are nil they are never discouraged, rising again and again after reverses seemingly unaware of defeat, also rarely showing emotion or feeling by any change of expression. This faculty of resistance makes them very popular as champions of the weak or oppressed, for they will face any personal danger or unpleasantness to help others, although they are often annoyed at the mental deficiencies and lack of self-reliance and moral courage of the weaker types.

When badly aspected the subjects of Scorpio are, however, most destructive, domineering, malicious, and restless, developing into scolds and unreasonable characters, with a taste for a wandering and unsettled life. When unafflicted by malefic planets the nature -is expansive, and their surroundings should be such that they may work off superfluous energy in some way beneficial both to mind acid body. Outdoor life is most necessary and beneficial, and those of this type forced by circumstances to sedentary occupations should take walking, riding, or gymnastic exercises whenever possible.

Their energetic, discerning, and powerful personalities are felt in every walk of life, whether in State, professional, or business capacities; as humanitarians or leaders of democratic circles their phenomenal and retrospective memories and inexhaustible argument and suggestion act as an energy of destruction or as a motive power to uplift humanity. Other professions for which they are suited are Magistrates, Detectives, Analysts, Principals of Schools and Institutions, Disciplinarians, Organisers, Engineers generally, and Marine Engineers in particular; they also make splendid surgeons and medical practitioners, usually in favour of drastic treatment for refractory patients. As authors they analyse and bring to the surface all the darkest corners in human life; they are also interested in handicrafts and intellectual progress, whilst their business capacity in driving a bargain or in buying and selling is remarkable.

The health defects of this House are generally of an uncommon nature, such as suppressed gout and rheumatism, painful and inflammatory ailments of the lower organs (which are governed by Scorpio); haemorrhoids, malaria, typhoid, angina pectoris, insomnia, and severe sick headaches. In temper they are electric and impulsive and inclined to take offence; but although an angry type have often great self-control, but when badly aspected their strong passions predominate, and like the Scorpion they sting with the tongue, and their expressions are sarcastic, lurid, and cruel.

In religion they believe in Divine justice being meted out to wrongdoers, and find no difficulty in administering punishment to transgressors according to their deserts.

In love and friendship they are very exclusive, having strong and intense affections for those to whom they are attracted, but are subject to sudden revulsions of feeling and are for this reason frequently unfortunate in marriage relations, being inclined to be exacting, mistrustful, and difficult to please, yet they always command respect, even from those who are unable to understand them. They will harmonise best with those of the Pisces, Cancer, Capricorn, and Virgo types, while those least in sympathy will be the Aquarian and Leo types.

The gems of this House are the Beryl, Aquamarine, Carbuncle, and Lodestone.

The Beryl.—The Beryl and Aquamarine are practically the same stone, differing only in colour, the Beryl varying from a bright blue to white, and the Aquamarine, as its name implies, coinciding with Pliny's description of "the gem green as the sea"; like the sea its colour varies from a pale cool green to a deep green. In quite recent years it has become common amongst jewellers and dealers in precious stones to describe all kinds generally as Aquamarines, and therefore it is not unusual to find one merchant describing the green stone as the Beryl, whilst his neighbour gives this name to the blue.

In their compositions these stones are almost exactly the same as the Emerald, and are found in India, Siberia, and Brazil. It has always been revered in the East as the stone of purity, and was considered to be particularly sensitive to personal influence, so that it is frequently given to brides at weddings that the auras of the newly-wedded may blend in the Beryl, preserving and increasing their mutual love. This belief was held by the Romans, and confirmed by Camillus Leonardus who says, "it renders the bearer cheerful and increases and preserves married love"; also, "it cures distempers of the throat and jaws, and is good for indispositions of the liver and disorders of the stomach."

It is appropriately regarded as the Stone of the Seer and Mystic, nearly all of whom will be found to have Scorpio strong in their horoscopes. It is mentioned by Aubrey as particularly favourable for clairvoyants because "it hath a weak tincture of red wherein magicians see visions." This effect, sometimes seen under the influence of changing light, is also noted by Rossetti in his ballad "Rose Mary," where, writing on the powers of the spirits of the Beryl, he describes the stone as—

"Rainbow hued through a misty pall,
 Like the middle light of a waterfall."

All varieties of this stone were considered beneficial to married people in keeping the affections true and constant and protecting from slander; and it was also regarded as a sovereign remedy against idleness, a sharpener of the intellect, and as being specially good for mariners and adventurers, preserving them from danger and sickness on sea and land, and efficacious in the discovery of all hidden things.

The Carbuncle.—The Carbuncle belongs to the same species of stone as the Garnet, the latter being cut with facets, while the former is cut en cabochon, or with a rounded surface. It is found in India, Ceylon, Brazil, and the Cape, and has been described by mediaeval writers (including Chaucer and Mandeville) as giving forth light in darkness, whilst in old legends a large Carbuncle is said to have served Noah as a lamp.

Shakespeare also refers to the light that comes from this stone, and these descriptions may have arisen from the fact that many very sensitive or psychic people are able to see a certain luminous effect surrounding the gem. It was a very popular stone with the Ancient Hebrews, who knew it as Baraketh, or flashing stone, which is derived from Barak, meaning lightning. Camillus Leonardus recommends it as a safeguard from poison, and in infectious illnesses, for repressing extrava-

THE COMPLETE BOOK OF TALISMANS, AMULETS AND MAGIC GEMSTONES

gance, and for mightily increasing the popularity and prosperity of its wearer.

During the Middle Ages it was believed to protect its owners from the plague, also to banish sadness, dispel evil thoughts, repress sensuality, reconcile differences between friends, and attract success to all undertakings, as well as to cure indigestion and sore throat if suspended round the neck.

According to Pliny there are male and female stones, the deep red being masculine and the lighter-coloured feminine, a belief also held with regard to other gems.

Amongst the tribes of Northern India and Africa it was believed to protect from wounds in battle, an idea also common amongst the Arabs.

The Lodestone.—The Lodestone is composed of proto-oxide and peroxide of iron, and from its magnetic qualities is known as Magnetite. This quality induced Dinocrates, a celebrated architect in the employ of Ptolemy Philadelphus, to plan a temple the roof of which was to be of Lodestone, so that the statue of Arsinoe, to whom the temple was dedicated, might remain in suspension, a plan which never materialised owing to the death of the architect and his patron. Claudius, a Roman poet who lived some 600 years later, mentions a statue of Venus made of Lodestone and one of Mars in Iron, placed in the same temple that they might be attracted together at the marriage ceremonies, the Romans believing that this stone kept husband and wife faithful and their love secure.

Orpheus attributes to the Lodestone the power of attracting the love of gods and men, and it was frequently set in wedding-rings for this purpose. In India it is believed to give vitality and health to those who wear it, and it is very popular amongst Mohammedans as a Talisman against evil spirits. In Elizabethan days mariners had great faith in this stone as a preservative from shipwreck, and also as an Amulet against gout if worn next the skin.

The Beryl, Aquamarine, Carbuncle, and Lodestone should not, however, be worn by those born in the Aquarius or Leo periods.

CHAPTER IX
SAGITTARIUS—THE HOUSE OF THE ARCHER

Period—The Constellation—The Bow in the Cloud—Mythology—Characteristics of the Type—Appropriateness of the Symbol—Fresh Air a Necessity—Professions—Ailments—Marriage Relations—Gem of the House—The Topaz—Nain-Ratan—Pliny and the Topaz—Discovery of the Stone—The Emperor Hadrian and his Ring—Appropriateness of the Stone to the Type—The Stone of Strength—As a Talisman against Asthma—Marbodus and the Topaz—Chrysolite also Favourable.

The Sun enters the Zodiacal House of Sagittarius the Archer on November 23rd and remains until December 21st approximately.

This House is symbolised by a Centaur armed with a bow ready to discharge an arrow (as shown in Illustration No. 9 of the coloured Frontispiece), and is ruled by the planet Jupiter.

Sagittarius the Archer forms one of the constellations of the Southern Hemisphere, situated between Scorpio the Scorpion and Capricornus the Goat. The bow of the Archer in the constellation contains three of the largest stars in this group, so that its form can be followed without much difficulty, affording a further illustration of Biblical history depicted in the heavens, as mentioned by Mr. R. A. Proctor the Astronomer. It will be remembered that in the previous chapter we noted that Libra was at one time symbolised by an altar, and Mr. Proctor says, describing this constellation:

"Next after the Altar (built by Noah after leaving the Ark), and in fact in the smoke from the Altar, is the bow of Sagittarius, and corresponding with this we read that God, after the savour of the Altar had reached him, said: 'I do set my bow in the cloud, and it shall come to pass when I bring a cloud over the earth that bow shall be seen in the cloud.' Close by the ship Argo (the Ark) again, is the raven, perched on Hydra (the great sea serpent), represented in the old sculptures immersed in the waves of ocean on which the Ark was floating."

The Greeks also adopted the Centaur as the symbol of this constellation, but according to their mythology the Centaur was Chiron the son of Saturn, who whilst living in the woods studied the medicinal virtues of herbs to such good effect that he became supreme as a physician. He was also famous for his skill in astronomy and proficiency in scientific knowledge, because of which he became in turn the instructor of Achilles, Hercules, and Aesculapius. In handling the arrows of Hercules, which had been poisoned by being dipped in the Hydra's blood, he accidentally let one fall upon his foot, inflicting a wound which in spite of his great skill in medicine he was unable to cure. Being born of immortal parents he could not die, so that to release him from his excruciating pains the gods translated him to the heavens to form this constellation.

"Midst golden stars he stands refulgent now
And thrusts the Scorpion with his bended bow."

One of the most noticeable characteristics of those born under the influence of Sagittarius is their acuteness of perception and accuracy in sensing the weak spots in the characters of those about them, resembling the Archer, who stands ready to shoot the arrow which seldom fails in hitting the mark. Sagittarians have a decisive way of expressing their opinion, which can never be mistaken as it exactly fits the case; behind their words is the intuition which gives them the power of inspiration. They are progressive, enterprising, and prophetic. With a clear knowledge and perception of what they wish to achieve, and their thoughts concentrated upon the goal which they are destined to reach, circumstances do not overcome them. They solve the many problems of life and get through the worst troubles with the least difficulty of any type.

Being lovers of freedom they will generally be found their own masters, or if in employment, in such position as gives them a maximum of liberty and independence, and they are seldom without money or the means of getting it. Their sense of justice and the fitness of things is very keen, and possessing great pride of family, any ill-treatment or harshness to those they are fond of amounts with them to almost personal affront, and in spite of the fact that as a rule they mind their own business, as regards outsiders, their sympathetic and loyal nature makes them quick to notice and resent any slight or interference on behalf of their families or the few they are attached to. The brain is clear and quick at assimilating new ideas and new modes of life, and the disposition naturally frank and honest, yet curiously enough there is at the same time a certain watchfulness and distrust of strangers which leads to deception, whilst disliking and trying to avoid it, for they are haters of secrecy and dissimulation. Their aspirations are lofty, exalted, and refined, and being hopeful, joyous, and youthful even in advanced years, they are generally popular and successful, although they seldom excel as students or in literary professions.

The manners of this type are usually affable and courteous, and the temper generally even, although apt to fly off unexpectedly at the smallest provocation when acting on the spur of the moment. Having an advantage over the slower-minded types, they aim in their anger at some vulnerable point, getting home every time, for when personal they are very personal, although never willingly malicious, often in this way saying more than they really mean or intended, and although quickly recovering from their petulant moods, the effects of their temper when roused are long-lasting.

When their environment and occupation is such as to enable them to lead healthy lives they make splendid characters, open air being most necessary to enable them to draw into themselves the vitality and energy they need. Otherwise they are apt to become restless, faultfinding, rebellious, exacting, domineering, and difficult to get on with, and should always be allowed to make changes in their professions without hindrance or objections, restraint of any kind being disastrous to their development, causing them to degenerate into uninteresting, weak, and undecided characters. Generally speaking, they have a clear conception of what they wish to achieve, and being naturally fond of sport and out-of-door exercise of all kinds, they are the less liable to weakness. Having ability and foresight above the average, forewarned is forearmed, and as children this type is frequently clairaudient as well as clairvoyant. They are lovers of hygiene, and having the greatest antipathy to cramped surroundings they naturally choose professions in which they can enjoy freedom of speech and action, with plenty of space, light, and air. They excel as Judges, Presidents, Generals, Commanders, Directors, Inspectors of Schools, Factories, and Workshops, also as Sanitary Inspectors, Managers, and Superintendents, etc., hating all subordinate positions.

These subjects are also fond of animals, so that it is not surprising that horses and dogs are their constant companions, and seem to respond readily to their wishes and desires with very little training; many keen sportsmen are found under this sign, who delight in tramping over long stretches of country, or find their most congenial recreations on breezy downs and hilltops. They are also frequently found as dog-fanciers, veterinary surgeons, horse-dealers, pigeon-fanciers, and other callings bringing them into touch with animals and an out-of-door life, and in consequence of this seem more liable than the other types to accidents in connection with horses.

The chief ailments to which these subjects are liable are bronchial and lung trouble, rheumatism, accidents to the thighs and hips (which are ruled by this sign), bruises, sprains, fractures, and diseases affecting the arterial system, apoplexy, and complaints which originate through a plethoric habit and corrupt the blood.

In married life they are not always fortunate, their demand for individuality and freedom of thought and action with an intense family pride frequently causing misunderstandings, and even jealousy. Being morbidly sensitive to coldness or indifference, slights fancied or real are keenly felt. Giving of their best they demand the best in return, and if once deceived seldom entirely forgive, although when unhappily mated they make the best of it as a rule to the outside world, shrinking from any publicity of their domestic differences, faults, or failings. They will be found to harmonise best with those of the Aries, Leo, Aquarius, and Libran types, and will find the Pisces and Virgo subjects the least sympathetic.

The gem best suited and universally accepted as most favourable for this type is the Topaz; and the Chrysolite is also fortunate for them.

The Topaz.—The Topaz is found in various colours—white, yellow, pink, green, and black; but it is in the first three colours that they are familiar in general use as gems.

The best stones come from Brazil and Mexico, but they are also found in Siberia, India, and many parts of Europe and Great Britain. The most valuable is the pink variety, which is found naturally in South America; but it has been discovered that some of the yellow species can be artificially changed to this colour under a special treatment of heat.

The white topaz of Brazil is found in pebble form, free from flaws, and is a very hard bright stone capable of receiving a very high polish. It is sometimes taken for a diamond, and is known in its native country as the Slave's Diamond, although it is not equal to the diamond in brilliancy and iridescence.

A saffron-yellow variety found in Ceylon, known as the Indian Topaz, has always been popular throughout India as a Talisman, being worn for health, caution, sagacity, and the prevention of sudden death. Because of these same qualities its favour is equally strong throughout Burmah, and it is always included in the Nan-Ratan, the sacred nine-stone jewel, which forms the most important ornament in the Burmese regalia, as may be seen in the jewels which are now on exhibition at the Indian Museum, South Kensington.

According to Pliny, the Topaz derives its name from the Island of Topazos in the Red Sea, where it was first found, and he says Topazein, in the Troglodyte tongue, means "to seek after," the island being so often lost amidst fogs. Some pirates who were weatherbound on this island and hard-pressed by famine, in tearing up roots for food accidentally discovered the stone. From the descriptions which have been handed down to us it is believed that the Chrysolite was frequently used in mistake for the Topaz, and as the Zodiacal Houses the two stones represent are in harmony with each other, the Chrysolite will also be a favourable stone for the subjects of Sagittarius.

Gabelschoverus mentions that the Emperor Hadrian, whose reign was one of the most prosperous and peaceful in Roman history, and who was most ardent in spreading Christianity, even writing an address to his soul on his death-bed (which inspired Pope's poem, "The Dying Christian to his Soul"), used as a Talisman an antique ring set with a Topaz which was engraved in Roman letters with the words NATURA—DEFICIT,—FORTUNA—MUTATUR,—DEUS—OMNIA—CERNIT, an expression of faith in the Almighty to overrule Nature and Fortune most appropriate to the owner of the ring.

Fresh air was as much a necessity to the ancient as to the modern subjects of Sagittarius, as is shown from the fact that the Romans wore this gem as a preservative from pestilential atmosphere, also to protect its wearer against perils and dangers in travelling, injuries from burns and scalds, and to avert all complaints of the chest and bowels.

The Topaz was called by Pliny "The Stone of Strength," and he describes as the most valuable, stones that have a predominating tint of orange in their colouring. Albertus Magnus recommends it as a cure for gout, and Camillus Leonardus as a charm against haemorrhoids; lunacy, and sudden death; also to bring riches to its wearers, and the favours of princes.

During the Middle Ages it was believed to dispel enchantments if set in gold and bound on the left arm or hung round the neck. It preserved from sensuality, calmed anger and frenzy, strengthened the intellect, brightened the wit, gave joyousness and contentment, and drove away broodings and apprehensions. It was also worn as a cure for asthma, and as a specific against insomnia, being sometimes powdered and taken in wine.

Marbodus renders its virtues in verse, translated by the Rev. C. W. King, as follows:

"The Topaz is a jewel rare
  And therefore must be bought full dear.
  Made up of hues of golden light,
  And with Celestial lustre bright,
  Here see the man on study bent,
  A life in contemplation spent."

The Topaz will not, however, be fortunate for the subjects born during the Pisces and Virgo period

CHAPTER X
CAPRICORN—THE HOUSE OF THE GOAT

Constellation—Period—Ruling Planet Saturn—Mythology—The Symbol of the Goat—Characteristics—Constitution and Health Defects—India under the Rule of Capricorn—Professions—Marriage—Saturn favourable for the Elderly—Gems of the House—The Ruby—Spinel—Qualities of the Gem—Sensitiveness for Good or Evil—The Malachite—Copper as a Talisman against Colic and Cholera—Black Onyx—Favourable and Unfavourable Influence of the Stone—Jet—The Afflictions of Saturn—Effects on other Types.

Capricorn, the tenth sign of the Zodiac, is situated in the Southern Celestial Hemisphere, the constellation being composed of fifty-one visible stars known to ancient Oriental nations as the southern gate of the Sun, because its entry into this sign on December 22nd marks the shortest day and the commencement of the winter solstice, when the Sun is farthest south of the Equator, after which its light slowly increases and correspondingly the days become slightly longer.

The Sun occupies this House until January 19th approximately, and as its Latin name, Capricornus, signifies, is symbolised by a Goat, as illustrated in No. 10 of the coloured Frontispiece. Saturn is the ruling planet of this House, and as he is sometimes depicted as an old man with a scythe (literally Old Father Time familiar to every one), this may explain the ancient Akkadian name for this month, Abba-uddu, meaning Old Father; and as the Greek words signifying both Time and Saturn differ only in one letter, in all probability the two may have been regarded as synonymous.

The Cornucopia, or Horn of Plenty, was also used as a symbol of this House, as in Ancient Mythology Saturn is believed to have introduced civilisation and the arts of husbandry, so that, as described by Virgil—

"With his mild empire peace and plenty came;
And hence the golden Times derived their name,"

the increasing length of the days promising a bountiful future.

Very frequently the Goat is shown with a fish's body joined to the shoulders, which is explained in classical literature as the result of an adventure of the god Pan. This deity, who was considered by the Greeks to symbolise the House, whilst feasting with other gods on the banks of the Nile was attacked by the monster Typhon. In order to escape Pan and his friends plunged into the river, assuming different shapes, Pan taking the form of a fish for the lower half of his body, and the head, shoulders, and forelegs of a goat for the other half.

The symbol of the Goat climbing a rocky eminence (as shown in the illustration), is very appropriate to well-developed subjects born under the influence of Capricorn who seem for ever persistently and patiently climbing upwards, and who are capable of great resistance in overcoming obstacles in the way, their dauntless energy and courage in facing difficulties reminding us of the goats kept by the owners of the great cattle ranches in Mexico, on account of their superior courage and intelligence to sheep, and who, if the latter are in danger of an attack by wolves, will face the foes, showing fight and fearlessness, collecting the sheep round them, and thus preventing a stampede, making their protection easier by the herdsmen.

Capricorn is an earthy sign, and its subjects are apt to exaggerate the importance of earthly life, and in youth suffer much furtive and fearful curiosity, regarding the mysteries of birth and death, and, as children, feel deeply any snub or reproof, and should never be brought up by coarse-minded people, as they readily take on the conditions of those around them, and although appreciative of commendation lose heart when indifferently treated.

This sign is typical of a remarkable continuity of purpose, and those born under its influence are deep thinkers and insatiable in their desire for knowledge, assiduous students, quick to seize and take advantage of any opportunity for self-improvement or advancement, indefatigable workers, and capable of planning out several schemes and thoughts at the same time.

The desire to make money is a marked characteristic, not so much for its own sake in the majority of cases as for the power and opportunities which wealth brings; but although thrifty and discreet in financial affairs generally it is difficult for them to economise in personal matters, and although they work harder and know better than most how to make both ends meet, yet the proverbial rainy day occasionally finds them unprepared.

They are generous by fits and starts, giving ungrudgingly of time as well as money where others bestow little, and nothing where others give much, and, in contrast to the Sagittarian type who give mostly to large institutions, the subjects of Capricorn prefer helping the individual.

The typical Capricornian takes life earnestly, and is much interested in the occult side of nature, as well as a great upholder of old customs and observances that bind the present with the past old-world traditions and antiquities generally having a great fascination for these subjects. When adversely aspected, however, this type degenerates sadly, showing great despondency and dread of failure in all they undertake, and without some outside stimulus becoming more and more apprehensive and mistrustful, avaricious and covetous until it is almost impossible to live with them. When the ruling planet Saturn is badly aspected by Mars, revolutionary tendencies and a cruel enjoyment of the sufferings of others is indicated; but so great is the love of work even amongst the most primitive of these subjects of Capricorn, that they are too much engaged to have time to be vicious, and when the malefic side of the Saturnian's qualities are very noticeable, it is often the result of too much solitude wherein the subject has brooded over troubles and anxieties.

The temper is strong and forceful, but generally well under control, although lasting when roused and bitterly resentful.

The constitution is remarkably strong, and these subjects frequently live to a good old age, the ailments to which they are liable being colds, deafness, affections of or accidents to the joints, especially the knees, which are ruled by this sign (and are often weak), colic, from flatulence, toothache, spleen, and liver trouble, also severe ear and headaches caused by nervous prostration, from mental and physical labour in excess. Endurance, Penetration, Caution, and Prudence being very noticeable in this type, they excel in all professions requiring shrewdness and acute discernment rising through personal merit to be recognised authorities in the various callings to which they are suited.

India, which comes under the rule of Capricorn, aptly illustrates the qualities and failings, for amongst the Indians we find profound learning, great power, rank, and a painstaking care of minute particulars; whilst the lower caste fittingly illustrate the debasement of the type. Subjects of this House are adapted for most professions and employments of a public or a governmental character. Being natural organisers, their concise methods are sought after by the weaker types they so often serve. Priests, Monks, Occultists, Organists, Statesmen, Editors, Authors, Designers, Architects, Builders, Mining Speculators, Land Surveyors, Agriculturists, Gardeners, are all professions and callings to which this type are attracted; also as Labourers, Miners, Carpenters, and woodcutters, it being interesting to note that Mr. Gladstone, who was born during this period, and who was an extremely good example of the highly intellectual subjects of this House, had also a fondness for tree-felling.

In marriage and friendship they are slow to form attachments, and are frequently unmarried; but when once attracted the influence is deep and lasting, although their love affairs are liable to great and fateful changes, for living, as a rule, solitary and self-centred lives, they create ideals beyond human attainment, and failing to realise their anticipations are often disappointed. Saturn, their ruling planet, being favourable to old rather than young people, they are advised not to marry early, the most happy and prosperous times in their lives being often between middle life and seventy, and they will harmonise best with those born during the Taurus, Virgo, Pisces, and Scorpio periods.

The gems of this House are the Ruby, Spinel, Malachite, Black Onyx, and Jet.

The Ruby.—The Ruby is one of the most precious of gems, when of a good size, free from flaws, and of the true pigeons'-blood colour, being more valuable than a diamond of the same size.

The finest rubies come from Burmah, and they are also found in Ceylon and Siam; their colour varies from light pink to the richest carmine. Until modern times the Spinel or Balas Ruby was included with the true Ruby, but they are quite different in their composition, Spinels being softer and not so brilliant, though more varied in colour, ranging from red, orange, green, and blue to violet. Amongst Oriental nations this stone has ever and still continues to be a great favourite as a Talisman; and throughout India, Burmah, and Ceylon it is considered to guard its wearers from the attacks of enemies, reveal the presence of poison by changing colour, and to attract friends and good fortune.

In China and Japan it is also worn to confer long life, health, and happiness. Pliny describes it as the Lychnis, and says the Star Rubies were considered by the Chaldeans to be most powerful in protecting from evil and attracting the favour of those in authority. Throughout the whole of the Orient the Ruby was believed to possess the power of foretelling danger by a loss of brilliancy and colour, a belief also common throughout Europe as confirmed by Wolfgangus Gabelschoverus, who writing in the year 1600, says, whilst travelling with his wife: "I observed by the way that a very fine Ruby (which she had given me) lost repeatedly and each time almost completely its splendid colour and assumed a blackish hue." He goes on to tell that the threatened evil was fulfilled by the loss of his wife, and that after her death the stone regained its colour and brilliancy.

Catherine of Aragon is reported to have also possessed a ring set with a ruby that indicated in the same manner the approach of misfortune.

Camillus Leonardus says that the Ruby gave control of the passions, drove out evil thoughts, secured possessions to their rightful owner, reconciled quarrels, brought peace and concord, also preserved bodily strength and health, and that the Balas Ruby (Spinel) possesses the power of averting danger of hail and tempest.

It was worn by the subjects of this House whose horoscopes were free from Saturn's afflictions to protect the body from plague, poison, and fevers, and to secure love and friendship, preserve health, vitality, and cheerfulness, against disorders of the liver and spleen, and to drive away evil dreams and spirits. It was also believed to be a very active and sensitive stone, and if the horoscope had Saturn badly afflicted would afford a ready channel for disappointment, bereavement, and other misfortunes incidental to the influence of this planet when malefic.

The Malachite.—Malachite is an opaque stone, its principal composition being carbonate of copper, which gives it a beautiful green colour.

The name is derived from the Greek Malaku, signifying the Mallow plant, as its colouring was thought to resemble that of Mallow leaves. The finest quality comes from Siberia, and it is also found in Australia, Africa, and Germany, and it is believed to be the Molochites of Pliny; it was also used extensively by the Egyptians, both for talismanic and ornamental purposes.

It is very popular in the East and throughout Russia, where it is regarded as a safeguard against colic and rheumatism, its benefits acting through the copper in its composition; and in connection with this, Dr. Alfred J. Pearce in his text-book of Astrology mentions "that workers in copper mines have escaped cholera when their neighbours died of it, also that copper is worn by the Hindus as a Charm against cholera."

Marbodus recommends the Malachite as a Talisman for young people because of its protective qualities and power in attracting sound sleep; it was also worn for protection from lightning and contagious diseases and for health, success, and constancy in the affections. During the Middle Ages it was customary to wear it engraved with a figure or symbol of the Sun as a preservative to the health and to avert despondency and depression of spirits to which the Capricorn type are liable.

Black Onyx.—The Onyx generally has been treated in the chapter on Leo when writing of the Sardonyx; but the stone peculiar to Capricorn is the black, or dark brown, which is generally marked with a decided white stripe across it, or the white stripe may appear in the form of a circle round the centre, in which case it is known as the Lynx-eye Onyx by the natives of India where the finest stones are found.

From very remote ages, particularly in India, the Black Onyx has been considered essentially the stone for rosaries, its attributes being to restrain passion, to give spiritual strength and inspiration, and to be beneficial in the cure of fits. It should not, however, be worn by any one born with Saturn unfavourable in their horoscope, which fact was known to mediaeval astrologers who, in such cases, as mentioned by Marbodus, assert that its wearer would be exposed to the assaults of demons and bad visions by night, and plagued with quarrels, law-suits, and melancholy by day; that it would nullify their labours, and even cause its owners to feel the pinch of poverty (all recognised Saturnian troubles and afflictions), only to be counteracted by the introduction of the Sun's brightening influence in the form of the Sard.

Jet.—Jet is of vegetable origin, being fossil wood, a variety of, but very much harder than ordinary coal, and capable of taking a very high polish. The finest is the well-known Whitby jet which was first discovered by the monks of the historical Abbey before the Reformation brought its ruin. Jet is also found on the coasts of the Baltic, and in the Middle Ages was known as Black Amber, being worn as a prophylactic against epilepsy and fits, and to prevent strangulation of the womb; taken internally, powdered in wine, it was considered good for the toothache, and mixed with beeswax was used for tumours. It was also well known and used by all ancient nations, the Greeks dedicating it to Cybele, the goddess of all things necessary to life produced by the earth, wearing it for her favours and especially for protection to travellers by sea and land. Boetius de Boot recommends it as a specific against nightmare, witchcraft, and melancholy apprehension.

Neither the Ruby, Malachite, Black Onyx, nor Jet should be worn by the Libra or Aries type, or indeed by any who have Saturn afflicted in their birth map.

CHAPTER XI
AQUARIUS—THE HOUSE OF THE WATER-BEARER

Constellation—Period—Symbol—Early Religious Teachings—The Glyph—Rulers of the House—Saturn and Uranus—Characteristics of the Type—Temper—Professions—Health Defects—Marriage and Friendships—Gems of the House—Garnets and Zircons—The Garnet and Ruby—Qualities of the Stone—Virtue, as a Keepsake—The Zircon—The Hyacinth—The Jargoon—The Jacinth as a Talisman for Sleep—Set in Gold for Restlessness—The Lyncurion of the Ancients: its Virtues.

Aquarius, the Water-bearer, is the eleventh sign of the Zodiac, and is situated in the Southern Celestial Hemisphere between the constellations of Capricornus the Goat and Pisces the Fishes. This constellation has only a few bright stars and is not easy to find, but with the aid of a good glass its shape as a pitcher or vase may be traced showing two star streams which How from its mouth, one towards the Goat and the other falling downwards. It can be seen best during the months of September and October, between the hours of 9 and II p.m., and is occupied by the Sun from January 10th until February 19th approximately each year.

The Pitcher or Vase, as the symbol of the House, was universally used by ancient nations, the Chinese describing it as the Vase full, the Chaldeans as the Watering-pot, the Arabians as the Pitcher or Urn, and the Greeks and Romans as the Water-pourer; it is illustrated in No. 11 of the Frontispiece.

In many old star maps the figure of a man is shown carrying the Pitcher; but at the present time, at any rate, the figure cannot be traced in the stars of the constellation and was doubtless entirely imaginary, being probably added to illustrate the early religious teachings of the Zodiac, the Arabic name for "a aquari," the principal star of this group, being "sadal melik," meaning "fortunate star of the King," the figure typifying the King, or Priest, who by his outpourings made his country fortunate or blessed. An interpretation which, at least, is in harmony with its qualities, is that Aquarius, being one of the airy triplicities and the period of its occupation by the Sun being a moist one (familiarly known to us as February Fill-dyke), the vapours and clouds borne on its air are appropriately symbolised by the figure of a water-bearer, and the two waved lines the most ancient pictorial illustration of water which form the Glyph of this House equally well expressed its qualities.

Ancient writers assign Saturn to be the ruler of this House as well as of Capricorn, and he is doubtless very strong when in occupation, but the consensus of opinion amongst modern astrologers is to replace Saturn by the planet Uranus as the ruler of this sign, appearing as he does to affect this House more than any other during his periodic stay of seven years. Being akin to Saturn in its nature, but unknown to the ancient authorities, they not unnaturally thought its qualities were of a Saturnian character.

Those born under the influence of Aquarius possess extremely complex minds and dispositions often unconsciously as well as consciously absorbing impressions and information on all kinds of topics and out-of-the-way subjects, their interests being widely spread and far-reaching; and, as their symbol the Waterbearer suggests, their diffusive natures give them an extraordinary facility in the passing on of knowledge to others in a manner easy to understand, their well-stocked minds full of reminiscence and anecdote making them most interesting companions when they choose.

Unlike those born under the influence of Capricorn, they do not run in any well-worn groove of thought nor use any established reason or method, preferring ways and ideas of their own to those of others. Despite their ability to succeed in almost any direction, their fluctuating moods incline them often to scatter their talents and energies, thus losing them many opportunities of advancement in a definite profession or occupation. Although acting from what seems to themselves well-defined motives, they frequently annoy their friends and relations by what appears to be a capricious restlessness. The perceptive faculty being stronger in the Aquarian type than in others, they are remarkably good judges of human nature and character, and, their analytical and reasoning powers being very pronounced, they see through the motives and actions of others very quickly and easily, often having a reply ready before the other has finished speaking. Although careful to examine the facts or truths of any matter before finally accepting it, they speak their minds freely or express their opinions forcibly when necessary. They are intelligent, independent, and progressive in their ideas, with a strong sense of justice and forethought in all they undertake. Contrary to the expectations of those about them, they often succeed where nothing but failure seems possible; their will-power, being firm even to obstinacy, continues to exert itself to the end of any achievement in spite of obstacles and difficulties which others consider insurmountable. They usually have more than one source of income, but do not show to the best advantage when born rich, for in their endeavour to get the best value for outlay and the best interest on investments, and being subject to sudden gains and losses, their dread of poverty makes money always more or less an anxiety, whether inherited or earned, which makes them very careful in financial affairs, giving outsiders the impression of meanness, although when wealthy they frequently leave large sums for the benefit of the community.

Extremes frequently meet in this type, which includes some of the strongest as well as some of the most erratic and indecisive characters who, when adversely aspected, become cantankerous, abrupt in manners, selfish, and obstinate, and through their eccentricity and peculiarity of temperament are often the creators of their own enemies and misfortunes.

The temper is quick and irritable, and they do not recover easily from its effect, surrounding themselves as it were with a barrier of reserve impossible to break through or approach.

The professions and occupations in which they are most successful are frequently of an uncommon nature, or of an advanced kind, noteworthy examples of subjects born during this period being Darwin, Dickens, Edison, Ruskin, and Sir Henry Irving. Many investors, metaphysicians, scientists, artists, authors, hypnotists, electricians, elocutionists, actors, art and literary critics, analysts, telegraphists are Aquarians, and having much resourceful and inventive genius are often successful where others fail.

The health defects of those born under this sign are usually complicated and sometimes incurable, including accidents from lightning and electricity, giddiness, neuritis, rheumatism, derangements of the digestive system, bad circulation, catarrh, eczema, bad chills, and sprains and injuries to the ankles which are ruled by this sign and are often weak in childhood.

In matters relating to marriage and friendship they arc difficult to please, being apt to demand a reason even for their ideals which makes them scrutinise the faults and failings of those with whom they come in contact, thoughtlessness and its resultant mistakes being to them incomprehensible. Although fond of living in towns and cities and mixing with others are often the most lonely of all the types; but if once deeply attracted are staunch and true, and will be most in sympathy with the Gemini, Libra, Aries, and Sagittarian types, and least in harmony with those of the Taurus and Scorpio signs.

The gems of this House are the Garnet and all the Zircons, which include the Jargoon, Hyacinth, and Jacinth.

The Garnet.—Garnets are found in many varieties, each being described by a special name; the Bohemian Garnet is a deep red, whilst the Cinnamon stone usually has its colour varied by a tinge of orange; Almandines have a violet hue and take their name from Alabanda, a town in Asia Minor, where, according to Pliny, this stone (which he describes as the Alabandicus) was in his time cut and polished. They are found in Brazil, Mexico, Bohemia, Australia, and North America, an uncommon bright green variety being also found in the Ural Mountains. The colour of the best stones approximates to that of the Ruby, fur which it was sometimes mistaken by the Ancients, and amongst modern jewellers it is frequently

THE COMPLETE BOOK OF TALISMANS, AMULETS AND MAGIC GEMSTONES

described as the Cape Ruby, although the Ruby is a much harder stone, richer in colour, and possesses much more fire.

Garnets have always been extensively used throughout the East and amongst the Greeks and Romans, the latter frequently using them for engraving, several fine specimens of Imperial portraits having come down to us in this way.

In India and throughout Persia it was known as an Amulet against poison and the plague, worn to attract health and cheerfulness, and as a protection against lightning. During the Middle Ages it was used as a remedy for inflammatory diseases, and to confer constancy, fidelity, and cheerfulness to its rightful wearers, but was said to cause discord amongst those having no right to it by birth. Like the Ruby, it warned its owner of approaching danger and trouble by changing its colour, and was much in vogue at one time as a keepsake between friends at parting.

The Zircon.—The Zircon includes Jacinth, or Hyacinth, and Jargoons, which, though differing in colour, are actually the same material species. As a rule amongst modern dealers in Precious Stones the White Zircon is known as the Jargoon, which is often found flawless and so bright as to closely resemble the diamond, being in fact often offered for sale as the diamond in Indian Bazaars.

Jacinths, or Hyacinths, are Zircons of deep orange or rich bright red colour, the Jacinth name being of Arabic origin, and the Hyacinth Greek, because it resembled the Hyacinth flowers which Apollo caused to spring from the blood of his favourite Hyacinthus whom he accidentally killed with a quoit. The remaining varieties of this stone, which are found in varying shades of yellow, grey, brown, and green, ranging from bright lively colours to dull cloudy shades, are described generally as Zircons, although very bright, clear, slightly coloured stones are described as pink or yellow Jargoons, according to the tint their colour may take. The best specimens come from India, Ceylon, Bohemia, France, and from Australia. Boetius de Boot recommends the Oriental Jacinth, "that comes from Calicut and Cambray," as a specific for promoting sleep; Marbodus says it makes its wearer attractive and agreeable, which Barrett in his "Natural Magic" confirms, adding that if set in gold and worn on the finger it is a desirable jewel as a solace for a restless brain. Camillus Leonardus, writing in 1750, says the Jacinth will strengthen weak hearts, dispel imaginary suspicions, allay jealousy, secure travellers from injuries and thieves, and protect them from pestilence, plague, and contagious epidemics.

It was well known to the Ancients, and is considered to be the Lyncurion of Theophrastus. The popularity of this stone in India is as great as ever, and at the present time it is worn as an antidote against poison, to attract riches, honour, and wisdom, and to drive away evil spirits.

The virtues attributed to it during the Middle Ages were that it attracted success, brought welcome to its wearer wherever he went, stimulated the appetite, and aided digestion, protected from fever, dropsy, jaundice, and noxious fancies, and restrained from excesses, its efficacy being greatly increased if set in gold. But neither the Garnet nor Zircon should be worn by those whose birthdays fall in the Taurus or Scorpio periods.

CHAPTER XII
PISCES—THE HOUSE OF THE FISHES

Period—Constellation—Precession of the Equinoxes—Icthyes, the Fishes—Mythology—Symbol—The Rulers of the House—Characteristics—Ailments of the Type—Professions—Friendship and Marriage—Harmonious and Inharmonious Types—The Gem of the House—The Amethyst—Virtues of the Stone—Talisman against Inebriety—Its Calming Influence—The Stone of St. Valentine—As a Lovers' Talisman—The Effect of Purple Rays—The Amethyst Beneficent to all Types—Real and Artificial Gems and how to select them.

The Sun enters the Zodiacal House of Pisces, the Fishes, on February 19th, remaining in occupation until March 10th.

The constellation of Pisces is situated in the Southern Celestial Hemisphere between Aquarius and Aries, occupying a large space near the Equator which the Sun crosses at the Vernal Equinox when entering the Zodiacal House of Aries.

At one time the constellations marked the actual Zodiacal Houses of the same name, but owing to the precession of the Equinoxes the constellations have moved forward, and Pisces occupies the space originally allotted to Aries; and this forward movement applies to all the Zodiacal Houses previously dealt with. The constellation can be seen best during the latter part of October and through November between 8 and 10 p.m., but owing to the absence of any important stars it is not easily traced.

It was known to the Greeks as Ichthyes, the Fishes, and as illustrating the connection of the Zodiac with religious teachings, it is interesting to note that the early Christians chose the Fish as the symbol of their faith because the Greek word IKhThYS, Fish, formed the initials of five words meaning Jesus Christ, Son of God, Saviour. In Ancient Grecian Mythology it is recorded that the two fishes were placed in the heavens by the goddess Minerva to commemorate the escape of Venus and her son Cupid who, whilst walking on the banks of the Euphrates, were attacked by the demon Typhon, described by Homer and Virgil as having a hundred dragon heads upon his shoulders, with devouring flames belching from the mouths and eyes, and with snakes issuing from his fingers. To escape this monster, Venus and Cupid transformed themselves into fishes and plunged into the river which afforded them safety.

This House is generally symbolised by two fishes connected with a band, as illustrated in No. 12 of the Frontispiece. Jupiter is usually considered to be the ruling planet of this House, or in the case of highly developed subjects the planet Neptune takes the rule.

The symbol of the two fishes attached yet turning in contrary directions seems an apt symbol of the characteristics of this type who are the most dual-natured of all signs, being liable to act on the impressions of their surroundings, showing at one moment extreme persistence and at another a want of determination. Like the two fishes represented back to back, their thoughts and actions are frequently at variance, and, although outwardly placid and docile, this sensitive, changeable disposition is soon ruffled by sudden impulse, resembling the shimmering water which is the native element of the fishes. Being receptive to the conditions around them Pisces subjects adapt themselves readily to any change of environment or circumstances fate may bring, but have a great dislike to anything that tends to ruffle their calm and placid temperaments. Hating suspense, uncertainty, or anxiety, and many-sided in their failings and weaknesses, they often appear to be a mass of contradictions.

The general characteristic of those born under the influence of Pisces is a strongly emotional, contemplative, facile nature with much artistic appreciation for beautiful scenery and surroundings. The pleasures of life have a great attraction for them, but from an inherent consideration of the possible demands of the future their expenditure in this direction is coupled with much prudence. Being susceptible to outside influences they are apt to rely too much on the advice and experiences of those with whom they come into contact, and are by turns too apprehensive and too venturesome. The mind is imaginative, philosophical, and acquisitive, and as a rule mechanical and accurate, although liable to become indolent and self-centred unless spurred on by those they are fond of, when they will persevere in their efforts towards a desired end with astonishing persistency. In spite of this spasmodic determination they are often lacking in self-confidence and fail to make the best of opportunities for their own interests and benefit. Very much appreciating any confidence in their ability to carry out work entrusted to them by others, which they perform with the utmost punctuality and precision; and having a liking for positions of responsibility and management, they frequently run two occupations at the same time. As children they are of a very observant and enquiring nature, continually asking questions, so that every advantage as regards education should be given them, a wrong start in life being more serious in its results to this type than to any other. They seldom change the profession or occupation on their own initiative, and although easily persuaded become obstinate when driven. Hating discord and strife, the temper is slow to anger but rebellious when roused, and although naturally of a peace-loving disposition they do not easily recover from its effects.

When adversely aspected they become selfish, secretive, discontented, and extravagant, and in business tricky and dishonest, and with a general want of balance and a tendency to intemperance.

This House ruling the feet, those born during the Pisces period are subject to ailments and injuries affecting these members, and are also liable to contract colds and serious illnesses from damp feet; they are also inclined to weakness of the back, abscesses and disorders of the blood, and irregularities of the general system, torpidity of the liver, and nervous breakdown, but they should never be encouraged to make much of any illness; being so susceptible, that suggestion alone will frequently cause its development.

In professions and occupations they are successful as actors, novelists, artists, teachers, travellers, musicians, examiners, and make good disciplinarians, also, being very resourceful in emergencies, they are extremely successful in the care and management of young people, interesting them and gaining their confidence and enthusiasm by original methods, yet exacting obedience without harshness or fault-finding. Illustrating the possibilities of this type when well developed, we may cite General Baden-Powell.

Being naturally fond of the water, they are successful as Captains, Sailors, and Fishermen; also in all businesses connected with liquids, such as hotel-keepers and caterers.

In friendship and marriage they are overcautious in some respects whilst imprudent in others, and being apprehensive of consequences they frequently weigh and consider before making any voluntary change in their lives and habits; so that although impressionable and affectionate, they are apt to drift aimlessly into circumstances, and, in many instances, marry late, although naturally inclined and fitted for home and family life. They will be found most in harmony with those born during the Cancer, Scorpio, Taurus, and Capricorn periods, and least in sympathy with those of the Gemini and Sagittarius periods.

The gem of this House is the Amethyst, a semiprecious stone in varying shades of purple which belongs to the quartz family and owes its colour to oxide of manganese and iron which forms part of its composition. The best variety comes from Siberia, Ceylon, Brazil, and Persia, and the Amethyst was originally regarded as a very precious stone, until the immense quantities received from Brazil reduced its value generally.

From the earliest dawn of history the occult properties of this stone as an antidote to inebriety have been recognised, by all writers, the name originating from a Greek word meaning "without intoxication," and according to Aristotle it was also the name of a beautiful nymph who invoked the aid of Diana to protect her from the attentions of Bacchus, which the goddess did by converting her into a precious gem, upon which Bacchus, in remembrance of his love, gave the stone

THE COMPLETE BOOK OF TALISMANS, AMULETS AND MAGIC GEMSTONES

its colour and the quality of preserving its wearers from the noxious influence of wine.

The Egyptians used these stones freely for Talismans, their soldiers wearing them as Amulets for success in their exploits and calmness in danger. Pliny says the Magi believed that if the symbols of the Sun and Moon were engraved upon the Amethyst it made a powerful charm against witchcraft, and procured for its wearers success to their petitions, good luck, and the favour of those in authority. Camillus Leonardus, confirming its efficacy in restraining intoxication, says:

"It also represses evil thoughts and all excesses, prevents contagion, and gives good understanding of hidden things, making a man vigilant and expert in business."

The Amethyst has always been associated with ecclesiastical decorations, its frequent use in episcopal rings giving rise to its description as "the Bishop's Stone," and rosaries of Amethyst beads were much in request in olden times to attract soothing influences in times of stress and to confer a pious calm on their wearers.

In religious art it was regarded as emblematic of resignation under earthly sufferings, patience in sorrow, and trust unto death, which Marbodus (translated by the Rev. C. W. King) expresses in verse:

"On high the Amethyst is set
In colour like the violet,
With flames as if of gold it glows
And far its purple radiance throws;
The humble heart it signifies
Of him who in the Saviour dies."

During the Middle Ages the qualities attributed to it were many: it indicated the presence of poison by becoming dim, also personal danger and ill-health by changing colour; it was, moreover, considered to give vigilance to business men, and to sportsmen and soldiers calmness in danger.

The Amethyst is the stone of St. Valentine, who is said to have always worn it; and in the days of romance and chivalry, if presented by a lady to her knight, or a bride to her husband in the shape of a heart set in silver, it was said to confer the greatest possible earthly happiness on the pair who would be blessed with good fortune for the remainder of their lives.

In connection with the soothing influence of this gem, it is interesting to note that according to modern research purple light rays have been found to exercise a calming effect upon nervous and hysterical patients and a consequent improvement in the vitality. Cases of neuralgia and sleeplessness have been relieved by an Amethyst rubbed gently over the temples. It is one of the very few gems that may universally be worn without adverse results.

REAL AND ARTIFICIAL GEMS AND HOW TO TEST AND SELECT THEM

The following notes are written in the hope that they may put readers upon their guard against some common deceptions and prevent disappointment which with a little knowledge can be avoided.

The qualities which make gems valuable are beauty of colour, brilliancy or fire, and hardness, in which they excel all other substances known.

A large variety of coloured stones come from Ceylon, and many tourists and travellers buy stones there in the hope of securing bargains, a hope that in the majority of cases does not materialise. Dealers in gems are amongst the shrewdest of mankind, and from continually handling and examining stones become wonderfully keen in judging them from their appearance and feel, and are very seldom mistaken in distinguishing the real from the imitation, and no novice will get the better of them in a deal, so that intending purchasers who have no practical experience of gems are advised to buy from established firms with a reputation to lose, or on the advice of an expert, rather than rely upon their own judgment.

Before the full beauty of a stone can be appreciated it has to be cut and polished, either with facets, or in the form known as cabochon. Practically all transparent stones are cut with facets, the best and most popular form being the "brilliant" cut (as shown in Illustration No. 1 of the Frontispiece) which has been. found so effective with diamonds that the term "brilliant" has become the recognised name for a diamond cut in this manner.

With oblong stones "trap" cutting is followed, Emeralds being the principal stones cut in this fashion (as shown in No. 4 of Frontispiece). "Rose" cutting is the form generally adopted with very small diamonds nowadays, although it is a much older form than the brilliant, and large antique stones are to be found cut in this fashion, culminating in a point formed by six triangular facets in place of the table of the brilliant. Semi-transparent and opaque stones, such as Moonstones, Opals, Agates, Turquoises, and Cornelians are usually cut en cabochon (as shown in the stones illustrated in Nos. 3, 6, and 7 of the Frontispiece), and Amethysts, Rubies, Emeralds, and Sapphires are also frequently cut in this fashion.

For years past scientists have been experimenting in the manufacture of precious stones, and with so much success that reconstructed stones have been put on the market and are now fairly universally used. These stones are made up from fragments of small genuine stones which are fused together by a continuous and very powerful flame directed on the mass whilst it is kept in motion, resulting in a solid lump that can be cut and polished in the same way as the natural mineral. This has been very successfully done with Rubies, some having been produced which passed every test save that of the microscope, which revealed numerous minute bubbles of a rounded shape invisible to the naked eye, and in greater quantities than would be found in the natural stones wherein the bubbles are more rectangular in shape. These Rubies, and also reconstructed Sapphires and Emeralds, are on sale everywhere at the present time, so that intending buyers of precious stones should ask their jewellers to guarantee that they are buying natural and not reconstructed stones.

All transparent gems may be roughly divided into two classes, singly and doubly refracting, a ray of light passing through being refracted or thrown back according to the nature of the stone. If, therefore, a lighted candle is placed in a darkened corner of a room and is looked at through a stone focussed between the eye and the candle, if the stone is a doubly refracting one two images of the flame will appear, and if it is singly refracting, one only will be seen. Stones that are doubly refractive are Ruby, Beryl, Topaz, Sapphire, Emerald, Tourmaline, Peridot, Chrysolite, Aquamarine, Amethyst, Jargoon, Zircon, and Crystal. Singly refracting stones are Diamonds, Spinels, and Garnets; glass also is singly refracting.

One of the simplest and most effective methods of testing the genuineness of a gem is to try if it is affected by filing with a small jeweller's file; care must be taken, however, in its use, as the facets of even some of the hardest stones are easily chipped. If the file scratches the stone it may be taken to be glass, or composition.

Combination stones, known as "Doublets," are frequently sold as genuine stones; in these the top part is made of the real stone and the lower part of crystal, glass, or composition, so that for their detection the bottom part as well as the top must be tried with the file. "Triplets" are another form of deception. In this case the tops and bottoms of the stones are genuine and the centre part is imitation: To detect this the gem should be held in a small pair of forceps, or corn tongs, in a cup of clear water, when the different parts of the stone will be plainly seen.

White Sapphires, Jargoons, and Aquamarines are sometimes mistaken for diamonds; but the White Sapphire will frequently have a suggestion of cloudiness, and the Jargoon or Zircon, though very hard, is brittle and chips easily, soon showing signs of wear. White Aquamarines usually have a slight bluish or greenish tint. White Topazes and Rock Crystal are not so brilliant and full of life as the other white stones, and all these are doubly refracting, whilst the Diamond is single.

Imitation Sapphires are as a rule harsher in colour than the real stone, which is soft and rich in the quality of its colour. Pearls are imitated with great skill, and are difficult to detect. They are usually lighter than the real Pearls, and if drilled the holes are seldom as small, and show marks of chipping and breaking round the edges. Pearls lose their lustre and deteriorate with age and the effect of gas and acids, and should be carefully wiped with a clean cloth after being worn, and in order to retain their brilliancy should be kept in dry magnesia.

Amber is imitated with glass and various compositions, glass being colder and harder to the touch and heavier than real Amber; whilst celluloid, which is frequently used, if rubbed briskly on a piece of cloth, will give off a noticeable odour of camphor which is largely used in its composition.

Opals and Turquoises, being porous, are affected by potash which is commonly used in the manufacture of soap, and also by oily or greasy substances; they should also be kept from contact with scent, as the spirit used in its. manufacture will very soon spoil the colour of Turquoises.

In conclusion, to ascertain if a transparent stone has any flaws it should be breathed upon until its lustre is temporarily dimmed, when any flaws or imperfections that exist can readily be seen.

BIBLIOGRAPHY

Aston, Wm. Geo., Shinto. The Ways of the Gods.
Aynsley, H. Murray, Symbolism of the East and West.
Barerra, Madame de, Gems and Jewels.
Barrett, Francis, The Magus.
Black, G. F., Scottish Charms and Amulets.
Boyle, Honble. Robert, An Essay about the Origins and Virtues of Gems.
Brand, John, Popular Antiquities.
Brinkley, Frank, Japan and China.
Budge, E. A. Wallis, M.A., LITT.D., The Papyrus of Ani, the Book of the Dead.
Carus, Paul, Chinese Philosophy.
Churchward, Albert, Signs and Symbols of Primordial Man.
Coleman, Charles, The Mythology of the Hindoos.
Deane, John Bathurst, The Worship of the Serpent.
Dennys, Nicholas Belfield, Folklore of China.
Elworthy, Fredk. Thomas, The Evil Eye. Horns of Honour.
Emanuel, H., Diamonds and Precious Stones.
Fraser, The Golden Bough.
Hazlitt, William Carew, Popular Antiquities of Great Britain.
Heath, Sidney, Romance of Symbolism.
Jones, Wm., Precious Stones.
King, The Rev. Chas. William, The Gnostics and their Remains. Antique Gems and Rings. The Natural History of Precious Stones and Gems.
Lang, Andrew, Custom and Myth.
Leo, Alan, Practical Astrology. Astrology for All.
Leonardus, Camillus, The Mirror of Stones.
Massey, Gerald, Ancient Egypt, the Light of the World.
Mawe, John, A Treatise on Diamonds and other Precious Stones.
Moor, Edward, The Hindoo Pantheon.
Pearce, Alfred J., The Textbook of Astrology.
Pinkerton, John, Voyages and Travels.
Smith, E. M., The Zodia.
Smith, Richard Gordon, Ancient Tales and Folklore of Japan.
Smith, Sir William, A Dictionary of Christian Antiquities.
Sykes, P. M., A Thousand Miles in Persia.
Waddell, Laurence Austine, The Buddhism of Tibet.
Waring, John B., Ceramic Art in Remote Ages.
Williams, Samuel Wells, A History of China. The Middle Kingdom.

THE COMPLETE BOOK OF TALISMANS, AMULETS AND MAGIC GEMSTONES

USING CHARMS, AMULETS AND RINGS TO ENHANCE YOUR LIFE
Creating Charms with Candles
Using a Wax Image to Charm
The Ancient Lucky Seven Love Ritual
A Ritual for Summoning a Spirit of the Dead
The Love Ritual of the Seven Knots
A Tree Charm to Gain Strength
The Incredible Magic In Stones and Gems:
How to Use Them in Amulets and Rings
By Brad Steiger
www.BradAndSherry.com

CASTING CHARMS WITH CANDLES

LOVE

SINCE the Middle Ages it has been believed that a candle formed in the image of a witch and burned with the proper incantation can bring love to the magician. Such witch-candles are easily available, especially around Halloween, and certain love-seekers might see fit to buy up a healthy supply from their local variety stores. According to tradition, a red colored witch candle brings about the best results.

First—goes the charm—anoint the witch-candle with perfume to signify femininity. Once this has been done, allow the candle to burn for ten minutes and offer this short invocation: "O loving spirits of Diana, let this offering to you help bring my lover (name) to me for now and forevermore."

The invocation should be made at sunset. It should be said once over the flame of the witch-candle, then the candle should be extinguished and the invocation repeated over the smoking wick. The spell should be repeated on consecutive sunsets until the candle has been consumed

DISPEL EVIL

A black candle formed in the shape of a skull (also readily available around Halloween) has long been utilized in ceremonial magic to dispel curses.

The skull-candle should be burned at midnight and a proclamation, which has been formally written on paper, is to be read above the flame: "In the name of the Mystic Skull, I (the magician's name), do hereby remove any curse that has been set against me." The candle must be anointed with oil and must be burned for exactly one-half hour, beginning precisely at midnight.

The process should be repeated on the following night, and this time, the proclamation should be burned near the end of the half-hour period. The ashes of the paper should be left before the sputtering candle for the remaining few minutes, then the flame should be snuffed.

POWER AND SUCCESS

Power and success may be gained through the ritual burning of a candle formed to the shape of a mummy's sarcophagus. One first anoints the candle with oil and sets before it an incense offering of sandalwood or myrrh. The candle is lighted to the following incantation:

"The Soul of the Gods is in Unas, the Spirit-Soul are with Unas and the offerings made unto him are more than those made unto the Gods. Unas is the Great Power, the Power of Powers, and this offering will bring his powers unto (the magician's name), who does it, and success shall be mine."

REMOVING A SPELL

If one should feel that he has become the unwelcome recipient of a candle spell, he may reverse its effect through an ancient Medieval candle burning ceremony.

The alerted victim should, for five nights in a row, light two large, black candles just as the sun is phasing into dusk. As the candles burn, the supplicant should recite this invocation:

"Beezlebub and all evil spirits, in the name of Astaroth and the Light and the Dark and the Gods of the Netherworld, remove thy curse and thy sting from the heart of (the supplicant's name), and whosoever shall be casting a curse against me, let he or she suffer his own curse. Let these candles be his candles, this burning be his burning, this curse be his curse. Let the pain that he has caused me fall upon himself!"

The two candles must be allowed to be completely consumed each night.

THE ANCIENT LUCKY SEVEN RITUAL

This ritual goes back to the early Middle Ages and has become a legendary magical method of gaining a desired lover's affection. It requires a cauldron of the first rain water in April (distilled water will do).

As the water boils, the following ingredients are to be collected and stirred into the Cupid's brew: seven hairs from a blood snake, seven feathers from an owl, seven scales from a snake, a hair from the object of love and a bit of his nail paring.

When all the ingredients have been incorporated into the cauldron, allow the magical "stew" to boil briskly for seven minutes. At the end of this time, you must permit the brew to cool before you sprinkle it upon your intended. It should be your desire merely to warm your lover up a bit, not to scald him.

(Author's note: All of the above ingredients seem relatively easy to obtain with the exception of the "seven hairs from a blood snake." After burrowing through several reference works, I found that "blood worm" was a slang term for sausage and bologna. It may be that "blood snake" was also a colloquialism for sausage prepared in the gut and/or hide of a pig. In that case, a "blood snake" could, perhaps, yield seven hairs.)

THE LOVE RITUAL OF THE SEVEN KNOTS

The expression "tying the knot" when one speaks of the marriage vows seems to have almost universal meaning. African friends have told me of similar "knot-tying" love spells in their own tribes. Somehow it seems the most natural kind of symbolism to visualize the binding of one's self to the object of one's secret love while the fingers weave the knots and the lips chant a soulful litany.

Here is how the ancient love spell of the seven knots was woven:

The magician would take a length of cord or ribbon which would sustain seven knots strung out at a distance of about an inch from one another. According to the ritual, the first knot was to be tied in the middle of the cord with these words:

"This First Knot ties up and encircles the physical being of (name of the loved one) so that he remains bound to me from this moment. The very utmost strength of my love and my will is within the circle and binds (name) to me."

At about the distance of one inch, the conjurer would form the second knot to the right of the first.

"With the Second Knot, I seize the will of (name) with my own, which is like the strength of steel. (name) will not say anything or do anything that shan't be in fullest accord with my wishes."

The third knot was tied to the left of the first knot.

"With the Third Knot I now encircle (name)'s love and clasp it firmly to mine. He will not be able to break away from me even though he might intend it. He will not be able to loosen my spell."

The fourth knot was to be placed to the right.

"The thoughts of my love will be completely held by my own. My love (name) will never be able to remove the image of my person from his mind. He will always execute my just desires as forcibly as I execute them now by the forces of our beautiful Diana and of the ardent prayer which I dedicate to all good spirits so that the Holy Light will ever be my counsel and keep me from bad intentions."

The fifth knot was done to the left.

"The Fifth Knot imprisons the heart of (name), and he will not be able to, nor will he try to, fall in love with any other woman. His heart will be devoted only to my happiness and my love."

The sixth knot was bound on the right.

The Sixth Knot binds (name)'s words, thoughts, doings, and desires to me alone from this day forward and forever more."

The last knot, the seventh, was secured to the left and with the speaking of the following words the spell, neared completion.

"The Seventh Knot makes (name)'s love completely mine, and with this knot I completely enclose him with the magic circle of this magic ribbon. With this shall I surround his heart; with this shall I love his heart; with this shall I love his entire physical being and will that his physical being shall be mixed with my own physical person. With the tying of the Seventh Knot, we shall stand together forever, and nothing, nor any one, will be able to tear us asunder or destroy our happiness."

The incantation completed, the maker of the ritual would then bind the two ends of the cord together and wear it in the manner of a garter upon her left arm above the elbow. The "seven-knot-love-garter" was to be worn to bed for seven alternate nights. Upon the fourteenth day, the charm was either to be burned in offering to Diana or to be hidden in a secret place.

A TREE-CHARM TO GAIN STRENGTH

Trees, an occultist explained to me, are a "... good source of radiant vitality on a very low-frequency scale" and may be drawn upon for "relief, and even cure, of backache conditions."

The prospective charm-maker is advised to select a suitable tree, "strong, upright, free from distortions, and of good size." Ash, spruce, and birch (definitely not yew) are recommended. For best results, the tree should be situated as far away from "human contamination" as possible.

Once a proper tree has been selected, the magician "makes friends" with it by "touching it, talking to it, and thinking into it." The tree should be circled nine times while the magi touches it gently with his fingertips or with the tip of his staff.

Upon the completion of the encirclement, take a final position to the North, lean back against the tree "firmly as if in the arms of a friend," and reach your hands behind you so that they might touch the bark of the tree. In this position, chant audibly:

O Tree;
Strong Tree; King Tree:
Take thou this weakness of my back.
Give me strength instead.
That I may be as upright as thyself
Between the Heavens (look up)
And the Earth beneath (look down)
Secure from storm
And blessed in every branch.
May this be so!

Repeat the incantation until you begin to feel a rapport with the tree. Once this has been sensed, relax, lean back against the tree, and allow it to work on your back for ten minutes.

"After a little while," the occultist said, "there should be a 'pulling out' feeling in the back which varies with individuals. When it is felt that the treatment is over, break contact gently, thank the Nature Spirits for their help, 'pay' the tree by sticking a pin into the bark, and take a small piece of the bark for a 'pocketlink' to carry with you.

THE INCREDIBLE MAGIC IN STONES AND GEMS

The Rev. Richard De A'Morelli has shared his arcane knowledge of the hidden magic in stones and gems and how best to use them in amulets and rings.

"Amulets can bestow complete control of the material plane and destiny; perhaps this explains why this knowledge has been forbidden for the uninitiated down through the centuries," Rev. De A'Morelli explained. Magical gems are not and can not be intended for use by the careless or foolish at heart.

"Perhaps the most popular amulets are the 12 birthstones. These semiprecious gems, mounted in rings and pendants, are usually sold to astrology buffs, but, also have widespread appeal. Because most people are familiar with these stones, the magic powers of each will be considered here."

Diamond—This precious gem is astrologically associated with the sign of Aries. A diamond amulet traditionally symbolizes enduring love and happiness in a marriage. Given as a gift, the gem strengthens emotional bonds and promotes loyalty. A diamond pendant may be worn to obtain honor and friendship. Mounted in a ring, the amulet insures lasting marriage and financial success.

Emerald—Traditionally associated with the astrological sign Taurus, this precious green gem possesses unique properties. An emerald pendant affords women protection against rape and defilement. Mounted in a ring, the stone promotes

THE COMPLETE BOOK OF TALISMANS, AMULETS AND MAGIC GEMSTONES

domestic stability and fortune. According to the legend, this amulet may be combat epilepsy, depression and insanity.

Agate—This stone may appear as striped or clouded quartz, and is astrologically associated with the sign Gemini. An agate amulet worn as a pendant promotes good health and fertility. An agate ring bestows wealth and honor; also, it can be used to obtain favors from people in high positions. Legend has it that any person who gazes upon this charm will be compelled to speak the truth and cannot maintain secrecy.

Ruby—This popular birthstone, which is associated with the astrological sign Cancer, reputedly promotes mental health and tranquility. A ruby pendant combats depression and enables the wearer to overcome sorrow. A ruby amulet worn as a ring bestows knowledge, health and wealth. This stone should never be given as a gift, as will result in discord and broken relationships.

Sardonyx—The birthstone of Leo people, this gem is a popular remedy for impotence. Ancient occultists believed that a sardonyx amulet could be worn to alleviate this affliction in less than a week. Mounted in a ring, sardonyx has no power; however, worn as a pendant, the stone combats sterility. Given as a gift, the sardonyx amulet guarantees the recipient's fidelity.

Sapphire—This deep blue corundum is astrologically associated with the sign Virgo. A Sapphire pendant is a reputed cure for fever, seizures, and delusions. Mounted in a ring, the gem bestows wisdom and compassion. When danger is imminent, this amulet reportedly takes on a chalky appearance, which remains until the hazard has subsided.

Opal—This semiprecious gem is associated with the astrological sign Libra. Worn as a ring, this amulet reputedly alleviates indigestion and other stomach disorders. Also, it instills tranquility and joy. An opal pendant is worn to attract happiness in love, fortune and favorable judgment in court. The opal amulet takes on a dull gray appearance when minor illness is forthcoming. A sickly yellow hue presages injury by accident.

Topaz—This semiprecious gem is the birthstone of Scorpio people. Some medieval occultists insisted that a topaz amulet promoted psychic sensitivity and facilitated control of destiny. A topaz pendant reputedly bestows honor, happiness and inner peace in addition to the above benefits. Mounted in a ring, the gem insures promotion and financial success.

Turquoise—This gem, which is the birthstone of Sagittarians, has been worn in amulets since the earliest times. American Indians considered the stone sacred, and medieval sorcerers used it in various magic rituals. Modern authorities claim that a turquoise amulet is an effective deterrent against illness and injury. Worn as a pendant, the stone also protects its bearer from a violent death. A turquoise ring may be worn to rekindle old love affairs and obtain emotional gratification.

Garnet—This semiprecious gem is the birthstone of Capricorn people. The stone was used extensively by early Egyptians and Phoenicians. It reputedly healed snake bite and food poisoning by absorbing alien chemicals in the blood through the skin. A garnet pendant is usually worn to arouse the passionate love of the opposite sex and to obtain physical gratification. A garnet ring reputedly combats fear and pessimism. Argument and eventual separation of two lovers results when garnet is given as a gift.

Amethyst—This gem, a purple variety of quartz, is traditionally considered to be the Aquarian birthstone. An amethyst ring is usually worn for protection against sorcery and the Evil Eye. An amethyst pendant prevents depression and supposedly bestows spiritual visions.

Bloodstone—Also known as heliotrope, this variety of quartz is the Piscean birthstone. Worn as a pendant, it prevents miscarriage and other illness during pregnancy. Mounted in a ring, the amulet reportedly promotes affluency and creativity. Worn to bed, bloodstone may bestow pleasant and clear visions of the future. In addition to the twelve birthstones described above, there are five other gems of magical significance which warrant consideration. These are as follows:

Amber—This gem, which has been used for magic purposes from time immemorial, is primarily a health aid. An amber pendant reportedly cures diseases of the blood, poor circulation and prevents heart attack. Mounted in a ring, this stone combats malfunction of the kidney and protects the wearer against heat stroke and suffocation.

Beryl—This opaque stone usually comes in yellow, pink, green or white. Worn as a pendant, it promotes happy marriage and honesty. Given as a gift, it is a popular deterrent to unfaithfulness. A beryl ring is frequently worn to insure good health during pregnancy.

Carnelian—This reddish quartz gem was highly popular with Old World occultists. Early Chaldeans gave the stone to enemies and thereby rendered them harmless. According to legend, the person who wore this stone, either as a ring

THE COMPLETE BOOK OF TALISMANS, AMULETS AND MAGIC GEMSTONES

or pendant, became sickly and listless, thus incapable of competition.

Coral—This stone occurs in a variety of colors and is allegedly invaluable to careless people. This amulet takes on a chalky white appearance when in close proximity with sick people. A coral ring or pendant may also be worn to promote health and wisdom.

Jade—Throughout history, man has used this gem as a deterrent to sorcery and demonic possession. Jade is therefore considered to be one of the most potent protective devices known to mankind. Modern occultists claim that a jade pendant may be worn to achieve the above effects, and that a Jade ring combats tragedy and depression.

Jet—Perhaps one of the most powerful amulets known, this lustrous black gem holds an important place in the legends of various cultures. In ancient Greece, occultists believed that it was a sacred substance, and in Assyria it was considered to be the gods' favorite jewel. Medieval legend credits the jet amulet with supernatural powers. The person wearing this stone supposedly attains complete control of the natural elements—fire, air, earth and water. To accommodate this purpose, a jet pendant is usually worn.

THE COMPLETE BOOK OF TALISMANS, AMULETS AND MAGIC GEMSTONES

On Talismans & the Healing Powers of Gems
By Shelley Kaehr, Ph.D.

"We find that the crystal as a stone, or any white stone, has a helpful influence – if carried about the body; not as an omen, not merely as a "good luck piece" or "good luck charm" but these vibrations that are needed as helpful influences for the entity are well to be kept close about the body."

Edgar Cayce, *the World's Greatest Psychic, Life Reading 2285-1*

In the past ten years I've written several books on the healing properties of stones and minerals. Since my first book *Gemstone Journeys* came out, I've been surprised by how many people are interested in this topic and how many people never heard of it before I mentioned it.

Ever since I was a child I carried stones around, collected them, wore them as jewelry, but it wasn't until I was an adult that I discovered they have real power you can easily access for a wide variety of purposes.

My take on gem healing is largely influenced by my first teacher, a Native American healer. He showed me that each stone carries a unique vibration and those vibrations can be used to enhance our daily lives in one of three areas – *love, health or money*. Let's face it; those three areas pretty much cover all we want out of life.

I've found when using stones by placing them on the body or wearing jewelry, you can tap into the frequency of the stone and begin to immolate it within your own energy field. Your body is a vast energetic system with a unique frequency. Stones and minerals have their own vibrations. Put the two together and you begin to get into a kind of rapport with the stone and therefore attract certain things to you depending on what you want.

Love

Rose quartz, for example, brings love to those who use it, so if you need more love in your life and you work with the rose quartz, you will begin vibrating at a frequency which naturally attracts love to you.

Health

Stones can be used for health concerns as well. Bloodstone is a particularly helpful remedy for all sorts of health issues. The stone is dark green with red flecks and I have seen countless times the person using it will suck the life out of the stone, leaving it either white or lighter than before.

Money

Citrine is a powerful stone for attracting financial prosperity. Put a couple of pieces in your purse or wallet and watch the results as you begin to carry a frequency that attracts cash.

The question remains, however; as to whether or not stones can be used as good luck charms or talismans. In my book *Edgar Cayce's Guide to Gemstones* I mentioned the fact that Cayce warned people about the use of any kind of talisman or charm. Why? I believe he was concerned the user would become too dependent on the stone instead of making his or her own luck.

If I carried a stone and was convinced it was keeping me safe, happy, peaceful, etc. and the stone got lost, I would be up a creek!

By the same token, many famous historical figures used stones and certain pieces of jewelry to protect them and bring luck. The most notable was the French Emperor Napoleon who is said to have worn a carnelian signet ring at all times in battle. He believed the stone protected him, and as it turns out, it did.

There is a lot of buzz these days about the Laws of Attraction and the simple fact we get what we think about. I've told people for years that although I have seen miracle after miracle with healing stones, I do not expect you to believe me. Try it yourself and see what happens!

I can't tell you exactly how or why it works, but I assure you, if you believe your rose quartz brought you the love of your life and your citrine is making you rich, then so be it! It shouldn't matter as long as the end result is favorable. The stone serves as a focal point of your intent.

So here's the toughest question of all – what do you want? Find the answer to that one question and then you'll be ready to read up and find the stone that's right for you. Anything you desire in this life is well within your grasp. Believe it, align energetically with it, and it's yours!

Shelley Kaehr, Ph.D. is known throughout the world for her work with healing gems. Visit her online at www.shelleykaehr.com

Gem Books By Shelley Kaehr, Ph.D.
Edgar Cayce's Guide to Gemstones
Gemstone Journeys
Lemurian Seeds: Hope for Humanity
Crystal Skull Consciousness
Gemstone Enlightenment

THE COMPLETE BOOK OF TALISMANS, AMULETS AND MAGIC GEMSTONES

GETTING THE MOST OUT OF YOUR FAVORITE GEMSTONES THROUGH MEDITATION

by Diane Tessman

Since 1981, Diane and Tibus have offered guidance to thousands of clients. Some clients have been with her since 1981 and have found Tibus to be an invaluable guide, through Diane. Indeed, these clients are now dear friends. Today, Diane lives in her native place in North Iowa, writes/channels 3 publications, and does personal, written counselings. She also personally fills all orders herself, choosing just the right crystal or gemstone for each client. An animal lover all her life, Diane has opened her ten-acre farm house to stray and abandoned cats and dogs. Feel free to ask Diane more about this aspect of her mission either over the internet or by writing to her at Box 352-BCJ, St Ansgar, IA 50472

Books by Diane Include — : ***SEVEN RAYS OF THE HEALING MILLENNIUM, THE COMING OF THE GOD CLOUD AND OTHER EARTH CHANGE REVELATIONS,* and *YOUR PASSPORT TO HEAVEN.***

www.DianeTessman.com <http://www.DianeTessman.com>

Crystals and gemstones are Mother Earth's infinitely diverse and magnificent energy, manifested in 3 dimensional form. They are millions of years old, having been created in catastrophic upheavals which compacted their mighty energy. They have held this power within as time has marched along on Earth. Centuries, millennia, eons: crystals and gemstones remain as they were created, powerful and infinitely beautiful. Gazing at them is a journey back in time.

The power within a crystal can be used scientifically to power computers and a variety of advanced technical devices. In the future, we will realize that a certain kind of crystal also powers star ships.

The power within a crystal and gemstone can also be used spiritually. It is this aspect which we will explore.

With crystals and gemstones, you can heal yourself or another, and you can facilitate communication with the higher realms of angels, extraterrestrials, and other-dimensional beings. My star guardian Tibus and I would like to give you four meditations using crystals. In meditating with crystals and gemstones, you will be empowering your own energy many-fold.

Before meditating with crystals and gemstones, you must realize a few spiritual truths.

Your relationship with your meditation crystal is a symbiotic one. There is a special energy within the crystal which is the life force of Gaia, the living spirit of Mother Earth. In a real sense, this special energy within the crystal is life. And of course you have a unique energy within yourself which is your spark of the Creator's flame - life.

Another spiritual truth to remember: Life is more far-spread, more diverse, and more wondrous than humankind has yet imagined it to be. The universe abounds with life which may be very different from humankind's narrow definition of life, but it is none the less - life.

Planet Earth herself is a living being with spirit, intelligence and even emotions. Earth is struggling for her life at present, mostly because of humankind's greed, selfishness, and insensitivity. When working with crystals, remember this sad truth. Bringing this truth to your meditation will enhance your ability to use the power within Gaia's crystals and gemstones.

When I meditate, I always devote part of my meditation to healing Mother Earth. I do not feel it is right to use her crystals and gemstones for other spiritual goals while ignoring her plight.; after all, she gave us these exquisite and powerful stones. Through crystals and gemstones, I find I can connect to her easily and communicate with her as a living being. I find that this mighty spirit needs my healing and companionship; she needs to know I recognize the fact that I am her human child, her creation. This aligns my energy and that of the crystal even more. Our energies become symbiotic and we are one.

Now, with in-put from my star guardian Tibus, I would like to give you three meditations with crystals and gemstones which I use and find very powerful and effective.

Meditation One:
Preferable for this meditation is a clear crystal of any size, shape, or hue. Many crystals are clear but there are a huge number which have astoundingly beautiful color. Use the one which feels best to you, best to your heart and soul.

Sit comfortably in a place where you can catch either the sun's light, the moon's light, or candle light. If the weather permits, I always prefer meditations outdoors in Mother Nature; I find them more powerful.

Clear your mind of daily cares and problems. Take 3 deep breaths. Relax and simply be. No thoughts need to be running through your head. Touch the earth, touch your soul.

Symbolilcally surround yourself with the golden white light of goodness. Feel peace and serenity settling upon you like light feathers. You are reaching higher consciousness.

The every day brain is now at rest. You are the whole you, the higher you. You are a part of Gaia and a part of the infinite Universe.

Feel the energy flowing through your crown, your third eye, your heart, your solar plexus, through your entire being. This is divine energy and this energy activates your crystal also.

Pick up your crystal and feel the warmth. Is it the warmth from your hand or is it warmth from the crystal? It does not matter because you are one with your crystal.

THE COMPLETE BOOK OF TALISMANS, AMULETS AND MAGIC GEMSTONES

Now hold your crystal up to the light and see the many facets within. Even if it is a very clear crystal, there is still volume, depth, and flow within. It is amazing, mesmerizing, and its powers are clear and vivid.

Now, the power of you and your crystal are at optimum force. Do not forget to send healing energies to Mother Earth. And what else is the goal of your meditation?

Healing? Or communication with angels or extraterrestrials or other dimension beings? Perhaps you simply want communication with them as an inspiration and exciting experience.

This meditation can be channeled into whatever goal you wish at this time. If you wish to heal yourself, another human, or an animal friend, after you have held the crystal up to the light, place it on the ailing area of the body. Keep your hand on it so your energies will continue to mingle and enhance its energies.

If you are healing, say these words: Energy of Gaia, emanate from this beautiful crystal. Energy of the Universal Creator, flow through me. Earth Mother, Sky Father, hear me! All energy is one, flowing, flowing. All-powerful One, heal this sick (or injured) being. Heal! Heal!

It is good if you continue expressing the feelings which come to you as you hold your crystal with your warm hand, on or over the area that needs healing. Say what comes from your heart regarding this individual (even yourself) and the need for healing.

If you wish to use thhis meditation for communication with other realms instead of healing, say the following words:

Higher beings of the universe, I wish to communicate.

Place your crystal directly in front of you, after you have mingled your energy with it by holding it. State whom you wish to communicate with: Fairies, extraterrestrials, angels, future humans, other-dimensional persona. Or if you have a specific being in mind, state his or her name. I often say, "Tibus, I am looking for you. My crystal beacon searches the skies for you. Are you there?"

Now, simply relax and see what thoughts come to mind. Telepathy will enter your being, emanating from the higher being you have summoned. You may be surprised at what he or she has to say, sometimes they have a joke or a humorous incident, sometimes they are sad about the plight of a specific endangered species or the planet herself, other times they wish to praise you for a kind act you have done, and sometimes they have a specific message for your life or to help someone you know.

Keep your focus on the crystal before you, but gently do so. You do not need to concentrate on the crystal, simply keep it in your gaze if your eyes are open. It is alright to close your eyes too.

By using your crystal in this meditation, you are not only using its power as well as your own, you are symbolically stating that you are a spiritual soul of goodness, who recognizes and uses the light and who acknowledges the wonder and diversity of the universe. You also acknowledge that Planet Earth is a sacred world which you love and protect. After all, you have taken her magnificent crystal creation on this meditative journey!

Here is a powerful meditation to use with your favorite gemstone.

Meditation Two:

THE COMPLETE BOOK OF TALISMANS, AMULETS AND MAGIC GEMSTONES

Follow your regular path to deep relaxation. Take three deep breaths. Clear your mind of worries and daily experiences.

Surround yourself with the golden white light of goodness.

Envision your gemstone as the globe of Planet Earth. It is she who gave this utterly beautiful object to you. Its energies are ancient, real, and powerful. Send unconditional love to this planet as you gaze on it. Know that she will soon reincarnate in a New Dawn of balance, peace, and beauty.

Now lift your head skyward, closing your gemstone into your warm hand. Close your eyes and feel the magical energies washing over your face from Mother Earth and Father Sky. You are cleansed, you have strength anew! This in itself is a small miracle.

Turning your head skyward is particularly effective if you are meditating at night and can look up at the stars glimmering overhead. See the stars! Hold your gemstone up to them; both your gemstones and the stars are made of universal molecules and there is universal consciousness within both, too.

Now bring your mind and heart back to your gemstone. Send a telepathic message to your gurardian angel or your star guardian. Do not hesitate to ask for help or to tell him or her about a specific problem or trouble you are having. Ask for a simply message which will guide you on your path, expressing that you wish more than anything to complete your purpose, your mission, here on Earth with love and goodness.

Continue holding your gemstone, feeling the symbiotic relationship you have with its unique energies.

You may be delightfully surprised as you receive your guardian's transmission. Other times, only a word or two will be received but they will mean something positive and will somehow be helpful. Do not feel disappointed if you do not receive an entire cosmic manuscript! The message may make little sense at the time but you will find sense in it in the next few weeks as your path unfolds.

If you do not feel you receive anything, do not become negative. Try again. Wear your gemstone or carry it in your pocket for a while. Think of it as a friend. Remember the beautiful experience of the starry night and of turning face to the sky and feeling cleansed and re-energized. This in itself is a tremendous gift.

You do not need to hear a thundering voice to be in touch with Spirit. The same goes for your connection to your crystals and gemstones. If your experiences are subtle but positive, it may well be that you are not in need of a thundering voice experience. If you listen to that small voice within, you may already have contact with your guardian - a shared consciousness between the two of you. By saying this, we do not detract from your own good intuition, but you may want to realize that your intuitive channels also pick up messages, thoughts, and feelings, from your guardian as well, and have for years.

The Creator Spirit can also reach you through your intuitive channels. Again, a message from God does not have to come in the thundering voice. Your gemstone can help this direct connection with God as well.

Your gemstone helps balance your energies also, so that all of this can happen, whether subtle or spectacular.

Consider again the miracle which created this gemstone: out of the violence and chaos of Earth's upheaval, came this exquisite stone with so much color, design, and power. Consider: no two are alike! What diversity Gaia possesses as she creates and creates!

THE COMPLETE BOOK OF TALISMANS, AMULETS AND MAGIC GEMSTONES

All of these thoughts and feelings, and more, will come to you as you become intertwined with the energies of your special gemstone. It must become natural to you for it to work at optimum.

Meditation Three:
This meditation is a very special Love Spell to use with the crystal or gemstone of your choice. Sometimes one crystal will be more of an angel vibration while another crystal seems more for healing just with its own powers. Yet another gemstone or crystal may speak to you personally, reaching your soul and feeling like it is yours. This is the crystal or gemstone you will want to use in this Love Spell.

This spell contains sacred words which speak of the power of love and of your love for Mother Earth. After meditating with the sacred words we are about to give you, you can add your own wishes of love for whomever you wish.

For instance, after you have completed the spell, you may want to add thoughts/words of healing for your mother. Or if you wish your husband or wife would love you more deeply, you can add that sentiment. If you wish to love and protect a stray cat you are feeding, you can add that to your spell. If you are concerned about your teenage son, you can include that in your Love Spell, surrounding him with protection and common sense. Or if you wish a certain man or woman would notice you and fall in love, seeing your many good qualities, you can add that.

Here is the sacred spell, given to my star guardian Tibus by his ancient wizard friend W'Vora. Use it wisely, for it has great power.

> *By the darkness of deep night*
> *And the bright sun of day*
> *Let love come to this troubled planet*
> *Let love mingle with the molecules of the sunrise air*
> *Let love spread like velvet in the black night*
> *Let love fill the oceans and spill through the lands*
> *Let all of this love then flow into the human heart and soul!*
>
> *Let light shine into the darkest of souls*
> *Let light fill even the hardest of hearts*
> *Let light dawn in the minds of those who are fragmented*
> *Let love and light BE on Mother Earth!*
>
> *Terra anima, soul of Gaia*
> *How do I worship thee?*
> *How I stand in awe of thy wonders!*
> *Terra anima, soul of Earth*
> *Embrace me for I am your child*
> *I love you as you love me.*

Now you can add to this, whatever wishes, prayers, spells, or hopes you have regarding love for any life form. Do you want another human to love you? Do you want to give

THE COMPLETE BOOK OF TALISMANS, AMULETS AND MAGIC GEMSTONES

love to a stray or abandoned puppy? Do you wish to show your father that you love him? Whatever love you wish to become reality, add it to this Love Spell as you hold your favorite gemstone or crystal.

Study and subsequent knowledge regarding gemstones and crystals is infinite because Mother Earth has created so many of them, all wondrous, all unique. One day, humankind will find even more gemstones and crystals on other worlds, other planets. They too will be helpmates for us, shining with their ancient powers, so that we can create a better reality for ourselves and for our world.

BIBLE SPELLS
WILLIAM ALEXANDER ORIBELLO

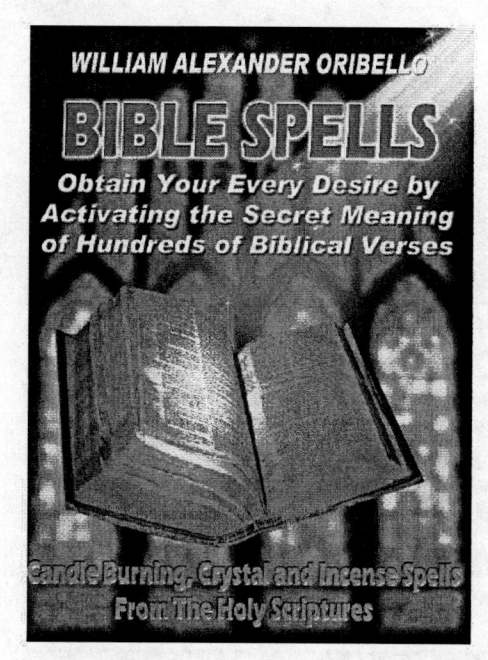

Obtain Your Every Desire by Activating the Secret Meaning of Hundreds of Biblical Verses

Candle Burning, Crystal and Incense Spells From The Holy Scriptures

The idea behind Bible Magick is simple; all verses in the Bible are charged with spiritual energies. This power of creation is called "LOGOS," meaning "WORD." It is thought that God the Creator used the LOGOS to initiate creation.

The Universe and everything within it are divine words that have solidified. You can imagine that they were once dissolved in the sound vibrations of the divine cosmic word. Each thing we see is a divine word become solid. ---------------------------$18.00

THERE IS A SECRET TO PERFORMING MAGICK!

This Unique, Very Personal, Book Of Shadows, Will Teach You This Closely Guarded SECRET, So That You Can Become Super Enpowered When Performing Any Spell Or Ritual.

$21.95

The Secret Book of Shadows
Cretarot

Add $5 for shipping and handling for up to 3 titles.

Place your order with:
Inner Light, Box 753, New Brunswick, NJ 08903
Credit Card Orders: 732-602-3407
PayPal Email: MrUFO8@hotmail.com

INNER LIGHT / GLOBAL COMMUNICATIONS
EXPLORING THE WORLD'S GREATEST MYSTERIES SINCE 1965

DISTRIBUTED BY GLOBAL COMMUNICATIONS

ORDER ALL TITLES FROM GLOBAL COMMUNICATIONS

Global Communications
Post Office Box 753
New Brunswick, New Jersey 08903

FOR OVER 40 YEARS Inner Light / Global Communications has brought to the world some of the best authors on Mysticism, Metaphysics, and the Unexplained. Our best recognized authors include: John A. Keel; Brad Steiger; Commander X; T. Lobsang Rampa; Tim Swartz; Timothy Green Beckley; William Alexander Oribello and Dragonstar.

OUR NUMBER ONE BEST SELLER!
OVER 50,000 COPIES IN PRINT!

THE LOST JOURNALS OF NIKOLA TESLA: HAARP—CHEMTRAILS AND THE SECRET OF ALTERNATIVE 4 by Tim Swartz

Discredited in his time, Nikola Tesla was made out by business competitors and the government to be nothing more than a crackpot. Nonetheless, these same conspirators later duplicated, and possibly even stole, many of Tesla's most famous inventions. Here is sensational data obtained from the inventor's most private papers and kept under wraps by military and big business concerns. Many of Tesla's most powerful and potentially dangerous scientific discoveries are being turned against ordinary citizens in programs of behavior and physical modification, including the seeding of clouds with mind and body altering chemicals. This book explores reverse gravity, free energy, contact with hidden dimensions, mysterious radio signals from space, earth changes, freak weather patterns, electric death rays, UFOs and particle beam weapons. ISBN: 1-892062-13-5 • $15.95

OTHER TESLA TITLES INCLUDE:
NIKOLA TESLA: FREE ENERGY AND THE WHITE DOVE by Commander X

Top Secret revelations by a former military intelligence operative regarding Tesla's secret propulsion system and how the Secret Government is flying anti-gravity craft. Reveals Tesla's "Cosmic Roots," and the existence of a remote underground site in Nevada where these craft are being hangared. ISBN: 0-938284-82-2 • $15.00

NIKOLA TESLA'S JOURNEY TO MARS—ARE WE ALREADY THERE? by Sean Casteel

Jules Verne wrote what was at the time considered to be far-fetched stories about the exploration of the moon and Mars. These classic literary works were based upon "wild rumors" circulating that such voyages had already occurred, with a group of scientists, all members of the same secret society. They had tapped into an unknown power source, using it to usher in the birth of flight years before the Wright Brothers flew their plane at Kittyhawk. Stranger than any fiction book could be, here is proof the NAZIs established colonies on the moon in the early 1940s; facts NASA doesn't want you to know! ISBN: 1-892062-31-3 • $14.95

INVISIBILITY AND LEVITATION—HOW-TO KEYS TO PERSONAL PERFORMANCE by Commander X—Utilized by occultists and the martial arts, these are not parlor tricks, but actual methods adopted by the ancients and now used by the military intelligence community to perfect invisibility as demonstrated during the Philadelphia Experiment and Stealth Technology. This book offers various techniques that really work, providing the reader with dozens of examples which takes the subject out of its mystical surroundings. ISBN: 0-938294-36-9 • $15.95

CONTINUED ON NEXT PAGE >

SUBTERRANEAN WORLDS INSIDE EARTH by Timothy Green Beckley
Is the earth hollow? Is our planet honeycombed with caverns inhabited with a mysterious race? Are there civilizations of super beings living beneath the surface? Here are strange and unexplainable legends of the "Wee People," the Dero, and long-haired Atlantean giants! ISBN: 0-938294-22-1 • $14.95

THE DULCE WARS: UNDERGROUND ALIEN BASES AND THE BATTLE FOR PLANET EARTH by Branton
In the corner of a small town in America's Southwest, something very strange is going on! An alien Fifth Column is already active on Earth and may be preparing for global conquest. Dulce, New Mexico is the epicenter of cattle mutilations; energy grids; secret societies; underground anomalies; conspiracies between townfolk and "outsiders;" unexplained legends; lost civilizations, as well as abductions and missing time. ISBN: 1-892062-12-7 • $17.50

UFOS, PROPHECY AND THE END OF TIME by Sean Casteel
Is this mankind's final wakeup call? Explores Terrorism in America! Violence Overseas! War In The Middle East! Natural Disasters Worldwide! Man versus Nature! Religious Jihad, and unholy perversion in the Church. But, perhaps most important, almost ignored, is the worldwide appearance of UFOs and the abduction of humans by what may well be the "gods of old." This volume draws from Biblical prophecy and reliable UFOlogical sources and represents a divine revelation from The Heavenly Ones On High. ISBN 1-892062-35-6 • $16.95

THE LONG LOST BOOKS OF T. LOBSANG RAMPA FEATURING: MY VISIT TO AGHARTA by T. Lobsang Rampa
For decades Rampa's books brought great enlightenment, comfort and joy to millions who have repeatedly clambered for more of his enchanting narratives, despite the fact that he has been deceased for more than a decade. Recently a "lost" manuscript was discovered detailing Rampa's journey to Agharta, the sacred underground land in the hollow earth. This previously unknown land is populated by enlightened masters of great wisdom. Also in this book are excerpts from some of previously unavailable works. Topics include: Death and Life on the "Other Side;" Other Dimensions; Astral Projection; Contact With The Space Brothers. ISBN: 1-89206-34-5 • $19.95

MJ-12 AND THE RIDDLE OF HANGAR 18: THE NEW EVIDENCE by Timothy Green Beckley with Sean Casteel
Stored away in a secret underground hangar are the remains of the UFO that crashed at Roswell. According to the author, the last eight presidents have been in on the ultimate deception...a "Cosmic Watergate!" Over 60 cases of crashed UFOs are documented, offering proof of the existence of MJ-12 and the Interplanetary Phenomenon Unit involved in the recovery of crashed UFOs and their occupants. ISBN: 1-892062-53-4 • $24.95

NEW MAGICK HANDBOOK: SIMPLE SPELLS FOR A COMPLEX WORLD by Dragonstar
Utilize everyday items to promote success: candles, crystals, herbs, gemstones, pendulum, charms, incantations and other proven methods of empowerment. The author is a mystic and occult adept who learned the science of alchemy and other universal laws. Here are spells and rituals to promote good health; encourage love; succeed in business; rid yourself of unwanted relationship and MORE! ISBN: 1-892062-19-4 • $14.95

A NEW BOOK OF REVELATIONS as Channeled through Tuella
This work corrects many of the misconceptions and inaccurate translations of the Old and New Testaments and lays the foundation for a New Book of Revelations as transcribed from the highest spiritual powers of the Universe. Shocking revelations include: The true meaning of 666; The special significance of the 13th Vortex; How the Primary Channel for this work was able to thwart the forces of darkness and facilitate the departure of the "Fallen Ones;" How God's rebellious son Jehovahn inserted distortions into the original Biblical Scriptures to create disharmony; How a legion of Angels will protect you personally during a global war. Tuella's other works include: Project World Evacuation and Ashtar, A Tribute. ISBN: 0-938-294-85-7 • $14.00

Global Communications, Box 753, New Brunswick, NJ 08903
Credit Card Orders 732 602-3407   MRUFO8@hotmail.com

INNER LIGHT PUBLICATIONS PRESENTS
A TRIBUTE TO TUELLA

PRIMARY CHANNEL FOR THE ASHTAR COMMAND

Though she has passed from the physical realm, the channel Tuella remains the primary source of messages transmitted from the *Ashtar Command*, a spiritually advanced group of ETS who guide and instruct from a huge mother-ship circulation the earth at the equator. Before her transition to heavenly realms Inner Light purchased the rights to her monumental works and have endeavored to make them available to the public. The following titles are available directly from the publisher.

Ashtar: Revealing the Secret Identity of the Forces of Light and Their Spiritual Program For Earth

Here are messages from Ashtar, spokesperson for the Solar Council whose mission is to assist in our growth as planetary individuals and to offer warnings and advice in these monumental times. A delightful read for advancing souls!

$15.00

Project World Evacuation (9th Printing)

Will we be lifted off the planet in times of global disaster by friendly space beings lead by members of the Ashtar Command. Is this the rapture spoke of in the Bible? Where will the rescued be taken. What are we expected to bring with us during the exodus?

$21.95

A New Book Of Revelations

Exposes the true meaning of 666. The special significance of the 13th Vortex. Corrects many inaccurate translations made of the Old and New Testaments and lays the foundation for a New World.

$16.00

🌒 *Cosmic Telepathy: A How To Manual*

A workbook and study guide to expand your inner clairvoyant powers. Now it is possible for humans to transport the barriers of time and space. Special material added by T. Lobsang Rampa. Large format, 8x11 edition.

$25.00

🌒 *Cosmic Prophecies For The Year 2000*

World chaos. World Changes. Freak Weather. Space Guardians. A cosmic symposium of 27 ET communiqués including 9 noted space commanders and representatives of the solar tribunal and spiritual hierarchy.

$14.00

🌒 *On Earth Assignment (Available Once Again!)*

The cosmic awakening of light workers, Walk-Ins, Star Children has begun! Are you a reincarnated soul? Were you on Atlantis? Find out what your miss on earth is. $21.95

🌒 *The Space People Speak*

While not a Tuella book, this Ashtar Command presentation is one of the original offerings of west coast channels and contains spiritually received portraits of some of the Ashtar representatives created by Carol Ann Rodriguez. $12.00

Rare Collectors Item Now Available!

🌒 *The Mystic Symbol Of The Solar Cross*

Believed "lost" this rare manuscript has been impossible to obtain. Limited reprint for serious students ONLY. Here are the key symbols that offer us the basic laws government every phase of our awareness. Here is the Great Awakening that will enable us to evolve toward a consciousness of the basic oneness of all life. Over 250, 8x11 pages in perfect bound format. Book comes with CD of a lecture given by Tuella. Many have been looking for this book!

$39.95 (counts as two books for purposes of shipping).

Add $5 for shipping and handling for up to 3 titles.
All items in this ad just
$139.95 + $10.00 shipping and handling.
Place your order with:
Inner Light, Box 753, New Brunswick, NJ 08903
Credit Card Orders: 732-602-3407
PayPal Email: MrUFO8@hotmail.com

If you would like more information about other spiritually enlightening books please write to:

**INNER LIGHT PUBLICATIONS
BOX 753: NEW BRUNSWICK, N.J. 08903**